Mahatma Gandhi National Rural Employment Guarantee Programme and Poverty in India

Mahatma Gandhi National Rural Employment Guarantee Programme and Poverty in India

P. Arunachalam

SERIALS PUBLICATIONS
NEW DELHI (INDIA)

First Published – 2011

ISBN: 978-81-8387-439-7

Published by

SERIALS PUBLICATIONS
4830/24, 1st Floor, Ansari Road
Darya Ganj, New Delhi-110002 (India)
Phone : 23245225. Fax : 91-11-23272135
E-mail : serials@sify.com
serialspublications.india@gmail.com
Website : www.serialspublications.com

Contents

Preface

Poverty reduction and its eventual elimination has been one of the major goals of development policy in India since Independence. Several poverty alleviation programmes have been in place for a long time now. There are numerous centrally-sponsored schemes (CSS), designed by the Centre, administered by the Ministry of Rural Development, but implemented by the States. Though there has been some reduction in the percentage of people below the poverty line since the 1970s, the problem still remains formidable with over 260 million people living below the poverty line. In fact, going by the World Bank's new yardstick to measure global poverty adopted last year, the number of people living on $1.25 per day (instead of the earlier $1 per day yardstick), India had 455 million people living below the poverty line in 2005. An overwhelming majority of the poor are in rural areas and continue to depend on agriculture for want of any other livelihood opportunities outside the sector. About 52 per cent of the country's workforce and over 60 per cent of the population depends of agriculture which now accounts for just 17 per cent of the country's GDP, thus perpetuating rural poverty and widening the rural-urban divide. The major weaknesses of the plethora of poverty alleviation programmes launched over the years have been the overlapping of schemes, thin spread of resources over a wide area, inadequate preparatory work before their launch, lack of proper co-ordination between the Central and State governments, inadequate funding by banks, paucity of trained staff at the ground level and poor governance and delivery resulting in widespread leakages and corruption. Apart from wage employment and nutrition programmes, and public distribution system, the accent over the past two decades has been on self-employment programmes to reduce rural poverty. The idea was to provide alternative livelihood opportunities to the surplus labour force that is forced to depend on agriculture. Self-employment programmes launched over the years have not been able to empower beneficiaries in the true sense of the term by enabling them to earn an income sufficient to lift them out of poverty.

Success of any sustainable Poverty alleviation Programme is based on increasing productive employment opportunities along with growth. The focus of Government of India relates to providing employment guarantee of 100 days of wage employment to every rural household, whose adult member(s) are willing to do unskilled manual work. Accordingly, the Parliament has passed the historic National Rural Employment Guarantee Act (NREGA) in the year 2005 that guarantees 100 days of wage employment in a year, to every rural household. This act was introduced with an aim of improving the purchasing power of the rural people, primarily semi or un-skilled work to people living in rural India, whether or not they are below the poverty line. The Government of India has renamed the National Rural Employment Guarantee Act (NREGA) as the Mahatma Gandhi National Rural Employment Guarantee Act. Prime Minister Manmohan Singh announced while addressing a meeting held to celebrate the Golden Jubilee the Panchayati Raj in October 2, 2009. The NREGA bill essentially guarantees employment for the unemployed through work such as building roads, improving water supply and works that are necessary to improve infrastructure in rural areas. The uniqueness of this bill is in the fact that it carries emphasis on issues like equality of wages for men and women, elimination of work contracting/middlemen, payment of wages only through bank and post office accounts to prevent corruption, creating transparency in workers muster rolls etc. Any individual, irrespective of his socio-economic status can ask for employment either in writing or verbally with the Gram Panchayat. The act guarantees that if work is not provided within a 15 day time frame including the eligibility verification and issuing of the job cards then the applicant is eligible for unemployment allowance. Work to be done is decided by the Gram Panchayat. Emphasis is given to unskilled manual labor focusing on building roads and other public village infrastructural facilities, water conservation, afforestation, land development & drought proofing. All adults in a house hold are eligible to work. If the work site is not within 5 kilometers from the applicant's residence then the applicant is eligible for an additional 10% of the wage. This law can be a big boost for nomadic tribal communities since locally domiciled but migrant population is also eligible for employment.

National Rural Employment Guarantee Act came into force on February 2, 2006 and was implemented in a phased manner. In Phase one it was introduced in 200 of the most backward districts of the country. It was implemented in an additional 130 districts in Phase two 2007-2008. As per the initial target, NREGA was to be expanded countrywide in five years. However, in order to bring the whole nation under its safety net and keeping in view the demand, the Scheme was extended to the remaining 274 rural districts of India from April 1, 2008 in Phase III. The Central government outlay for scheme is Rs. 39,100 crores ($8 billion) in FY 2009-10. Around one-third of the stipulated work force is women. The government is planning to open a call center, which upon becoming operational can be approached on the toll-free number, 1800-345-22-44. It was initially called the National Rural Employment Guarantee Act (NREGA) but was renamed on 2 October, 2009.

The National Rural Employment Guarantee Act, which came into force in February 2006, now covers all of rural India. It has generated over 450 crore person-days of employment, a major share going to women and Scheduled Caste and Scheduled Tribe families. Over Rs. 35,000 crore has been paid as wages. The remaining 266 districts were notified on September 28, 2008, and the scheme has now been extended to all the districts of the country. More than 4.47 crore households were provided employment in 20080-09. This is a significant jump over the 3.39 crore households covered under the scheme during 2007-08. Out of the 215. 63 crore person days created under the scheme during this period, 29 per cent and 25 per cent were in favour of SC and ST population respectively and 48 per cent of the total persons days created went in favour of women.The priorities of the work to be undertaken include watershed management and water conservation, drought-proofing, flood protection, land development, minor irrigation and rural connectivity. Such work is important to strengthen the ecological foundations of sustainable agriculture. The NREGA is probably the world's largest ecological security programme. A major weakness has been the absence of effective technical guidance and support from agricultural and rural universities and institutes. The Union Ministry of Rural Development has taken steps to achieve convergence of brain and brawn, by enlisting the support of Ministries and Departments. Such convergence of expertise for sustainable development will help to enhance farm productivity without causing ecological harm. What is now needed is a convergence for human development at NREGA sites. Few laws have had such stimulating economic, social and political impact so soon in India as the National Rural Employment Guarantee Act, 2005 – since renamed Mahatma Gandhi Rural Employment Guarantee Act. Think of the guaranteed employment to 4.47 crore rural households; additional income flowing to wage earners' hamlets to the tune of Rs.18, 155 crores; S.C., ST and women workers far outnumbering other sections of workers; 31.2 million poor families opening accounts in banks, post offices; India occupies the 132nd position among 179 countries in the UNDP's 2009 Human Development Index. That position may worsen. NREGA workers represent some of the most economically and socially underprivileged sections. Mostly, these workers are undernourished, with poor opportunities for healthcare. Hence, there is need to bring about a convergence of child care, nutrition, health (Rural Health Mission) and education programmes at NREGA sites. Education can be imparted in the evenings, using the joyful learning techniques available in computer-aided literacy programmes. Such a convergence in sustainable development along with convergence in human development will be creditable. There is also a need to raise the self-esteem of NREGA workers, making them feel proud of the fact that they are engaged in checking eco-destruction. Due recognition could be given to the NREGA groups that have done outstanding work in water harvesting, watershed development and soil healthcare with "Environment Saviour Awards". This will help spread awareness of the critical role NREGA workers play. To begin with, there could be 10 awards covering distinct agro-climatic zones, each worth Rs. 10 lakh. Since these will be group awards, the money could be divided among the workers, depending on how long they have worked. The NREGA will then help to improve both food security and human development index. There are uncommon opportunities to erase India's image as the land of the poor, hungry and illiterate. To utilise them, an import requirement is a change in the mindset from patronage to partnership and from undervaluing the human resource to considering our youthful population as our greatest asset.

I am very much indebted to the contributors for sending the papers within the stipulated period. The credit of this work undoubtedly goes to the contributors. I wholeheartedly acknowledge the immense encouragement and support given by my colleagues in CUSAT and Professor friends like Dr.K.C.Sankaranarayanan, Former Dean, Faculty of Social Sciences, CUSAT, Dr.Wolfgang Hoeltgen, German Indian Business-Center Hannover, Germany, Prof. Da Hsuan Feng, Senior Executive Vice President,National Cheng Kung University, Taiwan, Dr. Rafael A. Díaz Porras, Universidad Nacional Heredia, Costa Rica, Dr.Technimicel Musse, Professor, Winona State University, USA, Prof.Nicholas Aperigis, University of Piraeus, Greece, Prof. Erotokritos Vareleas, university of Macedonia, Thessaloniki, Greece, Dr.Muthukrishnan, City University, London, Dr.Malake, Professor, Asmara University, Eritriya, Ms. May Wong and Dr. Do from China, Dr. Hector J.Thyil from UK, Axel Dreher,

Professor of Economics, University of Goettingen, Germany, Dr. Gerard de Groot, Director, Development Research Institute (IVO), Tilburg University, the Netherlands, Dr.Wim Pelupessy, Senior Economist, IVO and all the IVO members, Tilburg University, the Netherlands, Dr.Job de Haan, Professor, Center, Tilburg University, the Netherlands for their help and encouragement I have received while doing my Post Doctoral Training Programme in the Development Research Institute, Tilburg University, the Netherlands during the period from 1999 to 2004, which made me strong and ultimately venturing into writing and editing books. Finally I would like to thank my colleagues, friends from Indian and abroad, my students and e.mail friends for their encouragement. I am also grateful to my son Saravanan Malhotra and daughter Pooja Gayatri for their moral support. I am also very much indebted to Serials Publications for bringing out this edited volume with care and interest.

Dr. P. Arunachalam
Faculty Member, Head (2004-07)
Department of Applied Economics,
Cochin University of Science
and Technology, Kochi-22.
E.Mail: arunachalam14@yahoo.co.uk,
09746770732 (Cell), 0484 2577741.

Poverty and MGNREGS

1

P. Arunachalam

Prof. Irma Glicman Adelman, an Irish Economist working in California University at Berkely, in her research work on 'Development Over Two Centuries', which is published in the Journal of Evolutionary Economics, 1995, has identified that India, along with China, would be one of the largest economies in this 21st Century. She has stated that the period 1700-1820 is the period of Netherlands (Holland), the period 1820-1890 is the period of England, the period 1890-2000 is the period of America and this 21st Century is the century of China and India. World Bank has also identified India would be a one the leading players of this century after China. India will be third largest economy after USA and China. India ($ 1,206,684 Million) will challenge the Global Economic Order in the next 15 years. India will overtake Italian economy ($ 2,313,893 Million) in 2015, England economy ($ 2,680,000 Million) in 2020, Japan economy ($ 4,910,692 Million) in 2025 and USA economy (14,441,425 Million) in 2050 (China will overtake Japan economy in 2016 and USA economy in 2027). India has the following advantages compared with other economies. India is 4th largest GDP in the world in terms of Purchasing Power. India is third fastest growing economy in the world after China and Vietnam. Service sector contributes around 57 per cent of GDP. The share of agriculture is around 17 per cent and Manufacture is 16 per cent in 2005-06. This is a character of a developed country. Expected GDP growth rate is 10 per cent shortly (It has come down from 9.2 per cent in 2006-07 to 6.2 per cent during 2008-09 due to recession. It is only a temporary phenomenon). India has $285 billion as Foreign Exchange Reserve as on today. India had just $1 billion as Foreign Exchange Reserve when it opened its economy in the year 1991. The size of the Indian economy is 4th largest and India ranks 13th among the richest countries in the world, she has the highest number of representatives among the countries in the top 20 list of world's richest persons, Indian cricket team is the richest in the world, the size film business in Bollywood has crossed even Hollywood, Europe and China, India among global top 10 in industrial production according to United National Industrial Development Organization Year book on Industrial statistics 2010 (China is now the World's second largest producer of manufactured goods).

India's high growth rates have been a matter of boastful self-congratulatory publicity for the Indian Government, with the recent recession being projected as a temporary setback, soon to be overcome. The latest Human Development Report released by the UNDP in India recently serves to confront and challenge the tall claims with the rude realities of India's sorry human development performance in the very midst of its much-touted economic success story. Undeniably, in the very phase when the Manmohan Singh Government is boasting of high growth rates, India's performance in terms of providing the basics required for a life of dignity continued to slide steeply.

India has been listed as one among 88 countries where people live with hungry. In the Global Hunger Index 2008, India occupied 66th position out of 88 countries listed by International Food Policy Research Institute, Washington, USA. It has stated that more than 200 million people in India facing hunger. According to the latest Human Development Index that was released globally on 5th October 2009 India ranks 134th out of 182 countries in the world, with the Human

Development Index (HDI) estimated at .612 based on 2007 data in terms of a long and healthy life, access to knowledge and a decent standard of living to its citizens. The Human Poverty Index (HPI-), focusing on the proportion of people below certain threshold levels in each of the dimensions of the HDI, is estimated at 28 per cent of Indians are living below the poverty line and placing the country in the 88th slot among 135 countries for which the index has been calculated.

Kevin Watkins, an Oxford academic, who edited the UN's human development report, has stated that despite growing prosperity brought on by a sustained boom, child malnourishment in India is higher than in Ethiopia and well above the African average of 28%. "India dominates the world hunger league,". "Economists like to debate the factors behind India's spectacular take-off. Perhaps they should be asking how a country can grow so fast with such a limited impact on child hunger." "I have no hesitation in saying that I do not envy China," "I want to emulate China. I want India to become an economic power, an economic superpower." When it comes to economic growth, India is a long way ahead of Bangladesh but when it comes to child survival rates, it lags behind. Bangladesh has been cutting child deaths at a rate some 50% higher than in India". Both Bangladesh and Nepal are far poorer than India, but India has a higher child death rate than either (Kathryn Hopkins, 2008).

For some time now, the Millennium Development Goals (MDGs) have been the organising framework for the activities of international organisations and donor agencies. The Millennium Development Goals are eight international development goals to be achieved by 2015 that respond to the world's main development challenges. The MDGs are drawn from the actions and targets contained in the Millennium Declaration that was adopted by 189 nations-and signed by 147 heads of state and governments during the UN Millennium Summit in September 2000. All 192 United nations Member States and at least 23 international organizations have agreed to achieve by the year 2015. In 2001, recognizing the need to assist impoverished nations more aggressively, UN member states adopted the targets. The MDGs aim to spur development by improving social and economic conditions in the world's poorest countries.

The eight MDGs break down into 21 quantifiable targets that are measured by 60 indicators.

- Goal 1: Eradicate extreme poverty and hunger
- Goal 2: Achieve universal primary education
- Goal 3: Promote gender equality and empower women
- Goal 4: Reduce child mortality
- Goal 5: Improve maternal health
- Goal 6: Combat HIV/AIDS, malaria and other diseases
- Goal 7: Ensure environmental sustainability
- Goal 8: Develop a Global Partnership for Development

United Nations Secretary General Ban Ki-moon has stated the world's main development challenges and to the calls of civil society, the MDGs promote poverty reduction, education, maternal health, gender equality, and aim at combating child mortality, AIDS and other diseases. Set for the year 2015, the MDGs are an agreed set of goals that can be achieved if all actors work together and do their part. Poor countries have pledged to govern better, and invest in their people through health care and education. Rich countries have pledged to support them, through aid, debt relief, and fairer trade. UNDP is working with a wide range of partners to help create coalitions for change to support the goals at global, regional and national levels, to benchmark progress towards them, and to help countries to build the institutional capacity, policies and programmes needed to achieve the MDGs particularly poverty.

In India, the first official definition of poverty was given in 1962. This pegged the rural poverty line at a monthly family income of Rs. 100 and the urban one at Rs. 125. In 1971, V.M.Dandekar and Nilkanth Rath used a different measure to estimate poverty. They used an average calorie norm of 2250 calories per capita per day for both rural and urban areas as a criterion to define the poverty line. The current poverty line was fixed in 1979, when a Planning Commission talk force defined the poverty line as the per capita expenditure level at which the average per capita calorie intake was 2400 and 2100 calories for rural and urban areas respectively. Different levels of calorie intake were fixed for rural and urban areas taking into consideration the fact that the calorie requirement in rural areas, where more people were engaged in manual labour, was more than in urban areas.

Nothing is easier than to recognise a poor person when you see him or her. Yet the task of identifying and counting the poor seems to elude the country's best experts. Take for instance the "headcount" of rural poverty – the proportion of the rural population below the poverty line. At least four alternative figures are available: 28 per cent from the Planning Commission, 50 per cent from the N.C. Saxena Committee report, 42 per cent from the Tendulkar Committee report, and 80 per cent or so from the National Commission for Enterprises in the Unorganised Sector (NCEUS) (Jean Drèze,2010).

The National Sample Survey Organization (NSSO) has used Monthly Per capita Consumption Expenditure (MPCE) to estimate what proportion of the population is poor. The MPCE Survey of NSSO divided the entire population into 11 expenditure classes. The calorie content of consumption baskets of each of these 11 MPCE classes was calculated. Then the money equivalent for the minimum calorie norm was ow3ked out and it was found that in 1973-74 the average amount of money needed to fulfill the basic calorie norm was Rs. 45.09 per capital for urban and Rs. 56.64 per capital for rural families. But the actual poverty lines would vary from state to state. The planning commission has been estimating the BPL population from MPE surveys conducted every five years. While the poverty line is defined in per capita terms, families and not individuals are identified as poor. The present poverty line based on the NSSOs 61st round survey done in 2004-05 is Rs. 356.30 capita for rural families and Rs. 538.60 per capita for urban families. In 2004-05, 28.3 per cent of rural and 27.5 per cent of urban families were estimated to be living below these poverty lines in India. The Planning Commission of India uses its own criteria and has estimated that 27.5% of the population was living below the poverty line in 2004–2005, down from 51.3% in 1977–1978, and 36% in 1993-1994.

According to the new World Bank's estimates on poverty based on 2005 data, India has 456 million people, 41.6% of its population, living below the new international poverty line of $1.25 (PPP) per day. The World Bank further estimates that 33% of the global poor now reside in India.

POVERTY REDUCTION TRENDS

South Asia is home to the largest number of poor in the world, and India accounts for the largest percentage of the region's share. The long-term performance of the Indian economy with respect to poverty reduction has been mixed, with poverty actually increasing in the first two decades after India became independent in 1947. However, there has been a sustained reduction in poverty since the 1970s.

The proportion of India's population below the poverty line has fluctuated widely in the past, but the overall trend has been downward. However, there have been roughly three periods of trends in income poverty.

1950 to mid-1970s: Income poverty reduction shows no discernible trend. In 1951, 47% of India's rural population was below the poverty line. The proportion went up to 64% in 1954-55; it came down to 45% in 1960-61 but in 1977-78, it went up again to 51%.

Mid-1970s to 1990: Income poverty declined significantly between the mid-1970s and the end of the 1980s. The decline was more pronounced between 1977-78 and 1986-87, with rural income poverty declining from 51% to 39%. It went down further to 34% by 1989-90. Urban income poverty went down from 41% in 1977-78 to 34% in 1986-87, and further to 33% in 1989-90.

After 1991: This post-economic reform period evidenced both setbacks and progress. Rural income poverty increased from 34% in 1989-90 to 43% in 1992 and then fell to 37% in 1993-94. Urban income poverty went up from 33.4% in 1989-90 to 33.7% in 1992 and declined to 32% in 1993-94 Also, NSS data for 1994-95 to 1998 show little or no poverty reduction, so that the evidence till 1999-2000 was that poverty, particularly rural poverty, had increased post-reform. However, the official estimate of poverty for 1999-2000 was 26.1%, a dramatic decline that led to much debate and analysis. This was because for this year the NSS had adopted a new survey methodology that led to both higher estimated mean consumption and also an estimated distribution that was more equal than in past NSS surveys. The latest NSS survey for 2004-05 is fully comparable to the surveys before 1999-2000 and shows poverty at 28.3% in rural areas, 25.7% in urban areas and 27.5% for the country as a whole, using Uniform Recall Period Consumption. The corresponding figures using the Mixed Recall Period Consumption method was 21.8%, 21.7% and 21.8% respectively. Thus, poverty has declined after 1998, although it is still being debated whether there was any significant poverty reduction between 1989-90 and 1999-00. The latest NSS survey was so designed as to also give estimates roughly, but not fully, comparable to the 1999-2000 survey. These suggest that most of the decline in rural poverty over the period during 1993-94 to 2004-05 actually occurred after 1999-2000.

In summary, the official poverty rates recorded by NSS are:

Year	*Round*	*Poverty Rate (%)*	*Poverty Reduction per year (%)*
1977-78	32	51.3	
1983	38	44.5	1.3
1987-88	43	38.9	1.2
1993-94	50	36.0	0.5
1999-00	55	26.9	7.4
2004-05	61	27.5	0.8

Source: http://en.wikipedia.org/wiki/Poverty_in_India

India remains the epicenter of poverty, both within South Asia and in the world, with as many as 259 million people below the national poverty line. In terms of the international poverty line of USD 1 per day (measured at 1993 purchasing power parity exchange rates), there are 358 million poor in India. If instead we use the norm of USD 2 per day, almost 80 percent of India's vast population is below poverty line, (World Bank (2003))

In 2005, one in three of the people in the world who consumed less than $ 1.25 a day (at 2005 purchasing power parity) lived in India–more than any other country. They accounted for about 40 per cent of India's population. Twenty-five years earlier, 60 per cent of India's population lived below the same real line. While this is clear progress, India's long-term pace of poverty reduction by this measure is no more than average for the developing world, excluding China OF the various measures devised to measure the incidence, depth and severity of poverty, the index most often quoted is the "head-count index". Unfortunately, changes in the methodology adopted by the NSS Expenditure Surveys prior to 1972-73 make estimates of the head-count index during the earlier years non-comparable.

However, allowing for this inadequacy, it appears that the following broad conclusions can be arrived at: first, that the incidence of poverty declined between the mid-1950s and early 1960s; second, that starting with the bad harvests of the mid-1960s we see a sharp rise in the incidence of poverty which touched a post-Independence peak by the late 1960s; third, that starting then and especially after 1975, India had witnessed a significant decline in poverty incidence till 1989-90; and finally, that the years of stabilization and structural adjustment have witnessed an initial sharp rise in poverty till 1992 and a subsequent decline in 1993-94, but that the 1993-94 figure appears higher than in 1989-90, pointing to a reversal of the earlier declining trend. An agricultural worker in Salegaon village, Orissa. Barring Kerala and West Bengal, no State in India has implemented radical land reform.

The literature examining the determinants of these poverty trends has identified three factors: first, agricultural output growth, leading to a rise in agricultural value added per head of the rural population and contributing to an increase in wages; second, price movements, especially movements in the price of food, which determine the value of the inflation-adjusted earnings of the poor; finally, government expenditure, which by directly and indirectly expanding non-agricultural employment, provides an impetus to a rise in money wages. While all three factors played a role in explaining the rise or decline in poverty incidence during different time periods, the relative significance of each and their directional effect varied across time. It has been argued that the decline in poverty incidence during the 1950s was due more to the stability of food prices (ensured in large part with PL 480 imports) and the rise in government expenditure. Inflation and a cutback in government expenditure after the mid-1960s contributed to the subsequent rise in poverty. However, the decline in poverty incidence after the mid-1970s appears to be attributable more to agricultural output growth and increases in state expenditure.

There is broad agreement on these trends and their determinants among economists in India today. However, disagreement increases as the focus of attention shifts to the years of economic reform. The disagreement on trends in poverty is based on the data set chosen. The most quoted estimates of poverty in India are based on data yielded by the "extensive" Household Consumer Expenditure Surveys, which since 1972-73 have been conducted once every five years. The two most recent surveys relate to 1987-88 and 1993-94. However, since 1986-87, the Government has revived an earlier practice of conducting consumer expenditure surveys on a more regular basis, with such surveys being available annually since 1988-89. The difference between these 'annual' surveys and the 'quinquennial' surveys is that the former are characterised by much smaller sample sizes. A smaller sample implies that the certainty with which the poverty ratio can be precisely identified tends to be lower purely because the range within which the actual poverty ratio can be estimated to lie tends to be larger than that for estimates based on bigger samples. Nonetheless, these estimates are of considerable value.

Disregarding this statistical truth, the Government, supported by sections of the media, has been claiming that the so-called 'thin' samples which the National Sample Survey Organisation (NSSO) surveys at substantial cost in the years between its larger quinquennial exercises should now be completely disregarded. The reason for this insistence is not hard to decipher. Using those annual surveys, economists have found that the poverty ratio had risen quite sharply during the early years of liberalisation. For example, even World Bank economists have indicated in a recent study (India: Achievements and Challenges in Reducing Poverty, World Bank, May 27, 1997) that based on the Planning Commission's poverty line (Rs. 49.09 and Rs. 56.64 at 1973-74 prices in rural and urban areas respectively), the poverty ratio which declined from 39.23 per cent in rural India and 36.60 per cent in urban India in 1987-88 to 36.43 and 32.76 per cent respectively in 1990-91, subsequently rose to 37.42 and 33.23 per cent in 1991 and 43.47 per cent and 33.73 per cent in 1992.

The massive increase in rural India suggests that even allowing for the greater variance associated with thin samples, poverty did increase in the early reform years. Further, even though the incidence of poverty fell in 1993-94 to 36.66 and 30.51 per cent, the figure for rural India is still higher than in 1990-91 (36.43 per cent) and 1989-90 (34.30 per cent). Not happy with that trend, the Government has decided to disregard the thin samples.

If we do include the thin samples in the analysis, the main conclusions that follow are: First, the rural poverty ratio at the all-India level, and in most States, fell sharply between 1973-74 and 1986-87 with subsequent years showing no clear trend in either direction. Thus if the liberalisation of the economy is dated back to the mid-1980s, the entire period since then is characterized by a slowdown in the pace of poverty reduction. Second, there was a marked increase in rural poverty in 1992 as compared with either 1989-90 or 1990-91. This was true of almost every State except Kerala where poverty fell continuously. At the all-India level, the number of poor increased by over 60 million between 1990-91 and 1992, or in the first 18 months of the reform period. Third, there was an appreciable moderation in poverty between 1992 and 1993-94 in both absolute and proportionate terms. Nonetheless, as compared with 1989-90, the rural poverty ratio was higher (36.7 as compared with 34.3 per cent) in 1993-94.

The 2005 ICP updates PPP rates last calculated in 1993 to produce an international poverty line of $ 1.25 a day. According to this, the proportion of the world's population living in poverty has fallen by approximately one percent a year since 1990. At this rate, it is unlikely that the developing world outside China will reach the MDG poverty goal. In this context, the article estimates India's poverty according to both the $ 1.25 a day international poverty line and India's national poverty line of $ 1.00 a day (at 2005 PPP) to find that: 42 percent of the population were living below $ 1.25 in 2005 (24 percent below $ 1.00) as compared to 60 percent twenty-five years ago (42 percent below $ 1.00) the number of people living below $ 1.25 rose from 421 to 456 million during 1981-2005 the number of people living in the 25 cent interval between $ 1.00 and $ 1.25 rose from 124 million to 189 million during 1981-2005 India's overall rate of poverty reduction during 1981-2005 according to both poverty lines was lower than the average for the developing world. India's share of poverty in the developing world outside China fell by just one percent since 1981 India's trend rate of poverty reduction during 1981-2005 according to both poverty lines is not sufficient to achieve MDG1-particularly in the context of rising food and fuel prices.

Biased estimates of poverty have been corrected by a clever idea, says Kaushik Basu, Professor of Economics at Cornell University. There is an old story of Stalin visiting a school in Moscow and asking the clever kid, Boris, "Who killed Julius Caesar?" Boris burst out crying, "Not me sir". A furious Stalin met the teacher and asked him to explain. The teacher, trembling, said, "Sir, I have now looked into the matter and can confirm that, incredible though it may seem, Boris did not kill Julius Caesar." An exasperated Stalin called on the headmaster. But the headmaster's response was the same. Boris had not done it. And this continued—the same question being asked of different authorities and the same answer. Finally, Stalin sent for the KGB chief and asked him to look into the matter. The following day, the chief returned to say, "Sir, the KGB has solved the problem. The boy has confessed." Has India's poverty as measured by the percentage of people living below the poverty line, gone down during the 1990s?

Baldev Raj Nayar, emeritus professor of political science at McGill University, counters critics who suggest that globalization has increased instability or poverty. By opening the door to multinational firms, India strengthened and diversified the country's economy. He admits that poverty is still a fact of life in India and that most benefits of globalization have gone to the top 20 percent of the population. India's macroeconomic performance from 1991 has in many respects been remarkable. Since the early 1990s, India has been among the fastest growing economies in the world, inflation has been relatively well contained, and the balance of payments has been maintained at comfortable levels. India's economic strength during the early and mid-1990s can be ascribed to the broad-ranging fiscal and structural reforms undertaken following the 1991 balance of payments crisis. These included reforms to the tax system, substantial cuts in the deficit of the consolidated public sector, liberalization and deregulation in the industrial sector, trade and tariff reforms, and measures to recapitalize and strengthen the supervision of banks and other financial intermediaries. Despite the gains in the area of poverty reduction since Independence – the poverty rate has fallen by over 20 percentage points since the 1950s and 1960s – roughly 35 percent of the population still remains below the poverty line. Moreover, poverty statistics during the 1990s generally stagnated or, in some cases, worsened, and per capita income in India still lags well behind that in other fast-growing Asian economies. Notably, rural poverty rates have tended to increase and the regional distribution of income has become more stratified. This has reflected both weak fiscal disciplines, constraining public development spending, and slowing structural reform, concentrating growth in the less-regulated services sector, which have left little scope for income gains for lower-skilled agricultural and industrial workers.

In key indicators used to calculate the human poverty index, India registers declining performance. The Human Poverty Index (HPI) has seen a steep decline from 62nd place among 155 countries in the last HDR. Confirming the findings of the National Commission for Enterprises in the Unorganized Sector (NCEUS) report headed by Arjun Sengupta, the HDR 2009 tells us that 41.6% of India's population earns below $ 1.25 a day, and 75.6% earns below $ 2 a day - a very different picture of poverty than that painted by the official estimate of 28.6% below the National Poverty Line. In the gender development index (GDI), India ranks 114 out of 155 countries. a staggering 46% of the country's children under 5 years of age are underweight. On this count, the "mighty" India (alongside Yemen and Timor Leste) ranks second only to Bangladesh at 48% - behind even the countries like Afghanistan (39%) and Niger (44%) which are otherwise at the bottom of the HDI ladder.

Dr. NC Saxena, Commissioner appointed by the Supreme Court, has stated that half the country's population of 1.15 billion is below the poverty line, which he apparently defines as a monthly per capita income of Rs 700 in rural areas and Rs 1,000 in urban areas. While a Planning Commission estimate puts the number of below poverty line (BPL) families at 62.5 million, state governments estimate that this number is closer to 107 million. Some experts feel that availing the public with more number of BPL ration cards help the state-level politicians to win elections through populist means. The World Bank's figure for the percentage of population below the poverty line in India is 42 per cent, based on 2005 data. The World Development Report 2008-Agriculture for Development, which has been brought out by the World Bank mentions that India presently faces the problem of depleting ground water level that makes agriculture unsustainable and poses risk to environment (Food Security Bill, 2009).

A number of emerging economies have encountered nutrition challenges similar to those currently facing India. For example, China reduced child undernutrition by more than half (from 25 per cent to 8 per cent) between 1990 and 2002;

Brazil reduced child undernutrition by 60 per cent (from 18 per cent to 7 per cent) from 1975 to 1989; Thailand reduced child undernutrition by half (from 50 per cent to 25 per cent) in less than a decade (1982-1986); and Viet Nam reduced child undernutrition by 40 per cent (from 45 per cent to 27 per cent) between 1990 and 2006. Four lessons can be learned from these countries' experiences: 1) Leadership at the highest level to ensure that priority is given to child nutrition outcomes across sectors and states, with large investments in nutrition interventions and successful poverty alleviation strategies. 2) Targeted nutrition interventions to prevent mild and moderate undernutrition and treat severe undernutrition as part of a continuum of care for children, particularly among the most vulnerable children: the youngest, the poorest, and the socially-excluded; 3) Reliance on community-based primary health care to ensure high coverage through community-based frontline workers; 4) Strong supervision, monitoring, evaluation, and knowledge management to provide the evidence base for timely and effective policy, programme and budgetary action. (Karin Hulshof, 2009)

In 'Incredible India', which sports a growth in GDP of 8 to 9 per cent, what is incredible is that it ranks 66th in a list of 88 countries on the World Hunger Index; almost 50 per cent of its children suffer from malnourishment and 75 per cent of its women from anaemia. Foodgrain-availability in rural India has fallen to 152 kg per capita, 23 kg less than in the 1990s, creating large-scale food insecurity in India's villages. The poorest 30 per cent of Indian households eat less than 1,700 kilo calories per day, per person, well below the international minimum standard of 2,100 kilo calories per day, even if they spend 70 per cent of their income on food. These are some of the findings of United Nations Special Rapporteur on the Right to Food submitted to the United Nations Human Rights Council in Geneva on September 22 by Jean Ziegler on "The Extent of Chronic Hunger and Malnutrition in India". He stated that falling agricultural wages, increasing landlessness and rising food prices have severely undermined the right to food in rural India.

Per capita foodgrain consumption in India declined from 476 grams per day in 1990 to only 418 grams per day in 2001. Aggregate calorific consumption per capita declined from just over 2,200 calories per day in 1987-88 to about 2,150 in 1999-2000, according to National Sample Survey data. Nutritional deficiencies remain huge - at least half the children in India (and possibly more in Pakistan) are born with protein deficiency. Anaemia and iron deficiency are also widespread and continue to be severe problems. Ironically, cultivators are suffering from the increase in food insecurity just as much as or even more than other groups. This is probably the most significant cause of the continued prevalence of widespread malnourishment. The macroeconomic causes of livelihood insecurity arise primarily from the effects of deregulating the market and reducing State expenditure-processes that have marked the last decade-and-a-half across South Asia. Land reforms and more equal property distribution remains the key to solving the structural problem of hunger. The more transient or temporary instances of hunger must also be dealt with through macroeconomic policies that firmly commit the government to a much greater degree of involvement, investment and regulation (Jayati Ghoshhttp,2006).

Food-for-education programme: To achieve cent per cent literacy, the food security need can be productively linked to increased enrolment in schools. With the phasing out of PDS, food coupons may be issued to poor people depending on their entitlement. Modified food-for-work scheme/ direct subsidies: With rationalization of input subsidies and MSP, the Central Government will be left with sufficient funds, which may be given as grants to each State depending on the number of poor. The State government will in turn distribute the grants to the village bodies, which can decide on the list of essential infrastructure, work the village needs and allow every needy villager to contribute through his labour and get paid in food coupons and cash. Community grain storage banks: The FCI can be gradually dismantled and procurement decentralised through the creation of foodgrain banks in each block/ village of the district, from which people may get subsidized foodgrains against food coupons. The food coupons can be numbered serially to avoid frauds. The grain storage facilities can be created within two years under the existing rural development schemes and the initial lot of grains can come from the existing FCI stocks. If culturally acceptable, the possibility of relatively cheap coarse grains, like bajara and ragi and nutritional grains like millets and pulses meeting the nutritional needs of the people can also be explored. This will not only enlarge the food basket but also prevent such locally adapted grains from becoming extinct. The community can be authorised to manage the food banks. This decentralised management will improve the delivery of entitlements, reduce handling and transport costs and eliminate corruption, thereby bringing down the issue price substantially. To enforce efficiency in grain banks operation, people can also be given an option to obtain foodgrains against food coupons from the open market, if the rates in the grain banks are higher, quality is poor or services are deficient. A fund can be set up to reimburse the food retailers for the presented coupons. This competition will lead to constant improvement and lower prices. It must also be mandatory to maintain a small buffer stock at the State level, to deal with exigencies. Eradicate extreme poverty and hunger. Target: Halve between 1990 and 2015, the proportion of people whose income is less than $1 a day. If all food produced worldwide were distributed equally, every person would be able to consume 2,760 calories a day (hunger defined as consuming less than 1,960 calories). India is home to the largest number of hungry people, 233 million, whereas Sub Saharan Africa has 183 million, China 119 million. The largest reductions have been in China.

Poverty reduction—and its eventual elimination—has been one of the major goals of development policy in India since Independence. Several poverty alleviation programmes have been in place for a long time now. There are numerous centrally-sponsored schemes (CSS), designed by the Centre, administered by the Ministry of Rural Development, but implemented by the States, with the States generally contributing 25 per cent to the cost. Though there has been some reduction in the percentage of people below the poverty line since the 1970s, the problem still remains formidable with over 260 million people living below the poverty line. In fact, going by the World Bank's new yardstick to measure global poverty adopted last year, the number of people living on $1.25 per day (instead of the earlier $1 per day yardstick), India had 455 million people living below the poverty line in 2005. An overwhelming majority of the poor are in rural areas and continue to depend on agriculture for want of any other livelihood opportunities outside the sector. About 52 per cent of the country's workforce and over 60 per cent of the population depends of agriculture which now accounts for just 17 per cent of the country's GDP, thus perpetuating rural poverty and widening the rural-urban divide. The major weaknesses of the plethora of poverty alleviation programmes launched over the years have been the overlapping of schemes, thin spread of resources over a wide area, inadequate preparatory work before their launch, lack of proper co-ordination between the Central and State governments, inadequate funding by banks, paucity of trained staff at the ground level and poor governance and delivery resulting in widespread leakages and corruption. Apart from wage employment and nutrition programmes, and public distribution system, the accent over the past two decades has been on self-employment programmes to reduce rural poverty. The idea was to provide alternative livelihood opportunities to the surplus labour force that is forced to depend on agriculture. Self-employment programmes launched over the years have not been able to empower beneficiaries in the true sense of the term by enabling them to earn an income sufficient to lift them out of poverty.

Success of any sustainable Poverty alleviation Programme is based on increasing productive employment opportunities along with growth. The focus of Government of India relates to providing employment guarantee of 100 days of wage employment to every rural household, whose adult member(s) are willing to do unskilled manual work. Accordingly, the Parliament has passed the historic National Rural Employment

Guarantee Act (NREGA) in the year 2005 that guarantees 100 days of wage employment in a year, to every rural household. This act was introduced with an aim of improving the purchasing power of the rural people, primarily semi or un-skilled work to people living in rural India, whether or not they are below the poverty line. The Government of India has renamed the National Rural Employment Guarantee Act (NREGA) as the Mahatma Gandhi National Rural Employment Guarantee Act. Prime Minister Manmohan Singh announced while addressing a meeting held to celebrate the Golden Jubilee the Panchayati Raj in October 2, 2009. The NREGA bill essentially guarantees employment for the unemployed through work such as building roads, improving water supply and works that are necessary to improve infrastructure in rural areas. The uniqueness of this bill is in the fact that it carries emphasis on issues like equality of wages for men and women, elimination of work contracting/middlemen, payment of wages only through bank and post office accounts to prevent corruption, creating transparency in workers muster rolls etc. Any individual, irrespective of his socio-economic status can ask for employment either in writing or verbally with the Gram Panchayat. The act guarantees that if work is not provided within a 15 day time frame including the eligibility verification and issuing of the job cards then the applicant is eligible for unemployment allowance. Work to be done is decided by the Gram Panchayat. Emphasis is given to unskilled manual labor focusing on building roads and other public village infrastructural facilities, water conservation, afforestation, land development & drought proofing. All adults in a house hold are eligible to work. If the work site is not within 5 kilometers from the applicant's residence then the applicant is eligible for an additional 10% of the wage. This law can be a big boost for nomadic tribal communities since locally domiciled but migrant population is also eligible for employment.

NATIONAL RURAL EMPLOYMENT GUARANTEE ACT

The Act came into force on February 2, 2006 and was implemented in a phased manner. In Phase one it was introduced in 200 of the most backward districts of the country.

It was implemented in an additional 330 districts in Phase two 2007-2008. The remaining 266 districts were notified on September 28, 2008, and the scheme has now been extended to all the districts of the country. More than 4.47 crore households were provided employment in 20080-09. This is a significant jump over the 3.39 crore households covered under the scheme during 2007-08. Out of the 215. 63 crore person days created under the scheme during this period, 29 per cent and 25 per cent were in favour of SC and ST population respectively and 48 per cent of the total persons days created went in favour of women. An allocation of Rs. 30100 crore has been made in the interim budget for 2009-10 as against 16, 000 crore in 2008-09 for NREGS. As per the initial target, NREGA was to be expanded countrywide in five years. However, in order to bring the whole nation under its safety net and keeping in view the demand, the Scheme was extended to the remaining 274 rural districts of India from April 1, 2008 in Phase III. The Central government outlay for scheme is Rs. 39,100 crores ($8 billion) in FY 2009-10.. Around one-third of the stipulated work force is women. The government is planning to open a call center, which upon becoming operational can be approached on the toll-free number, 1800-345-22-44. It was initially called the National Rural Employment Guarantee Act (NREGA) but was renamed on 2 October, 2009. Few laws have had such stimulating economic, social and political impact so soon in India as the National Rural Employment Guarantee Act, 2005 – since renamed Mahatma Gandhi Rural Employment Guarantee Act. Think of the guaranteed employment to 4.47 crore rural households; additional income flowing to wage earners' hamlets to the tune of Rs.18, 155 crores; S.C., ST and women workers far out-numbering other sections of workers; 31.2 million poor families opening accounts in banks, post offices.

SALIENT FEATURES OF THE ACT

- Adult members of a rural household, willing to do unskilled manual work, may apply for registration in writing or orally to the local Gram Panchayat

- The Gram Panchayat after due verification will issue a Job Card. The Job Card will bear the photograph of all adult members of the household willing to work under NREGA and is free of cost.
- The Job Card should be issued within 15 days of application.
- A Job Card holder may submit a written application for employment to the Gram Panchayat, stating the time and duration for which work is sought. The minimum days of employment have to be at least fourteen.
- The Gram Panchayat will issue a dated receipt of the written application for employment, against which the guarantee of providing employment within 15 days operates.
- Employment will be given within 15 days of application for work, if it is not then daily unemployment allowance as per the Act, has to be paid liability of payment of unemployment allowance is of the States.
- Work should ordinarily be provided within 5 km radius of the village. In case work is provided beyond 5 km, extra wages of 10% are payable to meet additional transportation and living expenses.
- Wages are to be paid according to the Minimum Wages Act 1948 for agricultural laborers in the State, unless the Centre notifies a wage rate which will not be less than Rs. 60/per day. Equal wages will be provided to both men and women.
- Wages are to be paid according to piece rate or daily rate. Disbursement of wages has to be done on weekly basis and not beyond a fortnight in any case.
- At least one-third beneficiaries shall be women who have registered and requested work under the scheme.
- Work site facilities such as crèche, drinking water, shade have to be provided.
- The shelf of projects for a village will be recommended by the gram sabha and approved by the zilla panchayat.

- At least 50% of works will be allotted to Gram Panchayats for execution.
- Permissible works predominantly include water and soil conservation, forestation and land development works.
- A 60:40 wage and material ratio has to be maintained. No contractors and machinery is allowed.
- The Central Government bears the 100 percent wage cost of unskilled manual labor and 75 percent of the material cost including the wages of skilled and semi skilled workers
- Social Audit has to be done by the Gram Sabha
- Grievance redressal mechanisms have to be put in place for ensuring a responsive implementation process.
- All accounts and records relating to the Scheme should be available for public scrutiny.

NREGA marks a paradigm shift from all precedent wage employment programmes. The significant aspects of this paradigm shift are captured below:

- NREGA provides a statutory guarantee of wage employment.
- It provides a rights-based framework for wage employment. Employment is dependent upon the worker exercising the choice to apply for registration, obtain a Job Card, and seek employment for the time and duration that the worker wants.
- There is a 15 day time limit for fulfilling the legal guarantee of providing employment.
- The legal mandate of providing employment in a time bound manner is underpinned by the provision of Unemployment Allowance.
- The Act is designed to offer an incentive structure to the States for providing employment as ninety percent of the cost for employment provided is borne by the Centre. There is a concomitant disincentive for not providing employment as the States then bear the

double indemnity of unemployment and the cost of unemployment allowance.

- Unlike the earlier wage employment programmes that were allocation based. NREGA is demand driven. Resource transfer under NREGA is based on the demand for employment and this provides another critical incentive to States to leverage the Act to meet the employment needs of the poor.
- NREGA has extensive inbuilt transparency safeguards
  - (a) *Documents:* Job Cards recording entitlements (in the custody of workers) written application for employment, Muster Rolls, Measurement Books and Asset Registers
  - (b) *Processes:* Acceptance of employment application, issue of dated receipts, time bound work allocation and wage payment, Citizen Information Boards at worksites, Vigilance Monitoring Committees, regular block, district and state level inspections and social audits
- The public delivery system has been made accountable, as it envisages an Annual Report on the outcomes of NREGA to be presented by the Central Government to the Parliament and to the Legislature by the State Government. Specifically personnel responsible for implementing the Act have been made legally responsible for delivering the guarantee under the Act.

Under Section 4 of the Act the Scheme to be formulated by the State Government will conform to the legally non-negotiable parameters laid down in Schedules I and II of the Act. In addition, the Schemes will conform to the operational parameters delineated in the Guidelines. The Scheme so formulated will be called the National Rural Employment Guarantee Scheme (NREGS), followed by the name of the State. The National level name and logo is mandatory. This logo will be used for all IEC materials and activities. The Scheme will be implemented as a Centrally Sponsored Scheme on a cost-sharing basis between the Centre and the States as determined by the Act.

NREGA is the first ever law internationally, that guarantees wage employment at an unprecedented scale. The primary objective of the Act is augmenting wage employment. Its auxiliary objective is strengthening natural resource management through works that address causes of chronic poverty like drought, deforestation and soil erosion and so encourage sustainable development. The process outcomes include strengthening grassroots processes of democracy and infusing transparency and accountability in governance.

With its rights-based framework and demand driven approach, NREGA marks a paradigm shift from the previous wage programmes. The Act is also a significant vehicle for strengthening decentralization and deepening processes of democracy by giving a pivotal role to the Panchayati Raj Institutions in planning, monitoring and implementation. Unique features of the ACT include, time bound employment guarantee and wage payment within 15 days, incentive-disincentive structure to the State Governments for providing employment as 90 per cent of the cost for employment provided is borne by the Centre or payment of unemployment allowance at their own cost and emphasis on labour intensive works prohibiting the use of contractors and machinery. The Act also mandates 33 percent participation for women. Over the last two years, implementation trends vindicate the basic objective of the Act.

Increasing Employment Opportunities: In 2007-08, 3.39 crore households were provided employment and 143.5 crore person days were generated in 330 districts. In 2008-2009, upto July, 253 crore households have been provided employment and 85.29 crore person days have been generated.

Enhancing Wage Earning and Impact on Minimum Wage: The enhanced wage earnings have lead to strengthening of the livelihood resource base of the rural poor in India; in 2007-2008, more than 68% of funds utilised were in the form of wages paid to the labourers. In 2008-2009, 73% of the funds have been utilized in the form of wages.

Increasing Outreach to the Poor: Self targeting in nature, the Programme has high works participation of marginalized groups like SC/ST (57%), women (43%) in 2007-2008. In 2008-2009, upto July, the participation is SC/ST (54%) and women (49%), strengthening Natural Resource Base of Rural India: In 2007-08, 17.88 lakh works have been undertaken, of which 49% were related to water conservation. In 2008-2009, upto July, 16.88 lakh works have been undertaken, of which 49% are related to water conservation.

Financial Inclusion of the Poor: The Central government has been encouraging the state governments to make wage payment through bank and post office accounts of wage seekers. Thus far, 2.9 crore (upto July '08) NREGA bank and post office accounts have been opened to disburse wages. The Ministry is also encouraging the NREGP workers to obtain insurance under Jan Shri Bima Yojana.

Initial evidence through independent studies indicates enhancement of agricultural productivity (through water harvesting, check dams, ground water recharging, improve moisture content, check in soil erosion and micro-irrigation), stemming of distress migration, increased access to markets and services through rural connectivity works, supplementing household incomes, Increase in women workforce participation ratios and the regeneration of natural resources.

The vision of the Ministry is enabling NREGA become a transformative vehicle of empowering local communities to enhance their livelihood security. The Ministry has taken several steps to ensure the Scheme is implemented effectively like encouraging decentralized participatory management, improving delivery systems and public accountability.

The Rozgar Jagrookta Puruskar award has been introduced to recognize outstanding Contributions by Civil society Organizations at State, District, Block and Gram Panchayat levels to generate awareness about provisions and entitlements and ensuring compliance with implementing processes.

To strengthen the capacity and give priority to the competencies required for effective planning, work execution, public disclosure and social audits the Ministry has been conducting training for NREGA functionaries, Thus far, 6.2 lakh PRI functionaries and 4.82 lakh vigilance and monitoring committees have been trained (upto July'08). The Central Government is also providing technical support in key areas of communication, training, work planning, IT, social audits and fund management at all levels of implementation to the state governments.

Web enabled Management Information System (MIS) is one of the largest data base rural households through their engagement in NREGP MIS places all critical parameters such as shelf of projects, sanctioned works, wage payments, number of days of employment provided and works under execution on line for easy public access. The data engineered software has been designed for cross verification of records and generation of alerts to support proactive response by management.

Monitoring and Evaluation: The Ministry has set up a comprehensive monitoring system. Around 260 National Level Monitors and Area Officers have undertaken field visits to each of the 330 Phase I and Phase II districts at least once. For effective monitoring of the projects 100% verification of the works at the Block level, 10% at the District level and 2% at the State level inspections need to be ensured.

Setting up of the Task force on Convergence: In order to optimize the multiplier effects of NREGP the Ministry has set up a Task Force to look at the possibility of convergence of programmes like National Horticulture Mission, Rashtriya Krishi Vikas Yojana, Bharat Nirman, and Watershed Development with NREGA. These convergence efforts will add value to NREGA, works and aid in creating durable efforts and also enable planned and coordinated public investments in rural areas. As Watkins has stated that government of India needs to become seriously committed to more equitable growth, strengthened provision of public services in health and action to tackle disparities based on gender, wealth and caste.

The National Rural Employment Guarantee Scheme (2005) differs from the other poverty alleviation measures in two significant respects. Where most welfare programmes cast the state in the role of benefactor offering handouts to the poor, the NREGS is built around notions of citizenship and entitlement. Secondly, the NREGS also facilitates disclosure by means of regular social audits. These audits, mandated to be done by the Gram Sabhas, are intended to identify and plug pilferage and corruption, which in turn, helps build awareness and confidence in beneficiaries who learn, over time, to become vigilant and assertive. Institutionalised social audits are vital if a programme of the dimensions of the NREGS is to succeed, and as much was the objective of a sample 10-day social audit conducted recently in Bhilwara by the Aruna Roy-led Mazdoor Kisan Shakti Sanghatan in close collaboration with the Rajasthan government. Over a fortnight, social auditors, fully backed by government machinery, minutely examined NREGS documents like job cards, muster rolls, and technical and financial sanctions and interacted with thousands of beneficiaries.

The Bhilwara social audit exposed irregularities; indeed it underscored the NREGS's susceptibility to corruption. Yet significantly, it also provided the answer to the problem. There can be no better certificate for the audit than the resistance it faced from the panchayat staff who obviously feared being held to account. The sarpanchs (village heads) sat in dharna, made their displeasure public at the 'jan sunwais' (public hearings), and demanded that they be spared punishment for wrongdoings. That the demand was backed by a Minister from the Rajasthan government points to the difficulties involved in breaching local power structures, now doubly more influential for the huge funds made available by the NREGS. Bhilwara alone got Rs.330 crore this financial year from the State's budget allocation of Rs.9, 500 crore. The monitoring mechanism under the NREGS must function robustly, not only to silence critics who argue that influx of funds on this scale can only lead to more corruption, but more importantly to reach the programme's numerous benefits, both financial and social, to the target group. Among other things, the Bhilwara audit team found that guaranteed employment had reduced distress migration by the Bhil tribal community, and raised wage levels across the private sector.

The National Rural Employment Guarantee Act, which came into force in February 2006, now covers all of rural India. It has generated over 450 crore person-days of employment, a major share going to women and Scheduled Caste and Scheduled Tribe families. Over Rs. 35,000 crore has been paid as wages. The priorities of the work to be undertaken include watershed management and water conservation, drought-proofing, flood protection, land development, minor irrigation and rural connectivity. Such work is important to strengthen the ecological foundations of sustainable agriculture. The NREGA is probably the world's largest ecological security programme. A major weakness has been the absence of effective technical guidance and support from agricultural and rural universities and institutes. The Union Ministry of Rural Development has taken steps to achieve convergence of brain and brawn, by enlisting the support of Ministries and Departments. Such convergence of expertise for sustainable development will help to enhance farm productivity without causing ecological harm. What is now needed is a convergence for human development at NREGA sites. India occupies the 132nd position among 179 countries in the UNDP's 2009 Human Development Index. That position may worsen. NREGA workers represent some of the most economically and socially underprivileged sections. Mostly, these workers are undernourished, with poor opportunities for healthcare. Hence, there is need to bring about a convergence of child care, nutrition, health (Rural Health Mission) and education programmes at NREGA sites. Education can be imparted in the evenings, using the joyful learning techniques available in computer-aided literacy programmes. Such a convergence in sustainable development along with convergence in human development will be creditable. There is also a need to raise the self-esteem of NREGA workers, making them feel proud of the fact that they are engaged in checking eco-destruction. Due recognition could be given to the NREGA groups that have done outstanding work in water harvesting, watershed development and soil healthcare with "Environment Saviour Awards". This will help spread awareness of the critical role

NREGA workers play. To begin with, there could be 10 awards covering distinct agro-climatic zones, each worth Rs. 10 lakh. Since these will be group awards, the money could be divided among the workers, depending on how long they have worked. The NREGA will then help to improve both food security and human development index. There are uncommon opportunities to erase India's image as the land of the poor, hungry and illiterate. To utilise them, an import requirement is a change in the mindset from patronage to partnership and from undervaluing the human resource to considering our youthful population as our greatest asset.

REFERENCES

Enakshi Ganguly Thukral, Bharti Ali, Saloni Mathur Children : Background & Perspective *infochangeindia.org/.../Children/.../Children-Background-Perspective.html*

Friedrich Huebler (2007), International Education Statistics: India has 21 Million Children, Tuesday, November 13...India has 21 million children out of school *huebler.blogspot.com/.../india-has-21-million-children-out-of.html*

India Progressing Towards Universal Elementary Education:: Where goes Missing 40% Efficiency? May-2007, *schoolreportcards.in/Media/m52.html*

Akshaya Mukul (2009), Sharp Decline in Out-of-School'Children,TNN, Sep 13, 2009, 01.47am IST, timesofindia.indiatimes.com › India

Siba Sankar Mohanty (2009), Union Budget 2009-10 Does Not Have A Pro Poor Orientation, 16 July, Countercurrents.org

V. Mohan Rao India and Its Literacy Mission, Monday, September 7th, 2009 *nvonews.com/2009/09/07/india-literacy-mission,*

Sushma (2009), Education Budget 2008-09, Viewpoint, Berlia President, Apeejay Stya Group & Vice President, Apeejay Education Society, New Delhi, Delhi, March 6, 2008/India PRwire/ —Summary www.indiaprwire.com/.../education/200803067868.htm

www.indiaedunews.com

Read more: http://www.ganpatinews.com/2010/02/27/budget-2010-allocation-of-25-more-funds-for-education-72930#ixzz0goI84NpF

Puja Marwaha (2009), "Right to Education Bill, 2009: Will It Help All Indians make the grade? http://www.thehindubusinessline.com /2009/07/24/stories/2009072450160800.htm

Jean Drèze,(2010), Poverty Estimates vs Food Entitlements, Tuesday, March 2, *newage.communistparty.in/.../poverty-estimates-vs-food-entitlements.html - 19 hours ago*

Karin Hulshof (2009), "Child Undernutrition in India is a Human Rights Issue"www.hindu.com/2009/12/10/stories/200912105 12 70900.htm

Food Security Bill (2009), India eIndia2007, Wednesday, July 22, 2009 http://eindia2007.blogspot.com/2009/07/food-security-bill-india.html

Jayati Ghosh (2006), "Introduction: Increasing Food Insecurity in South Asia" InfoChange News & Features, October, infor changeindia. org/2006-10225659/Agenda/Hunger-Has-fallen-Off-The-Map/Introduction-increasing-food-insecurity-in-South-Asia.html.

india.gov.in/citizen/health/national_rural.php

28,000 Health Centres Short In India Indian Economic Survey, Last Updated: 2009-07-02T16:20:47+05:30*www.india-server.com/.../national-rural-health-mission-allocated-8575.html –*

Karin Hulshof (2009), "Child Undernutrition in India is a Human Rights Issue" www.hindu.com/2009/12/10/stories/2009 121051270900.htm

www.unicef.org/india/media_3766.htm

UN (2007), Says India Must Reduce Child Mortality Rates, New Delhi 10 December 2007, *www1.voanews.com/.../a-13-2007-12-10-voa58-66534097.html*

thaindian.com India Worst in Cutting Child Mortality Rates Despite Fast Economic Growth http://www.thaindian.com/newsportal/south-asia/india-worst-in-cutting-child-mortality-rates-despite-fast-economic-growth_10018985.html#ixzz0h89ySKwD

Kathryn Hopkins (2008), The Guardian, Monday 28 July 2008 Human development: Child mortality stays high despite India's boom, *www.guardian.co.uk/.../india.internationalaidanddevelopment*

blog.taragana.com (2009), India's Neighbours Debunk Myths on Reducing Child Mortality, *October 5th, blog.taragana.com/.../2009/.../indias-neighbours-debunk-myths-on-reducing-child-mortality-12977*

www.unicef.org/india/overview_3705.htm

BBC NEWS | Health | Child mortality drop 'too slow'Child mortality drop 'too slow' *news.bbc.co.uk/2/hi/health/8249786.stm* –

India Needs Political will to Reduce Maternal Mortality: WHO http://www.thaindian.com/newsportal/health/india-needs-political-will-to-reduce-maternal-mortality-who_10033862.html#ixzz0hCEcN8GO

India Grapples with High Maternal Death Rate Mon Jan 26, 2009 6:in.reuters.com › Home › News › Top News

Ananta Basudev Sahu and Sandhya Rani Das (2007), "On Gender Issues and Empowerment of Women", Platinum Jubilee of Indian Statistical Institute, 1-2 February.

June Lennie (2002), Rural Women's Empowerment in a Communication Technology Project: Some Contradictory Effects, Paper published in Rural Society, Vol 12, No 3, 2002, pp.224-245.

Vinita Pandey (2005), Empowering Women in India: Changing Horizons—The Kalanjiam Experience, Journal of South Asian Women Studies,Vol:10, No.1 March, http://asiatica.org/jsaws/vol10_no1/empowering-women-india-changing-horizons-kalanjiam-experience/

www.awid.org , INDIA: Women's Political Empowerment, Yes; Better Lives, No... IPS News 26/11/2009 , www.awid.org/.../INDIA-Women-s-Political-Empowerment-Yes-Better-Lives-No

India Directory - Maps of India) india.mapsofindia.com › India Forum

www.wikigender.org/index.php/India -

Nageshwar (2010), *indiacurrentaffairs.org/political-empowerment-of-women-special-article-prof-k-nageshwar-2/* -

Lalit Kishore Where Do We Stand in Empowering Women in India? Dr., www.merinews.com › Lifestyle - Cached.

Raichel Matthai (2006), Political Status of Indian Women: Progress since independence VOL XLV No 01, Tuesday 24 April 2007, by www.mainstreamweekly.net › 2006 › December 23, 2006.

Rasheeda Bhagat (2009), Editorial, Women and Indian Politics, Business Line, Vol. 16, No. 229 Aug 18,

India.gov.in, *india.gov.in/sectors/rural/national_rural.php* –

National Rural Employment Guarantee Act- NREGA, *muktsar.nic.in/drda/nrega.htm*

S.D.Naik (2009), Empowering the Rural Poor, www. thehindu business line. com/.../20090703507009OO.htm

M.S.Swaminathan (2009), Synergy between Food Security Act & NREGA,www.thehindu.com/2009/06/01/.../2009060153 470800.htm

Editorial (2009), NREGS Under the Scanner, *www.thehindu.com/2009/10/29/stories/2009102954220800.htm*

MGNREGA Implementation in India: Problems, Prospects and Remedial Strategies with Special Reference to Kerala

2

P.K. Manoj

INTRODUCTION

In India, the implementation of MGNREGA (Mahatma Gandhi National Rural Employment Guarantee Act), or simply NREGA, as it was known since the enactment of the Act till getting rechristened in the name of Mahatma Gandhi–the father of the nation, has got tremendous potential to bring about far reaching improvements in the socio-economic life of the rural poor. Though Kerala has got one of the best profiles of socio-economic and educational achievements in the entire India, the unemployment is quite high. As such, the prospects of the Act should have been quite good. But, in spite of the high potentialities as above, MGNREA implementation in Kerala has been fraught with many problems. Similar problems have been there in many other states in India. In this context, this paper looks into the salient features of the Act and its major problems and prospects with a focus on Kerala state. Also, the paper makes suggestions for the smoother implementation of the Act, for faster socio-economic development of the nation.

MGNREAGA: SALIENT FEATURES

In fact, the National Rural Employment Guarantee Scheme (NREGS) which comes under the NREGA (now, MGNREGA) is a historic employment scheme in India for providing 100 days guaranteed wage employment for all employment seekers above 18 years of age and willing to do work. NREGS has come into force on 5th September 2005 in 200 districts in India and has been extended to another 130 districts later.

MGNREAGA IMPLEMENTATION: SOME PROGRESS, BUT MANY CONTROVERSIES

The ambitious NREGS scheme of the United Progressive Alliance (UPA) Government in India is embroiled in controversies ranging from embezzlement and misutilization of funds to defective implementation. In April 2010, the Supreme Court Vice-President, Parliamentary standing committee on rural development and Union Minister of state for rural development, Pradeep Jain, have all expressed concern over the state of affairs of NREGS implementation. Moreover, there are instances of bringing in political colour to the implementation of the scheme, the ruling UPA front accusing misutilization of NREGS funds, mostly against the states where opposition parties are in power. The gravity of the problem, however, is quite obvious from the remarks of a bench of Supreme Court comprising of Chief Justice K.G. Balakrishnan and Justice Deepak Verma and B.S Chauhan, according to which 'There is no uniform policy. The money is not reaching actual beneficiaries'. Expressing concern over the implementation of NREGS, the bench has commented that several projects under the scheme are failing as the funds allocated for them either remain unutilized or in many cases money lands up in wrong hands.

There has been a classic case in Haryana, the state bordering the national capital, where the funds meant for NREGS has been allegedly misutilized in Ambala district. Besides, instead of taking action against the responsible officers, the whistle blowers are being persecuted. Though it is envisaged that there should be maximum utilisation of all natural resources under NREGS to improve the living standards of rural population, there are widespread complaints that majority of work in Ambala district under NREGS existed only on paper. Despite the inquiry reports recommending registration of criminal cases against the erring officers, no action has been taken so far. The accused reportedly enjoys the patronage of powerful ruling politicians. Quite ironically, Ambala district has bagged a national award for spending a large sum under the scheme by the forest department, benefiting the poor. But the Forest department officials did not submit utilisation certificates of the expenditure incurred under the scheme.

Another instance of misutilization of NREGS funds has been reported by the Union Minister of State for rural development, Pardeep Jain, who has revealed that the funds meant for the scheme are being diverted to renovate bungalows of district collectors in Madhya Pradesh. Similar charges of misutilization of funds have been leveled against the ruling U.P Government headed by Chief Minister Mayawati, according to which regarding the funds earmarked for the schemes like MGNREGA no one knows what happened to the money. It has been reported that an amount of Rs.1,500 crore under NREGS scheme has not been utilized by the UP government, and that besides violating the NREGA, the non-admissible expenditure has deprived the rural households of wage and employment, the very objective of the NREGS. It has further been reported that even after utilizing the entire funds under the scheme as provided in the budget, the government has not been able to provide a minimum of one hundred days of employment to the needy households who demand work under the scheme.

In spite of some of the controversies in its implementation, MGNREGA has got tremendous potential for national economic development, particularly through empowerment of women and also the underprivileged classes. It has been officially declared by the Rural Development Ministry of the Government of India that women are contributing more than half the work force under this ambitious scheme. In fact, according to the Government women contribute about 52 percent of all households given employment under this scheme since 2008.

MGNREAGA IMPLEMENTATION IN KERALA: MAJOR PROBLEMS AND PROSPECTS

In Kerala, NREGS was implemented in Palakkad and Waynad districts initially on 5th February 2006. The scheme was later extended to the remaining 12 districts in the State also on 1st April 2008. Kerala being a small state in the Indian Union with very high unemployment - most of the unemployed being educated also - the prospects of the scheme are quite good. Around five lakh people among the unemployed in Kerala are estimated to have willingness to do physical labour. NREGS is a substantial boost in income and purchasing power.

Feature of NREGS in Kerala

- In Kerala, the Local governments are given a central role in the planning and implementation of NREGA and are the sole agencies responsible for implementation of local development projects under the scheme in Kerala.
- Engineering support is put in place. In addition to one diploma/degree holder working on contract at the level of the Village Panchayat, there is a system of accredited engineers. Such engineers are drawn from amongst retired engineers, staff working in Engineering Colleges, Polytechnics/ ITIs, engineers working in NGOs etc. These engineers are paid at rates fixed by Government for the work done by them. An engineer from a government department or agency, willing to help the Village Panchayat over and above his normal work, is allowed and paid at 50% of the rate applicable to others.
- Technical Sanction of the work is given not by individual engineers, but by a Technical Committee of engineers which includes a government engineer, a retired engineer and an engineer working in an academic institution for the purposes of transparency.
- An appellate system has been put in place at the district level to facilitate speedy sorting out of disputes.

- To mobilize the workers and the public and to assist the local governments in carrying out its duties, Village Panchayats have been given the freedom to identify one public servant of their choice having the time and inclination to do social work from any government department are posted on working arrangement as NREGS co-coordinators.
- Kudumbasree is given in the implementation of the programme. Under Kudumbasree every family below poverty line is organzied into a Neighbourhood Group (NHG) at the local level consisting of 15 to 40 families with each family being represented only by a woman. The NHGs are federated into an Area Development Society (ADS) at the level of the Ward of the Village Panchayat (a Village Panchayat Ward in Kerala has a population of around 1500 to 2000). The ADSs in a Village Panchayat are federated into a registered body called the Community Development Society (CDS). Each NHG, ADS and CDS has five volunteers carrying out different functional roles. • The ADS has been entrusted with the task of organizing public works under NREGS. Muster Rolls and other records are maintained by the ADS, implements are provided to labourers by them and the transparency and monitoring requirements are also carried out by them. Welfare amenities to the workers are also provided by the ADS. Since ADS is an organization of the poor and is basically a woman's group, there has been greater sensitivity and community participation in the implementation process.
- The estimates are summarized in the local language so as to be understood by ordinary people. At the beginning of every work, the nature of work, expected out turn and the likely wages are explained to the workers' groups.
- Since Kerala has limited public land, the eco-restoration works are selected for in degraded forest lands. Village Panchayats would implement the programme in forest areas with the technical supervision being done by field

level officials of the Forest Department representing a new kind of relationship between a Panchayat Raj Institution and a government department.

- The road works has been limited to 10% of the total expenditure and to give special priority to integrated watershed development works.
- In Kerala the women have outnumbered the men in MGNREGA activities, than any other state in India. As per statistics with the Ministry of Rural Development of the Government of India, women have constituted 85.05 per cent of the total 3,16,287 households which have been provided jobs under the Act since 2008.

Major Advantages of NREGS in Kerala

In Kerala NREGS now provides Rs 125 per person for a stipulated quantity of manual labour offered as registered worker in the local governments, as against a National wage rate of just Rs.60/- per person. Besides, compared to the earlier wage employment programmes such as NREGA, RLEGP, JRY, EAS, SGRY, IRDP, SGSY, there are significant achievements under NREGS due to the combination of transparent processes and procedures, local action and constant vigilance, the implementation of NREGA has been comparatively corruption free. The factors contributing to this situation, inter alia, include the following:

- In Kerala, a clear political decision has been conveyed to the Panchayats stating that the scheme has to be implemented strictly as per the laws in force. The argument for an asset focused programme ignoring the processes and conforming to the procedures on paper, has been rejected. Likewise, another argument that Kerala would lose out as the demand for unskilled labour is very limited and as the wages are much higher than the statutory minimum wages in more than 90% of the State, it would be better to go for public works, has also been rejected in the case of this state.

- The work is organized through the Kudumbashree system. Accordingly, the poor have got a stake in the NREGS activities, right from the beginning of its implementation.
- The technocratic power that is responsible to accord technical sanction, measure works and recommend payments has been made more spread out in the state and it is made accountable through the Committee system. In case of difference of opinion the appellate system would be resorted to.
- In Kerala, a special emphasis has been given to the rights of workers and they have been made fully aware of their entitlements. Further, it has been stipulated that all the payments are made only through the individual bank accounts of workers. This has been done to obviate corruption in its implementation.

Major Problems and Impediments of NREGS Implementation in Kerala

Though the Left parties (like, CPIM) are claiming that they have been instrumental in the enactment of the MGNREGA Act through sustained pressures on the ruling Government at the Centre, because of their commitment towards the upliftment of the poor, statistics show that in a Left ruled state like Kerala (and so also West Bengal) the implementation of the Act is lagging behind other states. As per the statistics compiled by the Government of India, while a job-seeking household under the scheme got over 40 days of employment on average nationally in 2008-09, in Kerala about 50 per cent of the rural poor did not avail even 15 days of employment during 2008-09. While a total of 6.3 lakh households availed jobs under the NREGA scheme in the state during the period, only 3.2 lakh sought more than 15 days of employment. In West Bengal, as high as 72 per cent of such households did not get even 15 days of employment. At the national level, over 66 per cent households availed more than 15 days of employment during 2008-09. In the fiscal year 2009-'10 too, employment provided to job seekers in Kerala and West Bengal is far behind the national average. While the data compiled by the Rural Development Ministry for the first five months of this fiscal year has showed that on average 39 days of employment has been provided to job-seeking households nationally, in West Bengal the average has been just 19 days while the same in respect of Kerala has been just 16 days.

Huge Potential of MGNREGA in Kerala: Vital Role in Women Empowerment

Because of the special features of MGNREGA implementation in Kerala, it has got high potential for women empowerment in the state, particularly because of the following reasons:

- As the work is organized by women's groups in Kerala, the gender perspective gets built in automatically. (This is because of the involvement of 'Kudumbashree' in MGNREGA)
- As women are comfortable working along with their neighbors, women constitute over 85 percent of the workers in Kerala - the highest women participation among all the states in India.
- For the first time equal wages are really paid and this has boosted the earnings of women.
- As the wages are paid into Bank accounts the habit of thrift which was already inculcated through the 'Kudumbashree' experiment has further been strengthened.
- As the Bank deposits are increasing, the intra-household status of the woman has also been improving commensurately as she controls substantial cash resources and withdrawal can be only on her decision.

Apart from the women empowerment point of view which is quite typical in Kerala, MGNREGA implementation has got tremendous potential for economic development of Kerala state, particularly through the socio-economic upliftment of the rural poor. Besides, NREGS has the potential to give a new dimension to the work culture in the state. While the workers have been hitherto controlled by contractors and their middlemen who know how to extract work. With the NREGS implementation the out-turn has been initially very poor as the workers could not be supervised properly. However, soon the workers have themselves realized that they would be losing collectively and a new internal dynamics evolved with peer pressure forcing workers to put in their maximum effort. Besides, a kind of social responsibility has also become evident as more capable workers have become more than willing to put in extra effort to make up for those who genuinely could not do hard work beyond a point, like the women and the elderly. In short, a new culture that promises far reaching benefits to the state in the future has begun to emerge.

Another implication of the MGNREGA implementation in Kerala has been the fact that public works have gained respectability. Hitherto such initiatives have been either highjacked either by a contractor or a local leader. At present, however, the workers consider it as their right. They tend to distinguish between wages provided by a contractor and wages directly given by the Panchayat. The latter is almost equated with a salary. This has motivated a large section of people who were hitherto unwilling to work into join the work force. There has been an interesting instance of a penurious descendant of the erstwhile Kollengode royal family in Palakkad District in Kerala taking an active part in NREGS and even motivating her relatives to join on the logic that self-help and access to legally entitled emoluments from a public source is better than charity from relatives

Yet another peculiarity of MGNREGA implementation in Kerala has been its integration with other developmental initiatives. Accordingly, strong natural resource management focus has been given to NREGS. For instance, the Bharathapuzha River rejuvenation with action plans emanating from the Village Panchayat as building blocks has been taken up as a mega project under the NREGS in Kerala.

[illegible]rala, there are attempts in the direction of integrating [illegible]vith People's Plan. Village Panchayats get more than [illegible]e on an average under People's Plan. If intelligently [illegible]ed it is expected that substantial improvement in quality of assets can be attained. In order to overcome the problem of shortage of technical staff, it has been decided to rope in voluntary services of reputed non-government organizations. Using the excellent network of Kudumbashree it has been decided in the State Employment Guarantee Council to develop a cadre of bare-foot technical volunteers from among the poor women. In order to develop the skills of the workers it has been decided to set up Labour Banks. A pilot has been launched in one Village Panchayat. The Labour Banks would be supported under People's Plan to take up other public works and even private works. It is well-nigh impossible to identify works in the plantation areas as well as in the coastal areas. It has been decided to seek the expert support from Government of India to come out with a shelf of projects which can be taken up in such geographical areas.

An innovative form of training has been developed by Kerala Institute of Local Administration (KILA) where there is a shift from the cascading model to a "ripple" model, according to which outstanding Panchayats become the master trainers and the neighbouring Panchayats formally learn from the experience of the best performers. Monitoring has been strengthened with the decision of the State Employment Guarantee Council to put in a system of State level and District level quality Monitors by identifying persons with reputation for integrity and competence. The State level Monitors would be of two categories–outstanding individuals whose views are widely respected by society and senior Technical Experts capable of giving authoritative feedback on the quality of implementation. Further the State Employment Guarantee Council has decided to request a team consisting of eminent experts to conduct an independent assessment of Kerala's performance and offer suggestions for improvement.

Strong Foundation and Markedly Superior Execution

In spite of a number of teething problems that MGNREGA has been facing in the initial phase of its execution, it is clear that the policy focus on natural resource management and corruption-free implementation would bring in good returns.

The administrative measures introduced in Kerala to implement the above Act with the active involvement of the Kudumbasree network have resulted in a strong foundation for it and has also opened up space for pro-poor innovations. The scheme has suddenly increased purchasing power of the poor and there is visible local economic development. This is particularly true of Wayanad District in Kerala which has been ridden with farmer suicides so far. The peasants have managed to get substantial relief from NREGS by getting over their inhibition in working as labourers in richer farmer's lands by moving on to the now-respectable public works.

A recent study conducted by Dr Jos Chathukulam and Dr K Gireesan, of Centre for Rural Management (CRM) has indicated that major defects identified during previous wage employment programmes in Kerala have been absent in the case of NREGS. The distinctive benefits of the scheme have been pointed out to be the provision of equal wages to men and women, non-involvement of contractors, very limited use of machinery, adherence to wage-material ratio etc. and also the absence of muster roll manipulations based on a study of its execution in the initial two districts of Palakkad and Wynad in Kerala.

SUGGESTIONS FOR SMOOTHER IMPLEMENTATION OF MGNREGA IN INDIA

For smoother implementation of MGNREGA in India, the model followed by Kerala appears to be quite advisable for the entire country. Apart from ensuring women empowerment in results in lesser instances of corruption and exploitation by the middlemen. However, except for a few states like Kerala and Tamil Nadu, many Indian states might not be having a strong machinery like 'Kudumbashree' (Kerala). This in turn results in MGNREGA implementation in such states less replicable from the Kerala model. However, other operational formalities (than ensuring the involvement of poverty alleviation programme like "Kudumbashree"), like ensuring better decentralization of powers in implementation activities, giving the central role of implementation to the local self government organizations, accrediting external technicians and engineers (ie. those from outside the regular job/contract employment under the scheme) on adhoc basis etc. seem to be quite desirable for any state in India. Regular monitoring and follow up of the system, minimizing the bureaucratic interventions are quite essential for the success of the scheme. Involving poverty alleviation programmes (like, "Kudumb-shree" in Kerala) acan make its implementation more meaningful.

CONCLUDING REMARKS

Concluding the paper, it may be opined that Kerala has got excellent potential to become a role model for the entire nation for systematic and corruption-free implementation of MGNREGA. The experience so far being satisfactory, the Kerala model can be replicated in other states. The Act as such is quite meaningful and powerful for rural development and women empowerment for the entire nation. The problem lies not in the Act per se, but in its defective implementation by the state governments. In many states its implementation is characterized by such defects like the involvement of the middlemen, political and bureaucratic exploitation, misuse of funds, muster roll manipulation, lack of transparency etc. which need to be strictly controlled. The prospects of the Act seem to be quite bright provided it is properly executed.

REFERENCES

Impact Assessment of NREGS in Kerala Evaluation of Systems and Processes by Dr Jos Chathukulam and Dr Gireesan Kottayam, Centre for Rural Management(CRM), April, 2008.

Vijayanand, S. M, *Implementation of NREGA: The Kerala Experience*, Department of Local Self Government, Government of Kerala.

Ministry of Rural Development, Government of India, New Delhi. Official website, www.nrega.nic.in

NCAER-PIF Study on Evaluating Performance of National Rural Employment Guarantee Act, New Delhi, NCAER, 2009.

"Kerala Seeks Flexibility in NREGA Rules", *The Financial Express*, dt. 04 Aug. 2009.

"NREGA: Red Marks for Bengal and Kerala", *The Indian Express*, dt.03 Feb. 2010.

Impact of Rural Employment Guarantee Programme and Poverty in India

3

P.M. Mathew, Bipasha Kalika

POVERTY IN INDIA: A BRIEF OVERVIEW

Poverty in India has reached abnormal heights, so much so that it has become almost impossible for the country to come out of the 'poverty-trap'. The problem of poverty is not just confined to rural India; urban poverty has been one of the most disturbing truths ever since India began treading the path of development and urbanisation. In the last five years (2004-2009) the number of people living below the poverty line has increased from 270 million to 325 million. This is an increase off 55 million people below the poverty line in just five years. Among the most important causes ascribed for the high level poverty in India are its history under the British rule, large population, low literacy, societal structure including the caste system and role of women, dependence on agriculture, and the economic policies adopted after its independence.

Poverty eradication in india, is considered to be a far fetched dream. Poverty alleviation is expected to make better progress in the next 50 years than in the past, as a trickle-down effect of the growing middle class. Increasing stress on education, reservation of seats in government jobs and the increasing empowerment of women and the economically weaker sections of society, are expected to contribute to the alleviation of poverty. However, it is incorrect yo say that all poverty alleviation schemes in india have failed. Since 1950s the Indian government and non-governmental organizations have initiated several programs to alleviate poverty, including subsidizing food and other necessities, increased access to loans, improving agricultural techniques and price supports, and promoting education and family planning. These measures have helped eliminate famines, cut absolute poverty levels by more than half, and reduced illiteracy and malnutrition.

HOW POVERTY CAN CRIPPLE A NATION

The impact of poverty in India has been very grave. Poverty cripples a nation. It is a shame for a nation if almost half of its population cannot meet the basic requirements of life. It is a shame if thousands of small children do not get access to primary education. It is a matter of great dismay, if more than half of the young Indian populace sit idle without contributing anything to India's growth story, because they are illiterate and cannot find a job. There have been various schemes to eradicate poverty and its adverse impact on a nation, however, poverty alleviation in India is a long term goal as already mentioned above. With poverty being as high as in India, we will have to wait for some more decades to actually see the results of poverty alleviation measures.

Poverty in India is one of the major concerns because even though India is one of the fastest emerging countries in the world, what is really slowing down India's robust growth rate is the prevalence of very high poverty. The rural poor depend on agricultural incomes which are highly unpredictable and the urban people rely on jobs that are, at best, scarce. Even though India is expected to grow at a double-digit rate in the near future, one factor that can pull India back is poverty. If the poor people from the rural areas are trained properly and made to work, they too can contribute in their own small way to India's incredible growth story. This is where we can rely on the effectiveness of schemes like the NREGA.

NATIONAL RURAL EMPLOYMENT GUARANTEE ACT (NREGA): AN INTRODUCTION

One of the most important.schemes that the Government of India adopted in 2005 to eradicate rural poverty is the introduction of the National Rural Employment Guarantee Act. The NREG Act is an act to provide for the enhancement of livelihood security of the households in rural ares of the country by providing at least one hundred days of guaranteed wage employment in every financial year to every household whose adult members volunteer to do unskilled manual work. It is the flagship programme of the UPA Government that directly touches lives of the poor and promotes inclusive growth. Enacted after a succesful struggle for an employment guarantee legislation, the NREG Act was a partial victory towards a full-fledged right to employment. The act became operational in february 2006, starting with 200 districts, and within three and a half years, has been extended to the rest of the country. NREGA is the first ever law that guarantees wage employment at an unprecedented scale. Dr. Jean Dreze, a Belgium born economist, has been a major influence on this project.

The major objectives of the act are:

- Augmenting wage employment.
- Strengthening natural resource management through works that address causes of chronic poverty like drought, deforestation and soil erosion.
- Encourage sustainable development.
- Strengthening grass-root processes of democracy by infusing transparency and accountability in governance.
- Strengthening decentralisation and deepening the processes of democracy by giving a pivotal role to the panchayati raj institutions in planning, monitoring and implementation.

AN ANALYSIS OF THE PERFORMANCE OF NREGA

Though, three and a half years is too short a period to gauge the impact of NREGA, it is worth mentioning that this important act is bringing about a silent revolution in the rual areas. This act has had repercussions at different levels, right from altering the socio-economic conditions of the affected districts to altering the social dynamics. Although well-intentioned, this act too faced the initial jitters. It received very half-hearted support from the states and the centre in implementation. A lot of debates and arguments have been doing rounds ever since this important legislation was passed. Despite this, the act has proven to be a good step towards rural poverty alleviation.

NREGA's record on the parameter of employment generation has been much better than its predecessors. Till 2008, about 25 million households have benefitted from about 857 million of person days employment generated. The act has brought about a lot of improvements in the spheres of financial inclusion and social security provision in the rural areas. Talking about financial inclusion, lets look at some numbers. As of 2008, 27.1 million bank accounts have been opened in rural areas with zero balance requirements for wage payments under the NREGA. Almost 80-90% of these are for households that have been included for the first time in the financial network of the country. Though financial inclusion was not an objective of the act, it still is an achievement. In terms of participation of the marginalized sections in the number of workdays created, more than 50% of total person days of employment generated have gone to SC and ST households.

In 2008-2009, the NREGA provided employment to almost 45 million rural people. Of those employed, nearly 50 percent were women and over 55 percent comprised of Scheduled Castes, Scheduled Tribes demonstrating the self-targeting nature of the programme. The NREGA has contributed immensely to the increased bargaining power of the agricultural labour. No longer are they prepared to settle for less than the notified wage. The average notified wage under NREGA has itself risen from Rs.65 per day in 2006-07 to Rs.87 in 2009-10. Also, there has been a commitment to provide a real wag rate of Rs. 100 under the NREGA. State governments are being encouraged to make wage payments under the programme through banks and post office accounts. Nearly 78 million such accounts have been opened till now. The government has also proposed to establish the institution of an ombudsman in every district for effective grievance redressal under NREGA.

One of the major objectives of the act has been to ensure one-third of women participation in total person days generated, the actual numbers have been close to an impressive 50%. Implementation of NREGA has contributed to very high levels of women empowerment, particularly in the following aspects.

- As the work is organized by women's groups, the gender perspective gets built in automatically.
- As women are comfortable working along with their neighbors, nearly 80% of the workers have been women.
- For the first time equal wages are really paid and this has boosted the earnings of women.
- As the wages are paid into Bank accounts the habit of thrift has further been strengthened.
- As the Bank deposits are increasing, the intra-household status of the women has also been improving commensurately as she controls substantial cash resources and withdrawal can be only on her decision.

There has been an increase in wages in almost all the indian states since the implementation of the act. Though the increase in the wage-level in rural india cannot be attributed to NREGA alone, but it would be foolish to ignore the role of this programme in the same. An ongoing study titled 'evaluation of NREGA' being conducted by the faculty of Institute of Development Studies, Jaipur, found that the act has shown great results in the rural areas in fields of economic empowerment, teamwork, has encouraged women in villages to come out of their veil and work, and has bridged the caste bias in rural india.

During 2008-2009, NREGA provided employment opportunities for more than 4.47 crore households as against

3.39 crore households covered in 2007-2008. the government is committed to provide a real wage of rs. 100 a day as an entitlement under the NREGA. In order to increase the productivity of assetsand resources under NREGA, convergence with other schemes relating to agriculture, forests, water resources, land resources and rural roads is being initiated. In the first stage, a total of 115 pilot districts have been selected for such convergence. The government of india has proposed an allocation of rs. 39,100 crore for the year 2009-2010 for NREGA which marks an increase of a mingboggling 144% over the 2008-2009 budget estimates.

CRITICAL ISSUES UNDER NREGA THAT NEEDS PROPER SURVEILLANCE

- Issue related to providing job-cards to the people on time.
- Issues related to selection of works.
- Issues related to the execution of works.
- Issues related to the measurement of the work done.
- Issues related to timely wage payments.

SOME LOOPHOLES IN THE ACT AND IN ITS IMPLEMENTATION

Though the NREGA has helped a lot of rural poor to get employed and become self-sufficient, this act and its implementation has some flaws too. Herein, we can talk about three issues.

- The first one is- why only 100 days of work? Since people do not get those 100 days fully, this proved to be an area of constant criticism. However, this year, according to the Finance minister Mr. Pranab Mukherjee, the Union government is looking to offer 50-60 more days of work to people who have already been employed for 100 days under the National Rural Employment Guarantee Act. He said funds for this could be drawn from the National Calamity Relief Fund, which has a corpus of Rs2,000 crore.
- The second issue is the rule of only one member per family being able to use it. Since poor families see themselves as a collective, splitting up is bad

economics. For instance, a day's wage at a brick kiln might be less than what it is for NREG work. But even though brick kilns are brutal and exploitative, all members of a family can work there-and for more than a hundred days.

– The last issue that we can talk about is the delay in payments. Though Andhra Pradesh seems to be ahead of many other states, this continues to be a problem. There has been instances when people have actually waited for more than four months to get an amount much lesser than what was owed to them. There have been many recording errors, when people who work do not get recorded and people who haven't worked, get recorded. The planning commission has sought the reserve bank of India's intervention in streamlining the mechanism of paying wages under the NREGA. In a letter to the central bank, the commission said that the BRI should give directions to banks to ensure that payments to the beneficiaries of the NREGA are made only through banks or post offices (mentioned above).

The focus of NREGA has always been right which is- work must be provided on demand. The NREGA has always made sure that the assets created should benefit the poorest and the marginalised communities first. The work itself has created and sustained favourable conditions for providing minimum wage employment in transparent and an accountable manner. Despite all the criticisms with respect to corruption and leakages, the NREGA has actually drawn attention to the weaknesses of the delivery mechanism.

A CRITICAL ANALYSIS OF THE IMPACT OF NREGA

NREGA has given rise to a new work culture. The workers were hitherto controlled by contractors and their middlemen who knew how to extract work. Public works have now gained respectability. NREGA has suddenly increased purchasing power of the poor and there is visible local economic development. This is particularly true of Wayanad in Kerala which was ridden with farmer suicides. The peasants have managed to get substantial relief from NREGA by getting over their inhibition in working as labourers in richer farmer's lands by moving on to the now-respectable public works

It is true, however, that the achievements of the NREGA have been uneven. If we look at NREGA's state-wise impact, Andhra Pradesh has fared better than most states, thanks to the growing awareness of the people of their rights. This is one state where, some 2.7 million people applied for job-cards in the first month after the programme was announced and everyone received them. And in many states the job-cards are yet to be issued. Rajasthan is the state after Andhra Pradesh which has gained the maximum from the NREGA. However states like Maharashtra has benefitted very abysmally from the NREGA.

The act's foundations still being weak, any immediate changes must not burden the fragile success and infact must strengthen its basic structure. With all its shortcomings and failings, the limited benefit provided by the NREGA has been an important support structure for the poorest and most marginalised rural communities. Wage work has been open to all those who offer to do casual manual work on eight categories of work—most of which are designed to strengthen the natural resource base of those who are most dependent on such community assets for their livelihoods.

So, lets examine why NREGA has been more succesful than any other poverty alleviation schemes and what ensured better targeting. Unlike the other programmes which have been made toothless by anchoring them to below poverty line (BPL) cards, NREGA is a self-targeting programme. It is no wonder that the distribution of beneficiaries by social groups is almost similar to the distribution of poor obtained from the NSSO (National Sample Survey Organisation) consumption surveys. Evidently, the self-targeting inherent in NREGA has a better score in targeting the poor than the officially conducted but flawed identification of BPL households. In fact, the self-selection nature of NREGA has persuaded the finance ministry to classify workers in the programme as poor, for inclusion in the Janashree Bima Yojana. Similarly, the case of extension of Rashtriya Swasthaya Yojana to the NREGA workers.

The NREGA has ben more or less succesful in energising, mobilising, empowering and delivering to india's poorest and most marginalised rural people. It has also been somewhat succesful in providing the rural poor a measure of dignity, tangible economic benefit and a motivation to participate in local action. The NREGA stands apart from the employment and poverty alleviation programmes in many significant ways. It is the first national programme of consequence which has woven transparency and accountability into the mundane fabric of daily interaction of people with the government. It also gives an opportunity to break the feudally enforced silence of its victims. Through transparency and social audit measures, NREGA allows anyone, anywhere, to be a part of the monitoring of the delivery system. It also gives the poor an opportunity to realise the constitutional sovereignty, the power of the people, considering India is the largest democracy in the world.

CONCLUSION

Although a programme of this magnitude will take time to be of any relevance in changing the landscape of rural India, initial reports of evaluation studies by various institutions and individuals has documented the processes of revival and resurgence largely driven by NREGA as an axis of struggle by the rural poor. It has neither been claimed nor was envisaged that NREGA is the key to successful rejuvenation of rural areas. This requires many such efforts particularly towards ensuring the broken linkages of the growth process to include the rural areas as engines of growth. Nonetheless, it does offer an opportunity for the rural poor to stake claim to the fruits of the growth. Moreover, NREGA success stories provide opportunities for mainstreaming and legitimizing the struggle for other social security legislation.

Independent India has to acknowledge the critical role the NREGA has played in providing a measure of inclusive growth. It has given people a right to work, to re-establish the dignity of labour, to ensure people's economic and democratic rights and entitlements, to create labour intensive infrastructure and assets, and to build the human resource base of our country. For the first time, the power elite recognises the people's right to fight endemic hunger and poverty with dignity, accepting that their labour will be the foundation for infrastructure and economic growth. The entitlements paradigm is still to be established in many States in the country. Second generation issues like the expansion of the categories of permissible works needs to be taken up with labour and the deprived continuing to be the central focus. The improvements must be to strengthen, not divert from these basic tenets. In the midst of the current economic slowdown, there is enough evidence that this kind of commitment can work to help reduce the slowdown.

NREGA's success is as much a hope for civil society activists fighting for the rights of the poor as it is a critique of the developmentalist state in case it fails to deliver.

REFERENCES

http://nrega.nic.in/circular/Minutes_meeting7Aug09.pdf

http://www.tribuneindia.com/2009/20090918/

http://www.indiaenews.com/business/20090909/219776.htm

http://www.theindiapost.com/2009/02/08/survey-to-study-the-impact-of-nrega/

www.thehindu.com

http://www.livemint.com

Inclusive Growth in Economic Development With Regard Rural India

4

G. Paramasivan, J. Sacratees

INTRODUCTION

India is a country of villages and about fifty per cent of the villages have very poor socio economic conditions. Since the dawn of independence, concerted efforts have been made to ameliorate the living standard of rural masses. So, rural development as an integrated concept of growth and poverty elimination has been of paramount concern in all the consequent five year plans. The second element of India's poverty reduction strategy is the targeted poverty alleviation programmes. The rationale for introducing the targeted programmes for the poor came to the fore in the late 1960s when the government policies had to face severe criticisms because the much anticipated benefits of economic growth was not percolating to the poor and the disadvantaged. The targeted poverty alleviation programmes are basically supply-side interventions on the part of the state in response to the needs of the poor and the disadvantaged. The notion of poverty that has been used in targeted poverty alleviation programmes in India is primarily based on lowness of income or purchasing power or in terms of calorie consumption below and above norm. However, any discussion on poverty and its alleviation would remain incomplete if one fails to take note of the development literature that emerged in the 1980s.

Poverty is one of the main issues, attracting the attention of sociologists and economists. Poverty in India is widespread with the nation estimated to have a third of the world's poor. It indicates a condition in which a person fails to maintain a living standard adequate for a comfortable lifestyle. Though India boasts of a high economic growth, it is shameful that there is still large scale poverty in India. Poverty in India can be defined as a situation when a certain section of people are unable to fulfill their basic needs. India has the world's largest number of poor people living in a single country. Out of its total population of more than 1 billion, 350 to 400 million people are living below the poverty line. According to the criterion used by the Planning Commission of India 27.5% of the population was living below the poverty line in 2004–2005, down from 51.3% in 1977–1978, and 36% in 1993-1994 While poverty rates in India are high, they are not on a par with what neighbouring Pakistan and Bangladesh experience.

Poverty in India is reducing but it is still a major issue. Millions of people in India are unable to meet these basic standards, and according to government estimates, in 2007 there were nearly 220.1 million people living below the poverty line. Nearly 21.1% of the entire rural population and 15% of the urban population of India exists in this difficult physical and financial predicament. An estimated 260.3 million are below the poverty line, of which 193.2 million are in the rural areas and 67.1 million are in urban areas. More than 75% of poor people reside in villages. Poverty level is not uniform across India. The poverty level is below 10% in states like Delhi, Goa, and Punjab etc whereas it is below 50% in Bihar (43) and Orissa (47). It is between 30-40% in Northeastern states of Assam, Tripura, and Mehgalaya and in Southern states of TamilNadu and Uttar Pradesh.

Since the early 1950s, government has initiated, sustained, and refined various planning schemes to help the poor. Eradication of poverty in India is generally only considered to be a long-term goal. Poverty alleviation is expected to make better progress in the next 50 years than in the past, as a trickle-down effect of the growing middle class. Increasing stress on education, reservation of seats in government jobs and the increasing empowerment of women and the economically weaker sections of society, are also expected to contribute to the alleviation of poverty. It is incorrect to say that all poverty reduction programmes have failed.

POVERTY REDUCTION PROGRAMMES AND EMPLOYMENT GENERATION PROGRAMMES

Since the 1970s the Indian government has made poverty reduction a priority in its development planning. Policies have focused on improving the poor standard of living by ensuring food security, promoting self-employment through greater access to assets, increasing wage employment and improving access to basic social services. Launched in 1965, India's Public Distribution System has helped meet people's basic food needs by providing rations at subsidized prices. The largest credit-based government poverty reduction programme in the world, the Integrated Rural Development Programme (IRDP) provides rural households below the poverty line with credit to purchase income-generating assets. Launched in 1979, the programme has supplied subsidized credit to such groups as small and marginalized farmers, agricultural laborers, rural artisans, the physically handicapped, scheduled castes and scheduled tribes. Within this target population, 40% of the beneficiaries are supposed to be women. Although the programme has reached 51 million families, only 27% of the borrowers have been women. The programme has significantly increased the income of 57% of assisted families.

Other programms include the Integrated Rural Development Programme, Jawahar Rozgar Yojana, Training Rural Youth for Self Employment (TRYSEM) and to the credit of the government, other on-going initiatives. Government has introduced a number of antipoverty programs since independence to alleviate poverty. These include various employment guarantee programmes such as National Rural

Employment Programme, Rural Landless Employment Guarantee Programme etc. Recently, Government has initiated National Rural Employment Guarantee Program (NREGP). As per NREGP, the government will provide 100 days of employment per year to whosoever is willing to work. NREGP is considered as a landmark program in poverty alleviation measures. One of the major problems with poverty alleviation programs is their implementation. Rajiv Gandhi once said that out of 100 paisa allocated for poor only 14 paisa reaches them. But in spite of their weaknesses, poverty alleviated program can be credited for their success in alleviating poverty to an extent. Greater public-private partnership and committed and efficient bureaucratic machinery is required to tackle poverty. In 1982-83, Development of Women and Children in Rural Areas (DWCRA) was launched as a sub-scheme of IRDP. The focus of DWCRA was on economic activities for rural women to be taken up in groups. The concept of the group was to enable women to take a larger amount of loan, so that by pooling their individual loans they could start viable non- farm activity. DWCRA too met with limited success.

PERFORMANCE OF NREGA IN INDIA

The National Rural Employment Gaurantee Act (**NREGA**) has now been in operation for over three years, and is extended to all the rural areas of the country. In a relatively short span of time, it has already become one of the most avidly studied programmes of the Central Government. The National Rural Employment Scheme (**NREGS**) is an important strategy in the current economic context of global economic crisis and national economic slowdown, where raising aggregate demand is a major task for the government. Fiscal policy that provides more wage income directly to unskilled workers in the rural areas is likely to be much more effective in increasing aggregate incomes than other forms of public spending.

The draft proposed by the National Advisory Council envisaged legal guarantee to every household in rural areas for 100 days for doing casual manual work. Thus, NREGA was notified on September 7, 2005. The Act came into force on

February 2, 2006 when 200 selected districts of the country were brought under its purview (phase I, 2006-07). NREGA was extended to additional 130 districts in phase II during 2007-08. The remaining rural areas were notified with effect from April 1, 2008. NREGA now covers all rural areas of the country.

The pioneering programme saw its budget outlay increase to Rs 39,100 crore in the interim budget for 2009-10. In the last fiscal, the same stood at Rs 16, 000 crore. In 2007-08 the budget outlay The NREGA aimed at generating jobs in the rural areas, provided employment to over 4.47 crore households, in the previous fiscal. During the first year of implementation (FY 2006-2007) in 200 districts, more than 2.10 crore households were employed and 90.5 crore person days were employed. In 2007-08 3.39 crore households were provided employment and 143.59 crore person days were households have been provided employment and 215.63 crore person days have been generated across the country. According to the NREGA website, as on March 2009, out of total 99 million households that demanded employment, the number of households working under NREGA is only 14 million and the cumulative number of households that have competed 100 days of employment is about 4 million. Still, the scheme has managed to touch and improve the lives of close to 5 crore rural people more effectively than most of the anti-poverty programmes in the country.

According to C.P. Chandrasekhar and Jayati Ghosh, "The NREGA is necessarily 'inclusive' at the most basic level in economic terms, because is self targets those who are willing to engage in arduous physical work for a daily wage, in other words, the poorest sections of society. But it is also socially inclusive as well, that is, it disproportionately involves women, SCs and STs as workers in the scheme. Many analysts feel that the programme is boosting the purchasing power of the rural poor and it has led to a stable income for the rural population. The most eligible rural families that the NREGA hope to benefit are those of the landless-labours as well as the small and marginal farmers.

CONCLUSION

The importance of developing infrastructure has long been recognized as central in promoting economic growth. In rural areas it has wide ranging impacts on individuals, households and communities both in terms of income and other quality of life indicators. There are both direct and indirect benefits from infrastructure development and it is important to consider the indirect benefits in decision-making about infrastructure projects. Education, for example, can affect income and health both of that in turn affect quality of life. There are also strong social benefits from infrastructure that need to be taken into account. Economic benefits such as increased income, employment, productivity gain, better income distribution and opportunity for diversification are obvious. Social benefits such as time savings, school enrolment levels, access to health services, environmental improvement, skill development, capacity building, improved information and gender impacts are less transparent, but in the longer term may be as or more effective in poverty reduction because they lead to sustained improvements in quality of life independent of income sources.

NREGA is already making a difference to the lives of the people. Yet there is a long way to go. Without a doubt, NREGA has the potential to change the socio-economic landscape in rural India in the long term. Socio economic uplift of the masses has been the watchword of the rural development schemes being implemented in the district. It is very interesting time in the history of independent India, when the government is taking steps to provide its citizens with rights that it has never given before. NREGA is one of the greatest experiments undertaken in India to eradicate rural poverty. Ever since its launch, NREGA is playing the role of a catalyst in rural economy. It is true that corruption and lack of adequate preparation in implementing NREGA have led to some setbacks. Is spite of the some few shortfalls in the programme, the programme is successful but it requires more transparency in its implementation.

REFERENCES

Madheswaran, S., & Dharmadhikary, A. (2001), Empowering Rural Women through Self-Help Groups: Lessons from Maharastra Rural Credit Project. Indian Journal of Agricultural Economics. 56(3): 427-443.

World Bank (2003), Microfinance in India: Issues, Constraints, and Potential for Sustainable Growth. Washington, DC.

Gopal Singh et al. (2003), Economic Empowerment of Rural Women in India, RBSA Publishers, Jaipur, p. 25

Mishra K.C. (2008), Rural Development in India: Challenges and Task-Ahead, Southern Economist, Vol.47, No.8, p.5

Munian. A. (2009), Micro Finance Poverty Eradication: Analytical Issues, Southern Economist, Vol.48, No.1, p.43

Annural Report 2006-2007, Ministry of Rural Development, Govt. of India

Collier, Paul (1998), "Women in Development: Defining the Issues." Policy, Planning and Research Working Paper 129, Population and Human Resources Department, World Bank, Washington, D.C.

Sadik, N. (1988), "Women, the Center of Development", Development, Vol. 1, 30-31.

Rainer Kuhnle, Rural Infrastructure Development and Poverty Reduction in Bangladesh

World Bank (1990), Poverty-World Development Indicators, World Development Report

Mahatma Gandhi Rural Employment Guarantee Scheme and Trends in Women Empowerment 5

V. Preetha, D. Mavoothu

In a rural agrarian economy, which is also labor surplus, the population depends on the wages they earn through unskilled casual manual labor. They are vulnerable to the possibility of sinking from transient to chronic poverty in the event of inadequate labor demand or in the face of unpredictable crisis like ill health and disaster. In a context of poverty and unemployment workfare programme have been important intervention in developed as well as developing countries for many years. This programme typically provide unskilled manual workers with short-term employment on public work such as irrigation, infrastructure, forestation, soil conservation and road construction. The rationale for workfare programme provide incomes transfer to poor households during critical times and therefore enable consumption smoothening specially during slack agriculture seasons or years. In countries with high unemployment rate transfer benefit from workfare programmer can prevent poverty worsening especially during lean periods. Durable asset that these programme may create have the potential to generate a second round of employment benefit as necessary infrastructure is developed.

The need for evolving a mechanism to supplement existing livelihood sources in rural areas was recognized during development planning in India. The government implemented workfare programme that offered a minimum wage on public Works. The wage employment was started in different forms as a pilot project like Rural Manpower Programme (RMP), Crash Scheme For Rural Employment, Pilot Intensive Rural Employment Programme, National Rural Employment Programme, The Jawahar implemented by state government with central assistance was self-targeting, and the objectives was to provide enhanced livelihood security, specially of those depends on casual manual labor. At the state level the Government of Maharashtra formulates the Maharashtra Employment Guarantee Act in1977 to provide wage employment to those who demand it[1] .The united Progressive Alliance (UPA) Government made landmark legislation by implementing National Rural employment Guarantee Act (NREGA) in 2006. The NREGA built on the experience of Maharashtra Rural Employment Guarantee Act which shown possibility of putting permanent system of employment.

MAHATMA GANDHI RURAL EMPLOYMENT GUARANTEE ACT

Soon after assuming power the UPA Government took an impressive step. NREGA was formed by redesigning food for work Programme of 2004. NREGA is unique in the sense that it aims to provide rural employment on a large scale; it is the first expression of the right to work as an enforceable legal entitlement. The UPA government renamed NREGA into Mahatma Gandhi Rural Employment Guarantee Act (MGREGA) on October o2, 2009, when the country celebrated 140th birth anniversary of our Father Of Nation[2].

The economic architecture of MGREGA was Jean Dreaz[3]. In July2004 a draft of MREGA was prepared and sent to the National Advisory Council (NAC). Within a month NAC revised the draft and sent to the government for urgent consideration. In August 2005 Parliament passed the landmark legislation the NATIONAL RURAL EMPLOYMENT GURANTEE ACT. It is a national law funded largely by the central government and which guarantee 100 days of wage employment per year per households. The act placed an enforceable legal obligation on the state and gives bargaining power to the labours[4]. It calls for provide minimum statutory wages to the workers. The most remarkable feature of MGREGA is that it completely denied the role of contractors in its any stage.

MGREGA was a wise movement for improving rural households[5]. It can be seen as one element of a large vision for social policy. The vision involves both a major increase in government spending and a radical improvement in the composition. This vision is the reflection of the idea that government is the largest Employer of Last Resort as put forward by many economists like, J.M Keynes, David Ricardo and Karl Marx etc.

OBJECTIVES OF MGREGA

The primary objective of MGREGA is to provide not less than 100 days of employment of guaranteed employment in a financial year to every rural household who are willing to do unskilled manual work. The secondary objectives are the creation of durable community asset and development of infrastructure. The choice of work suggested in the act addresses causes of chronic poverty like drought, deforestation and soil erosion. The scheme has additional objectives of providing 1/3 rd of employment to women with a purpose of empowering them. Since the act lay on constant and consistent audits it call for quality of work as a central objectives. The local government is legally bound to provide employment to the applicant.[6]

FEATURES OF MGREGA

The following are the salient features of MGREGA [7]

- The MGREGA is open to all rural households who are in need of wage employment,
- Those who are willing to do unskilled manual work may submit an application form to the local Grama Panchayat, which issue job card that is valid for a period of five years,

- As far as possible employment should be provide within a radius of 5 Kilometer of the village where the applicant resides at the time of job application
- Every person who has done work is entitled to receive agricultural minimum wages as notified by the states government,
- Panchayat shall distribute wages on a weekly basis through individual account opened at scheduled commercial banks or post office,

The applicant is entitled to get unemployment allowances if the Grama Panchayat fails to provide employment within 15 days,

- The women get priority and 1/3 rd of employment must provide to women.

  (8) Panchayat Raj Institution plays a very important role in planning and implementation in the ratio of 50:30:20 for Grama Panchayat, Block Panchayat and District Panchayat,
- Equal wages should be paid to both men and women,
- There must be crèche facilities at the worksite to take care the children of women workers,
- The act emphasized on Social Audit
- It ensures Right to Information to the Public and the scheme completely banned the role of contractors

OUTLAYS AND FUNDING

The funding programme will be such that it is implemented as a centrally sponsored scheme under cost sharing basis between center and state is 90:10.The central government bears the cost of wages of unskilled manual works, 75%of cost of wages of skilled and semi-skilled workers, administrative costs such as salaries and allowances of programme officers and the supporting staff and expenses of employment guarantee council. The state government is entrusted to bear the cost of certain item like 25% of cost of materials and wages of skilled and semi-skilled workers, unemployment allowances and administrative expenses of state employment guarantee council[8].

The Concept of Women Empowerment

The topic of women empowerment has been discussed elaborately at various international conference from1975 onwards. The first united Nation General Assembly passed a resolution to eliminate all forms of discrimination against women. It emphasized the need for ensuring freedom and equity for women in civic, cultural, economic, political and social areas of the activities. The 1993 Vienna Conference on Population and Development and the Beijing Women's World Conference also highlighted the need for the promotion of women empowerment programme at all over the world[9]

Empowerment is the process of increasing the capacity of individual or groups to make choices and to transform those choices into desired actions and outcomes. Central to this process are actions, which build individual and collective asset and improve the efficiency and fairness of the organizational and institutional contexts that govern the use of these assets[10].

Empowerment is a kind of personal power...it's a sense of purpose where even supersteous belief can have a positive effect on our mind[11]

Empowerment means strengthening or the power and delegating authority to subordinate and give them the feeling that they are masters of their own work[12].

According to Kabeer," empowerment is the process by which those who have been denied the ability to make strategic life choice acquire such an ability of women to control resources, to determine agendas and make decisions"[13].

According to Moser, "Empowerment is the capacity of women to increase their own self-reliance and internal strength. This is identified as the right to determine choices in life and to influence the direction of changes, through the ability to gain control over materials and non-materials resources."[14]

Empowerment is commonly described as a process whereby women become able to organize themselves to increase their own self-reliance, to assist their independence to make choices and to control resources that will assist in challenging and eliminating their own self

MGREGA AND ITS IMPACT ON THE SOCIETY

MGREGA is a paradigm shift from programme to action. It provides a statutory guarantee of wage employment. It emphasized a legal basis for wage seekers in the application for employment. The legal guarantee has to be fulfilled within the time limit prescribed and thus mandate is underpinned by the provision of unemployment allowances. MGREGA is a demand -driven employment scheme and not supply- driven the act is designed in such a way of provide incentives for the state for granting employment by supllying90% of the cost by the central government. Resource transfer under MGREGA from center to state is based on the demand for employment and there is another incentive to state government to meet the employment need of the economy. Because of all these reason MGREGA is a unique in its implementation. It brings an empowering effect on the beneficiaries in particular and community in general which can be analyzed under following heading:

MGREGA BENEFICIARIES

About 4.5 crore households were benefited from MGREGA in a financial year 2008-09. The total number of beneficiaries were 2.1 crore and 3.39 crore in the financial year 2006-07 and 2007-08 respectively. Thus an increase is taking place in providing employment to rural folk. In percentage terms 32% increase took place in the financial year 2008-09as compared to 2007-08.[15]

IMPACT ON INCOME

The MGREGA empowers each state government to fix a statutory minimum wages to the employees on the basis of minimum wage Act of 1948. Since MGREGA wage is higher than that of wage in agricultural work, it increases income of the beneficiaries for example the wages for women workers is 60or 70 in Kerala for agricultural jobs. But MGREGA works bring wages of Rs.125 per day during off and peak seasons. The Report of Comptroller and Auditor General of India has pointed out that the government has spent more than Rs.40, 000crores in implementing MGREGA, out of which more than 25,000 crores has been paid as wages to those millions of manual workers. It reveals that more than half of expenditure was going to the pocket of beneficiaries[16].

IMPACT ON POVERTY

MGREGA ensures food security and protecting rural households from hunger. The main purpose of the scheme is to bring the landless families into the social safety net. Under this scheme the government has offered a modest gainful employment, which will fetch Rs. 500 -/-per month for a family. Thus it gives a necessary push to the purchasing power of the rural poor. An additional income of approximately Rs.6000 a year is sufficient to pull a section of family above the poverty line. A study conducted by E.M. Thomas by taking into account the MGREGA beneficiaries of vadakkanchery Panchayat in Palakkad district of Kerala reveals that MGREGA employment reduced poverty in the study areas. It helped 90% of beneficiaries to clear their debts.

IMPACT ON MIGRATION

The Act makes a dent in migration. Migration for work within and between states is common in the countryside and cities. When work is made available in the village, many rural families are likely to stay back instead of going to the cities in the slack seasons. For example a report prepared by Samathan -center for Development support[17], based on the monitoring report 2006-07 reveals that migration has considerably decreased due to availability of jobs at local level. The guaranteed employment increase incomes of labor which can be used to meet daily needs like food, cloth etc and ensure dignity of laborers. The response is collected from the beneficiaries of Maharashtra, Uttar Pradesh, Jharkhand, Chhattisgarh and Bihar. MGREGA increase bargaining power of labourers if they migrate because they have the opportunity of going back to home and will able to get jobs at a reasonable wage rate.

IMPACT ON PANCHAYAT RAJ INSTITUTION

Governments keenness to involve Panchayat raj institution directly in the scheme is laudable. Grama Panchayat and Gramasabha would decide types of works to be undertaken in the village and the use of funds earmarked under the scheme. Since the scheme calls for significant involvement of local people and Panchayat raj institution is absolutely essential to impart comprehensive training for transferring various skills. It is also essential that the implementation process needs to be reviewed and monitored rightly at the Panchayat raj institution level.[18]

IMPACT ON INFRASTRUCTURE

The act is concerned with the development of social infrastructure. The Act calls for steps towards growth through higher investment in rural infrastructure. The labor-intensive public works such as watershed management, land regeneration, restoration of tanks, protection of forest, etc increase productivity of agriculture. It may also lead to enhanced opportunities for the poor through fishing and other water related production.

IMPACT ON EDUCATION AND HEALTH

Second monitoring Report of MGREGA in Uttar Pradesh, Maharashtra, Madhya Pradesh, Jharkhand, Chhattisgarh and Bihar reveals that villagers spend their income to improve quality of education of children by paying admission fees, purchasing books, providing tuition fees, buying school uniform etc. Due to construction of connectivity of road, children get opportunity of go to school by vehicle or foot and children's more regular in attending class.

The study also reveals that some of the beneficiaries using MGREGA payment for treatment of family members. Since employment generation increases income, the village people have more money at their hand and hence they are able to spend on health of family.

IMPACT ON ACCESS TO BANKING SERVICES

Till the implementation of MGREGA despite the spread of rural banks large number of rural households does not have any access to banking service over 7.33 crore MGREGA bank and post office account have been opened so far. This MGREGA helped to bring rural poor under organized banking service. In addition to that the workers are provided with medical and health care insurance. Certain innovative experiments in the form of smart card and biometric signature for wage payments in remote villages are also implemented. Close to 5 crore saving bank account have been opened with post office and banks across the country just for the payment of wages under MGREGA. States like, Anthra Pradesh, Karnataka,, Himachal Pradesh and Kerala have opened saving bank account for all MGREGA employees, while others like Orissa, Jharkhand, Chattisgarh, Madhya Pradesh and Rajasthan have made substantial progress in providing banking services to rural folk[19]

IMPACT ON INCLUSIVE GROWTH

MGREGA provides employment to marginalized groups like Scheduled Caste /scheduled Tribes and women. The participation percentage of Scheduled /Scheduled tribe were 55% in 2008-09 53% and upto July 2009.Women has surpassed the statutory minimum requirements of 33% in 2008-09 . It was 48%in 2008-09 and 52% in 2009-10 (up to July).

MGREGA and Women Participation

The female unemployment rate was slightly higher than that of male for the world as a whole. It was 6.4%for female and 6.1%for males (Report of Inter National Labor Organization 2004) Many of the studies reveals that workers participation rate of women were fall short of men. As against 51.6% for males, it was only 22.7% for females. The corresponding worker participation in Kerala was 50.6% and 15.3% for males and females [20]

The table below reveals that worker participation rates favours male both in urban and rural areas. The worker participation rates among females in rural areas are higher than that of urban females. For example rural female participation rates is 32.7% in 2004-2005, but it was only 16.6% in urban areas

As per the record of International Labor organization, in an economy where agriculture provide employment to larger share of population, women are more likely to find employment in the informal economy than men.

Table 1
Worker Participation Rates in India

Category	*Year* 1993-94	1999-2000	2004-2005
Rural male	55.3%	53.1%	54.6%
Rural female	32.8%	29.9%	32.7%
Urban male	52.15%	51.8%	54.9%
Urban female	15.5%	13.9%	16.6%

Source: Economic Review2008[21]

Since the above table reveals large share of female worker participation rates in rural areas as compared to urban areas the decision to implement MGREGA in the rural areas was right and good in every sense. The analysis of following table reveals that a large share of MGREGA employment generated are enjoyed by women

Table 2
MGREGA Employment and Women Participation

Year	*Total Number of Days of Employment (in crore)*	*Women Share in MGREGA Employment (in %)*
2006-07	2.1	40
2007-08	3.39	42.52
2008-09	4.5	47.88
2009-10(up to October 2009)	3.42	51.05

*Source.*www.nrega.nic.in

From the above table it is clear that women worker participation was increasing over years under MGREGA work.

For example it was 61.09 lakh (42.52%) in 2007-06 which increased to 103.57 lakh (47.88%) in 2008-09 and 51.05% till October 2009

Thus as against over all worker participation MGREGA, women worker participation share a positive trends.

MGREGA AND WOMEN EMPOWERMENT

Gender equality has been considered as one of the essential components of human development in rural areas over several years. Empowerment is a goal of action and process of reflection. Many studies revealed that MGREGA have great empowering effect on the women. Because it incorporates special provision that lead to better standards of living for women India is a rural economy where a large share of population depends on agriculture. A report of International labor Organization stated that agriculture job is shared largely by women workers but their mobility to job is limited by many factors like they have to take of their children, they are confined to surrounding of their home due to ideology of seclusion and they are vulnerable class and caste related sex abuses. In addition to that rural womens have less access to information on job opportunities because of the lower literacy level, less access to mass media and interaction with the market place. Introduction of mechanized cultivation has displaced women who have hardly been trained in the use of machine series and have thus remained confined to manual tasks.

As compared to previous wage employment programme MGREGA employment, are attractive for women. Since MGREGA employments are locally available, being government work there is regularity and predictability of working hours, less chance of work condition being exploitative and work is considered socially acceptable and dignified. It is better paid than any other work to women. The Act stipulated that work is provided locally, within five Kilo Meter of the residence. This makes participation in MGREGA work is logistically feasible for women. Since women have to bear the main responsibility of households works traveling any distance for paid work is makes more difficulty to women. The MGREGA was regarded acceptable because of another important reason that it promises the statutory minimum wages. In addition to the fact that the local government rather than private employees offers MGREGA work, it frees potential women workers from the caste and community based structures related to who they can and cannot work. Moreover, MGREGA employment offers a new sense of independence for women. Many studies reveal that the women working in MGREGA is benefited in many senses because they do not have to go through a potentially embarrassing and humiliating conversation to ask anyone in the village for work

The empowerment of MGREGA on women can be analyzed with the help of following trends on different aspects.

Government figures indicate an impressive participation in the MGREGAwork.In2008-2009, 103.57 lakhs of women workers were engaged in MGREGA. It was only 61.09 lakhs in 2007-2008. In percentage terms it was 42.52% and 47.88% respectively.[22]

Employment at MGREGA worksite seems to have raised both enthusiasm and expectation among women workers. Women workers unanimously affirmed that the benefit from MGREGA employment were high and therefore they would like to get more days of work in a year

A survey conducted in May-June 2008 in six north Indian states reveals that a large majority of (79%) women workers collect their own wages and they keep their wages. It is true that what really matters are not who keep the money but who has control over it. Interview with women suggest that in a larger number of cases women have substantial share in deciding how the money is to be spent.[23]

A study of National Federation on Indian Women[24] under MGREGA reveals that there is a positive trends in migration in sample states-Chattisgarh,Madhya Pradesh,Orissa, and ThamiNadu. It seems that hopes and works generated by MGREGA has made the poor citizens able to remain in their own villages. 73% of the respondents in the study area reveal that neither they nor their family used to migrate in 2007. This will certainly have significant impact on the questions of security, health and children's education.

Since MGREGA works concentrated on water harvesting and irrigations it puts an end to the water scarcity problem in the village areas, which in turn help, the rural women. A study by Digumarti Bhaskara Rao[25] and others found that the proportion of rural woman affected by water scarcity is estimated by 32%in Asia. The median time for collecting water in the dry season is 1.6 hours per day and in wet seasons .6 hours. Collecting water from rivers and springs takes more than other sources. Thus water scarcity forces women to spend more time in water collection than employment. A study of Ministry of Rural Development for the year 2003 shows that 54% of work undertaken was related to water conservation on which in turn reduce the time required to collect water and can create a favorable situation to engage in other economically advantage works.

Widows are the other major group who enjoy the benefit of MGREGA employment. As per 1991 census there are about 33 millions widows in India. The proportion of widows in the female population rises sharply with age reaching 60- 70 and above [26]. A study report from Uttar Pradesh reveals that the life of widows had undergone many changes because they can earn more than that of earnings under other works. In addition to those widows who are not getting widow pensions MGREGA employment offers relief and confidence. Studies also reveal it improved credit-worthiness importantly for some women and especially for women heading households.The MGREGA has made loans more easily available and women say they have been able to repay at least a part of their loans.

Several respondents stated that work provide under the MGREGA has allowed them to stop doing hazardous work or work they did not want to do.

Many of the respondents opined that payment through banks and post office could benefit them greatly. Because it will increase the possibility of saving and a reduction in the possibility of being cheated away by those who distribute wage in the village. It is an effective tool for increasing control over the resources use by women

CHALLENGES AND PROBLEMS

The MGREGA is a revolutionary legislation. It has led to the payment of a hundred days of employment and wages in many parts of the country and has created awareness amongst workers about their rights. But there is much that still needs to be improved upon. In many states the implementation is faced with many challenges. These challenges are different for different states. Some of the most notable problems in the implementation are discussed below:

UNAWARENESS

Most women were aware about the fact that each households is guaranteed 100 days of work in a year. But awareness about operational guidelines, households' registration, the job card distribution process, work application and entitlements such as worksite facilities and unemployment allowances were inadequate. A study of National Federation of Indian Women has find that only less than half of Indian women workers have made a formal application for a job card. Most people just applied orally or gave their names when asked whether they wanted a job card in addition to various labor sectors such as street vendors, cobblers, auto rickshaw drivers etc were unaware of the law

LACK OF PROPER PLANNING

A Report of Comptroller and Auditor General stated that many districts lack proper perspective plans and annual plans for the implementation of the scheme. As a result most of the work is undertaken rashly at the end of each year and the people didn't get 100 days of employment. For example, Chattisgarh produced employment of just 35 days per households per year on an average in a fiscal year 2007-2008 under MGREGA and it was 41 days in 2006-07. In Bihar till February 2009 only an average of 35 days of employment was provided

Delay in Wage Payments

Though the Act stipulated payment of wages within 15 days of the work done, huge delay was made in payment of wages and several people were also deprived of unemployment allowances. There were delays even up to 326 days in certain states like Chattisgarh and Bihar.[27]

MGREGA AS A BARRIER TO ECONOMIC DEVELOPMENT

The World Bank has described that much acclaimed MGREGA is a barrier for economic development since it prevent internal mobility (World Bank Report 2009). According to the report the internal mobility is necessary, as lifting people out of poverty requires shifting population from village to cities. The bank said that the process of migration should be encouraged. It opined that negative attitude led by the government and ignorance of the benefit of population mobility has caused migration to be overlooked as a force in economic development[28].

LACK OF PAYMENT OF MINIMUM WAGES

Many of villagers forced to conduct agitation and protest against the payment of wages, which is less than that of minimum statutory wages. At the same time there are certain states, which pay more than that of minimum wages

CORRUPTIONS

The Study of National Council of Applied Economic Research reveals that there are several cases of corruptions in MGREGA. Cases of corruptions, discrepancies in workdays and payment have been reported in almost all studies. The study said that several cases of over reporting, discrimination, and significant delays in providing job cards and inflated wages[29]. The whole process become very bureaucratic which involves lot of paper work and causing undue delays. A study of Bimal Jalan,former Governer of Reserve Bank of India reveals same facts.

INTER-STATE VARIATIONS

There is considerable inter-state variation in providing employment and the distributing wages. States that pay compensation include Madhya Pradesh, Orissa, Maharashtra, West Bengal, Kerala, Manipur and Jharkhand.

POOR WORK-SITE FACILITIES

MGREGA is committed to ensuring a workplace conducive to productivity and workers welfare. With this in mind MGREGA have been allocated for the purpose of providing safe drinking water, shade for period of rest, first aid and child care facilities at the worksites. But studies reveal that these facilities are routinely absent from worksites. In addition to the report of Comptroller and Auditor General Report (2007) has pointed out that in Bihar as 8.99 lakhs was paid as wages to fictious labor in respect of 7 days of work reduced, the names of same workers were recorded twice or thrice. It also pointed out shortcomings in the maintenance of job card and muster roles in many places.

LACK OF ATTAINING GOAL

According to the MGREGA websites as on March 2009, out of total 99 million households that demand employment the number of households working under MGREGA is only 14 million and the cumulative number of households that have completed 100 days of employment is about 4 million, thus there is lack of attaining goal. In most of the states the mandatory biannual social audit is not taking place.

UNAVAILABILITY OF ADMINISTRATIVE STAFFS

Social audit in many states reveals inadequacy of administrative staff, which is, affected MGREGA implementation.

LOW QUALITY OF ASSET CREATED

As far as quality of projects being undertaken under MGREGA is concerned, the Director of Center for Environmental Concern, K.S.Gopal has pointed out that all the asset created under the scheme are waste and by and large unproductive. He also pointes out that quite correctly the work becomes an asset only if it has any of the productive use and majority of the MGREGA projects ends up with being unproductive. The ponds,lakes,canals etc. were remained as an useless things with no one take responsibility for further maintenance.

SUGGETIONS

Based on the above analysis following important suggestions that have to be undertaken to reap the fruit of MGREGA are given;

- Intensive efforts should be made to increase awareness among employees through media and short duration classes,
- The Panchayath Raj Institution should lay down proper planning based on the need of locality,
- Efforts should be made for implementation of planning within a stipulated time periods.
- Required administrative staff should be appointed as early as possible to ensure smooth implementation,
- The government should seriously considered to recognize a one year diploma courses conducted by wide range of Government and non government training institution spread across the country
- Special recruitment for office staff through Union Public Service Commission and State Public Commission can be made. Such officers can be appointed only after at least six months of training,
- Delay in wage payment should be avoided because most of the MGREGA beneficiaries are those from socially and economically disadvantaged sections, (8)Bi-annual monitoring should be undertaken and necessary steps should be made to overcome drawbacks revealed by the monitoring report,
- Most of the MGREGA reports are published through Internet are not accessible to the beneficiaries because of lack of knowledge about it's operation. So short-term classes can be provided to beneficiaries for such purpose,
- Effort should be made to ensure adequate worksite facilities envisaged by MGREGA,

- Central Government should pay attention for the efficient implementation of MGREGA in all states especially poorly implementing states,
- Attempts should be made to ensure quality of work undertaken under the scheme,
- Social audits can be conducted to ensure transparency in procedure,
- The decision of Ministry of Rural Development for starting an independent redressal mechanism through Lok Adalath and a National Helpline to lodge complaints against corrupt practice is good and it should be made in practice as early as possible and
- Establish the village knowledge center which serve as a means for check whether they are actually receiving the promising benefits and to complain against corrupt government functionaries

CONCLUSION

To conclude we must have faith in what our Prime Minister Dr. Manmohan Singh has described "MGREGA as a landmark in our history in removing poverty from the face of nation". We should not forget that MGREGA is a single largest rights based social protection initiative in the world. It is the first ever law internationally, that guarantees wage employment at an unprecedented scale. The law is a big boost for nomadic tribal community since locally domiciled but migrant population is also eligible for employment. In spite of many challenges,the reports from certain states show that there is a significant leap forward in employment . Several features like Right To Information and monitoring, etc put together signals the possibility of inaugurating a wholly new chapter in rural governance of India. It also provides an opportunity for improving gender relation in some of the most remote areas of the country. By taking inspiration from the gains that MGREGA made effort should be made to strengthen these gains by removing barriers for achieving goals. The achievement of some state can be taken as a good model for non-achieving states for the flagship program to be effective

ENDNOTES

1. 'National Rural Employment Guarantee Act', A Report prepared by Ministry of Rural Developmentt2006-2007
2. The Hindu,Coimbatore, October3,2009
3. Fadhel Kaboub (2007), 'Employment Guarantee Program: A Survey on Theories And Policy Experience', Working Paper
4. Jean Dreze(2005)', Employment Guarantee Promise and Demise',Yojana, Volume 49,,pp.4-8
5. The Hindu,,Coimbathur,October 14,2009
6. National Rural Employment Guarantee Scheme at a Glance A Report Prepared by District Program Co-ordinater, Palakkad.2007
7. Government of India, National Rural Employment Guarantee Act: Operational Guidelines (2006)
8. [6]
9. Empowerment Definition, Available at http://translate google.com in/translate?hl=en&s1=es=u=http://www.wikilearning.com/monografia/empowerment-definition
10. Empowerment, available at http://web.worldbank.org/WESITE EXTERNAL/TOPICS/EXTPOVERTY/EXTEMPOWERMENT/0,,contentMDK20245753~PAGE PK:210058~pipk210062~the site PK:486411html
11. Empowerment Available at http://www.achieving-life-abundance.com /cmpowerment definition.html
12. [11]
13. [11]
14. [1]
15. Official Data of MGREGA implementation status Available at www.nrega.nic.in
16. The Hindu, Coimbatore, May25, 2009
17. Status of NREGA Implementation: 2nd Monitoring Report Prepared by Samarthan Center For Development Support
18. Amrit Patel, 'Role Of PRI in Implementing Rural Employment Guarantee Scheme', Kurukshetra, Volume54, NO: 10,August2006, pp 24-33
19. (15)
20. Worker Participation Rate Available athttp://www.napsipag-researchorg/pdf/Em-THOMAS.pdf
21. Economic Review 2008,Prepared by State Planning Board TVM, KeralaPage. 443
22. [15], New Delhi
23. Reethika Khera et al(2009),Women workers and Perception of the National Rural Employment Guarantee Act, Economic And Political Weekly,VolumeXLIV,NO:43,PP 49-56
24. 'A Study on Socio-Economic Empowerment of Women under NREGA,(2008),A study by National Federation of Indian Women
25. Digumarti et.al(1999),Status of World's Women, Discovery Publishing House p.28

26. C.S. Prasad et.al.(2007),Sixty Yeares oF the Indian Economy(1947-2007),New Delhi,Centurey Publication,pp.716-742
27. Samu,(2009),Labour: NREGA/Employment.Human Rights Documentation, Indian Social Institute,NewDElhi
28. The Hindu, Coimbatore 2009
29. All-India Report on Evaluation of NREGA: A Survey of Twenty Districts (2007), Prepared by Institute OF Applied Man Power Research

Implementation of NREGS in the Narasannapeta Mandal of Srikakulam District of Andhra Pradesh 6

M. Sundara Rao, B. Lakshamana Rao

During the period of planned economic development the Government of India is initiating and implementing a series of Wage Employment programmes. According to researchers the earlier rural employment programmes are not able to deliver the expected results due to the constraints like: lack of awareness, lack of planning, quality of assets created not always of requisite standard, reports of false muster rolls, problems in Payment: often less than prescribed wages, disparity between wages paid to women and men, contractors persisted, no comprehensive database, inadequate capacity of implementing agencies and lack of public accountability. India's long experience of employment generation programmes has lessons to offer. The lack of comprehensive planning, improper targeting of beneficiaries, and leakages in implementation are some of the major deficiencies. An employment scheme for rural India should go beyond the present scope of public works projects, and address urban demands. While taking into account the above constraints the Governemnt of India launched National Rural Employment Guarantee Scheme (NREGS) which is an offshoot of National Rural Employment Act-2005, which was enacted by parliament in September, 2005.

SPECIAL FEATURES OF NREGS

The objectives of NREGS are to provide hundred days of wage employment, unskilled manual work to any adult, who seeks work, Livelihood security to rural Households and creation of durable community assets. The NREGS should be viewed as a demand driven programme but not a supply oriented one. The Government has a statutory obligation to provide employment to every household, or, if unable to do so, to provide on the fringes of hunger, disillusioned by government schemes and unfulfilled promises will able to asset their right in the existing scenario of politico-bureaucratic nexus.

The newly introduced dimensions in NREGS as the compulsory stipulations are: hundred days of wage employment on demand in a financial year to the registered households, payment on weekly basis, equal wages to men and women, ban on contractors and labour-displacing machines, only works identified by Gram Panchayat, Mandal Parishad and Zilla Parishad. The special provisions to be provided for the benefit of workers are: engaging aaya for taking care of children at work site, engaging water persons for supply of drinking water at worksites, providing shade and floor sheet at work site, first aid box at worksite and medical facilities and compensation for accident s and deaths The priority works to be undertaken under NREGS arte identified as: water conservation and water harvesting, drought proofing including a forestation, irrigation canals including micro irrigation works, provision of irrigation facilities to SC/ST, renovation of traditional water bodies, land development, flood control and protection works, rural connectivity and any other works approved by Government of India..

The officials involved in NREGS are: at village level are Field Assistant, Grama Panchayat Secretary and Grama Panchayt. At the Mandal level PO, MPDO and MPP will take part and at District level PD DWMA, District Progamme Coordinator, DPC (Dist. Collector) and ZP and at Tribal Areas PO, ITDA. The Panchayat Raj Institutons play an important role in planning and implementation. Nearly 75per cent works are to be managed by Gram Panchayats, 15per cent by Mandal

Praja Parishads and the remaining 10 percent by Zilla Praja Parishads. As a whole the Grama Panchayat is the implementing agency for all the NREGS works. Regarding the administrative staff, at village level - Field Assistant, at Mandal Level-3 Tech. Assistants, 2 Computer Operators, 1 Programme Officer and at District level - Project Director, Additional Project Director, 3 Programme Managers and At State level Director one State Project Manager and 7 Project Managers will be there to look after the management of the NREGS works. This study mainly focuses upon analyzing different dimensions relating To the implementation aspects of NREGS works in the Narasannapeta mandal of Srikakulam district of Andhra Pradesh while selecting a sample of 150 NREGS beneficiaries from the selected two villages.

THE IMPLEMENTATION ASPECTS OF NREGS IN THE STUDY AREA

In the state of Andhra Pradesh the implementation of NREGS in the state of progress. The information given in Table 1 shows that since its inception in the state 1129294 job cards are issued in which the number of individuals covered are recorded at 25369548. During 2008-09 1596940 job cards are issued in which the number of individuals recorded at 3041973. Under NREGS during 2008-09 wage employment is provided to 65516106 households and the individuals consist of 9569900. An amount of Rs. 16450154 lakhs were spent towards labour wages and a total amount of Rs 21955893 lakhs were spent on different aspects of NREGS. At the state level the average number of days of employment during 2008-09 is recorded as 36.17 and the number of households completed 100 days of work is recorded as 342422.

In the selected Srikakulam district of Andhra Pradesh also the implementation of NREGS in the state of progress. The information given in Table 1 shows that since its inception in the district 473838 job cards are issued in which the number of individuals covered are recorded at 1061568. During 2008-09, 53117 job cards are issued in which the number of individuals recorded is 12698. Under NREGS during 2008-09 in the Srikakulam district the wage employment is provided to

Table 1

Implementation Aspects of NREGS : 2008-09 (Upto Feb 2009)

Item	*State*	*Distract*	*Mandal*
	Andhra Pradesh	*Srikakulam*	*Narasannapeta*
No.of Job Cards issued(since inception)	11296294	473838	12466
No.of Individuals in Job Cards(since inception)	25369548	1061568	28879
No.of Job Cards issued during 2008-09	1596940	53117	272
No.of Individuals in Job Cards during 2008-09	3041973	12698	515
Wage Employment Provided during 2008-09			
a) No.of House Holds	65516106	269722	6315
b) No.of Labour	9569900	423961	9469
Expenditure on Labour Wages(Rs in lakhs)	16450154	715139	186
Material -Skilld Wage (Rs in lakhs)	4601114	42188	7
Contigency (Rs in lakhs)	904625	31844	7
Total expenditure(Rs in lakhs)	21955893	789171	200
Avg days of Employment	36.17	33.94	38
No. of House Holds Completed 100 Days	342422	11099	276

Source: Department of Rural development, Govt of Andhra Pradesh, 2008-09.

269722 households and the individuals consist of 423961. An amount of Rs. 715139 lakhs were spent towards labour wages and a total amount of Rs 789171 lakhs were spent on different aspects of NREGS. At the district level the average number of days of employment during 2008-09 is recorded as 33.94 which is lower than the state average of 36.17 days and the number of households completed 100 days of work are recorded as only11099.

In the selected Narasannapeta mandal the implementation of NREGS is in the initial stages. The information given in Table 1 shows that since its inception in the mandal 12466 job cards are issued in which the number of individuals covered are recorded at 28879. During 2008-09(up to Feb) only 272 job cards are issued in which the number of individuals recorded are 515. Under NREGS during 2008-09 in the Narasannapeta mandal the wage employment is provided to only 6315 households and the individuals consist of 9469. An amount of Rs.186 lakhs were spent towards labour wages and a total amount of Rs. 200 lakhs were spent on different aspects of NREGS. At the mandal level the average number of days of employment during 2008-09 is recorded as 38 which is lower than the state average of 38 days which is higher than both the average of state and also selected district. The number of households completed 100 days of work is recorded as only 276.

Socio Economic Features of the Selected Households

The demographic profile of the sample households shows that, a major proportion of sample households are having the family size with 4 members only and more than 6 members are in very lower proportion. The structure of the family size of the selected sample households ultimately reveal that due to the effective implementation of family welfare programmes in the study area the extent of the family size of the households is recorded low. The statistical information relating to age composition of the family members of selected households shows that the family members below the age group of 0-14 and above 51 are very limited. On the other hand the number of family numbers who are in the age group of 15-30, which is very effective age group are in higher proportion and more than 75 per cent of family members lies in the age group of 15-50 years.. The information relating to the levels of literacy of family members show that major proportion are found illiterates. Among the educated family members higher extent are in the stage of primary education.. The information relating to occupational structure of the family members of the selected households indicate that more than 90 per cent of them are participation in labour works. Only 4 percent of them are involved in cultivation activity.

The Management Aspects of the NREGS in the Study Area

In this study an attempt is made to assess the participation levels of the respondents in the NREGS works. In this context different implementation aspects and workers responses about the existing practices under NREGS works are carried out. The important issues like the source through the workers came to know about NREGS works, whether they received employment letter or not, the number of working days of the workers in the NREGS works, the reasons for their limited participation in NREGS works, the average number of annual working days, the average daily wage received by them, different particulars about the nature and payment of wages, the selection procedure supervision aspects are carried out in this study.

The analysis pertaining to the source of information about NREGS reveals that 26.43 percent of the respondents came to know about NREGS through local sources like village leaders and 19.44 percent are aware through sarpanches. However nearly 20 percent of respondents are aware of this programme through village level field assistant who is specifically appointed for this programme. The analysis relating to the number of days waited by the respondents to get the job cards shows that, nearly 60 percent of the respondents receive their job cards in less than 10 days of their registration. Similarly nearly 30 percent got their job cards in less than 25 days. This information indicate that majority of the respondents are able to get their job cards before the stipulated time of two weeks.

It seems that the concerned are able to fulfill their duties promptly in giving job cards. A higher proportion of nearly 90 percent of the sample respondents are able to get information about their employment through field assistant who is specifically appointed to implement the NREGS at the village level. This indicates that the involvement of local leaders and the village level institutions is very limited in the implementation of NREGS. It is very interesting to note that only 30 percent of the respondents received their employment letters and 70 percent of respondents are reported that they have not received any employment letter.

Though the respondents are offered with a minimum of 100 days of work under NREGS, out of total respondents, only 35 percent are able to avail the opportunity of working for a stipulated period of 100 days and also more than that. That proportion of respondents who worked for less than 50 days or recorded minimum. A higher proportion of nearly 53 percent respondents availed only 50-59 days work.. Hence, an attempt is made to identify the reasons for the non-availing of the respondents minimum 100 days of work provided under NREGS. The analysis pertaining to identify the reasons for their inability to avail 100 days of stipulated work is carried out. Among the sample respondents who are not able to attend full days of work under NREGS, nearly 30 percent of respondents reported that due to attend their own works, 15 percent reported sickness as the reason for not fulfilling complete full days of work. The analysis reveals that though the respondents are offered with a minimum of 100 days under NREGS, they are not able to avail the guaranteed days of work because of their personnel reasons.

Respondents Views on Implementation of NREGS

An attempt is made to know the reaction of the respondents what will be their reaction if they are being denied in providing the guaranteed 100 days of work under NREGS. Nearly half of the respondents stated that they will report that matter to the concerned field assistant who is associated with the scheme. Only 10 percent of the respondents stated that they will place the issue before the Village Panchayat. The available statistical information on this issue reveal that the respondents are well aware about to whom they have to report the irregularities took under NREGS. An attempt is also made to estimate the average daily wage received by the respondents during their work period. It is noticed that though the worker is to be provided with a daily wage of Rs. 80 under NREGS, it is found that in the study area by and large the respondents are provided with peace rate of wage, rather than daily wage, due to the prevalence of peace rates of wage, the respondents received different wage rates on daily basis. In the study area only 15 percent of total respondents are able to receive more than Rs.80 as average daily wage. It is also noticed that a major proportion of the total respondents have received an average daily wage in between Rs. 50-80 and nearly 10 percent of respondents have received an average daily wage which is less than Rs.50. The average daily wage received by the respondents is quite lower than the stipulated daily wage of Rs.80 offered under NREGS. This may be attributed as a reason for the inability of the major proportion of respondents for not availing the guaranteed 100 days of work under NREGS.

The average hours of work per day contributed by the sample respondents are estimated. It is found that only half of total respondents are able to contribute the stipulated 8 hours of work per day on an average. It is noticed that nearly half of the selected respondents have contributed only 6 hours of work per day on an average. The analysis relating to average hours of work contributed by respondents per day is found relatively low. The statistical information relating to the frequency of payment of wages shows that under NREGS the respondents have to be provided with only payments. However, in the study area it is found that nearly 15 percent of the respondents are not able to receive weekly payments. They are being provided with monthly payments because of delays taking place in the submission of bills and in their processing. The analysis relating to the place of wages to the respondents covered under NREGS shows that, three forth respondents reported that wages are paying through post offices according to the norms of NREGS. However, 20 percent of respondents are paid their wages through SHGs, where there is the scope for recovery of the old loans of the respondents.

The information relating to the procedure followed for the selection of workers is extracted from the sample respondents. It is noticed that, large number of respondents are selected through SHGs; Village Secretary, ward members and with the officers help. The extent of political support is only recorded at 10 percent. It shows that the selection of workers is largely conducted on official lines rather than political and other aspects. In the study area it is observed that the concerned officials following strictly regarding muster rolls and all respondents reported that muster rolls are taken every day on regular basis. The collected data relating to the different sources of supervising officials who have coordinated the different activities undertaken by the workers reveal that a major proportion of the activity of the workers is being supervised by the concerned field assistant. Generally according to the norms of NREGS, each household will be provided with one job card. In the study area it is found that a higher proportion of the households is provided with single job card. However, 15 percent of the households are provided with two existence of more number of workers in the households. The number of working persons under NREGS from each household is estimated. It is founded that higher proportion of the selected households are having two workers. The households with single worker are recorded at 33 percent and remaining households are having either 3 or more than 3 workers.

CONCLUSION

The above analysis ultimately reveals that in the study area the ongoing National Rural Employment Guarantee Scheme (NREGS) has achieved success in promoting employment opportunities in the interior villages of the Narasannapeta mandal of the backward Srikakulam district in Andhra Pradesh. The success of the NREGS is set against the rural-specific milieu characterized by poorer educational attainment levels, lower levels of economically active population, declining employment opportunities in the It is noticed tha t the NREGS is able to succeed in the study area because of its important feature of the involvement of local bodies, as they are closer to the problem. Empowering local bodies to create jobs in education and healthcare, and other public services, will cater to the varied requirements of rural employment seekers and serving as an efficient starting point. However, wage employment schemes like NREGS which are supported by government can only offer transitional solutions. The government should simultaneously address skills-shortage and create the environment necessary for fostering economic development

REFERENCES

Jean Dreze, Financial Implication of an Employment Guarantee Act: Preliminary Estimates, Note prepared on behalf of the National Advisory Council.

C.P. Chandrasekhar and Jayati Ghosh "How Feasible is a Rural Employment Guarantee" ?in India: An Economic Agenda for 2004

Jayati Ghosh (2004), "Paying for Employment Guarantee" Frontline October.

Kalar Khera " Rural Employment Scheme a Hit in Northern India, Feb 28, Yahoo News.

Arghyam: "National Rural Employment Guarantee Act: Water Shed Programme".

Government of India: National Rural Employment Act - 2005

Ministry of Rural Development, New Delhi. (2006): *"NREGA 2005 Operational Guidelines"*.

Adult Education – An Instrument of Poverty Alleviation

7

K. Sudha Rani, T. Ananda

Poverty can be defined as a social phenomenon in which a section of the society is unable to fulfill even its basic necessities of life. Poverty in India still remains unabated. The country has hardly been able to establish her identity free from the age old impression 'India is a poor country'. Despite decades long effort most of our population are still struggling below poverty line. The Gandhiji's dream to provide each and every Indian poor an access to basic needs of life is yet to be materialized. Although the planning commission of India has added qualitative parameters to the concept of basic needs, in terms of minimum food, clothing and shelter, our country has failed to provide the same to its citizens.

POVERTY SCENARIO IN INDIA

Millions of people in India are unable to meet these basic standards, and according to government estimates, in 2007 there were nearly 220.1 million people living below the poverty line.

Nearly 21.1% of the entire rural population and 15% of the urban population of India exists in this difficult physical and financial predicament. The following chart presents the poverty situation:

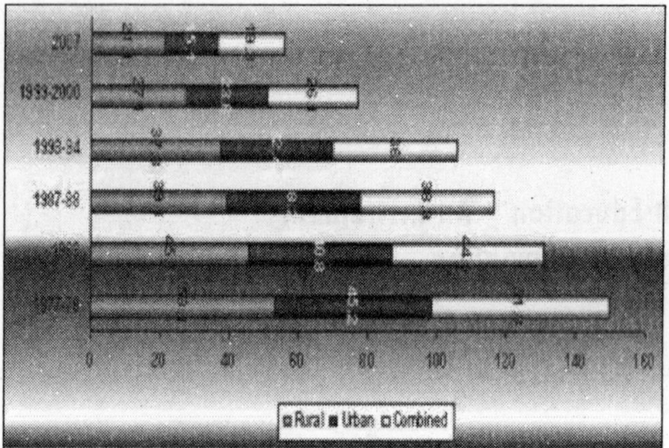

Source: World Development Indicators database, April 2002

Fig 1: Poverty Scenario in India

The division of resources, as well as wealth, is very uneven in India–this disparity creates different poverty ratios for different states. For instance, states such as Delhi and Punjab have very low poverty ratios. On the other hand, 40-50% of the populations in Bihar and Orissa live below the poverty line.

POVERTY IN INDIA- FRESH FIGURES

Despite sustained high GDP growth in India, latest estimates of global poverty by World Bank suggest that India has more people living below US$ 2 than even sub-Saharan Africa. These new figures should compel political leaders and policymakers to devise fresh strategies to reduce poverty.

None other than the World Bank (WB) has busted the hype about India's post-liberalization success. According to the Bank's new estimates not only is India home to roughly one-third of all the poor in the world, it has a higher proportion of its population living on less than $ 2 a day than even sub-Saharan Africa.

Compared with India's 828 million people, or 75.6% of the population living below US$ 2 a day, sub-Saharan Africa, considered the world's poorest region, ranks better with 72.2%

of its population - about 551 million people - below the US$ 2 a day level.

India has 456 million people, or around 42% of its population living below the new international poverty line of $ 1.25 a day. The number of Indian poor constitutes 33% of the global poor-pegged at 1.4 billion people.

NEW ESTIMATES

The new estimates are based on recently re-calculated purchasing power parity (PPP) exchange rates that make comparisons across countries possible. The new PPP has been arrived at as "the average poverty line found in the poorest 10-20 countries," according to the Bank's briefing note.

In other words, nearly five out of 10 Indians live below what the world's poorest countries consider the poverty line.

These sobering figures have emerged from the World Bank's latest estimates on global poverty, and clearly hint at the fruits of economic benefits having failed to trickle down to India's poor.

The data available shows that the rate of poverty decline in India was faster between 1981 and 1990 than between 1990 and 2005. The poverty rate - those below $ 1.25 per day - for India declined from 59.8% in 1981 to 51.3% by 1990, or 8.5 percentage points over nine years. Between 1990 and 2005 it declined to 41.6%, which is a drop of 9.7 percentage points over 15 years, clearly a much slower rate of decline.

PROVISIONS

Right from the independence our Government started a number of poverty eradication programmes. Swarnajayanti Gram Swarojagar Yojana (SGSY), Drought Prone Area Programme (DPAP), Tribal Area Development Programme (TADP), High Yield Variety Programme (HYVP), Minimum Needs Programme (MNP), Training of rural Youth for Self-Employment (TRYSEM) etc. Though some of the above programmes recorded appreciable progress in some areas, by and large all programmes and their approaches were selective, sporadic, and sectorial in nature and suffered from several defects.

However there is no denying the fact that our progress is very slow and most corresponding adequately to the extent of our need. Although there is a lot of provision for the poverty stricken masses of our country the former always fails to reach the latter properly. This may be attributed to the procedural and attitudinal rigidities in government machinery, corrupt practices, and lack of proportionate distribution on the part of clients, misuse of government benefits by the clients etc.

It can hardly be said that the government is not doing enough for the poor. There is no doubt in the fact that a lot of need based schemes are in progress for the eradication of poverty and the uplift of the poor. However our achievement is still insignificant. The reasons are tow dimensional. On the one hand governmental schemes are not properly reaching the poor. On the other hand the latter are not able to receive the benefits due to their ignorance or lack of awareness. Thus there is a wide gap between need and supply which in turn allows poverty to prevail as poverty with a little variation from time to time.

Concept and Chronology of Adult Education in India

Approaches	*Cycles/Periods*	*Key Concepts*	*Programmes*
Traditional	First cycle (1882-1947)	Basic Literacy	Night Schools
Life-oriented	Second cycle (1949-1966)	Civic Literacy	Social Education
Work-oriented	Third cycle (1967-1977)	Functional Literacy	Farmers Functional Literacy Programme and Shramik Vidyapeeths
Social Change	Fourth cycle (1978 to till date)	Developmental Literacy	NAEP, MPFL, TLC,CEP.

Creation of awareness, dissemination of information on government programmes, vocational training and increase the income of the labour may be measures that would help to bridge the gap between the need and supply. This can be achieved through certain specified levels of educational preparation among the masses. Adult education is such a type of education which provides the instruments for liberation form ignorance and important input for human development as the quality of human factors determine the quality of development.

Adult Education is a package of educational programmes for adults out side the formal education system aiming at providing more information and better knowledge and skills for improving their life style and also their earning capacity. Adult education helps the adults to become aware of themselves and their society to come to some understanding about the problems which they face and to encourage them to select their own task. Knowledge and skills is then the secondary part of adult education to make available the knowledge and skill they need to tackle the problems which they face and to encourage them to select their own task. Knowledge and skills is then the secondary part of adult education to make available the knowledge and skills they need to tackle the problems. This understanding will come slowly. Action-integral to the acquisition of knowledge and skills will be true encouragement to act in some way or another-thus the adult education has been a major tool and important input for human resource development.

It is possible to discern a pattern and certain cyclical trends in the history of Indian Adult Education. Broadly, there are four cycles which represent the four major approaches and concepts of adult education in India. While the traditional approach to literacy adopted the view that learning the traditional approach to literacy adopted the view that learning to read and write had an innate goodness in itself. Manifested during the face of social education, the life-oriented approaches continue even today. It goes beyond the acquisition of knowledge and the emphasis is on the application of learning to daily living. The work-oriented approach dominated during the phase of functional literacy. Based on Paulo-Freire's philosophy conscientisation, the social change approach made its debut during the phase of NAEP and it continues even to day.

Thus recognizing the role of literacy and education in all-round development of the individual and nation as a whole, the Government of India has launched the above programmes and continuously improved in terms of its quality based on the experiences and research findings. To create a learning society by providing for life-long leaning opportunities which may result in the release of creative energies of the people, the National Literacy Mission has been implementing the Continuing Education Programme by establishing Continuing Education Centres and organizing the programmes which are multifarious, far reaching and essential for the upliftment of quality of life.

ROLE OF ADULT EDUCATION IN POVERTY ALLEVIATION

Poverty alleviating programmes in the country are the first level of response to overcome the problem of poverty. The second level response consists of meeting the needs of the people through supplementing and complementing the large formal educational system through non-formal and open learning systems of education. Adult education is a type of non-formal education in this direction has an important role in this regard. Some of its important dimensions are discussed in the context of the objective of poverty alleviation.

INCREASING EFFECTIVENESS OF DEVELOPMENT PROGRAMMES

It is widely recognized that the successful implementation of any developmental programme needs the participation of its target group at various stages of the programme implementation starting from planning to evaluation. Due to their ignorance the people does not come forward to receive the assistance that are offered to them. The access to information is so limited that they do not know about the programme designed to promote their development. Information window is one of the important activities of CECs, provides information about various development schemes formulated by the Government, new agricultural practices, legal rights etc. will ensure that their benefits actually reach the target groups.

PROMOTION OF EMPLOYMENT

Education of the right type increases quality of labour and inculcates a sense of self-confidence among the recipients. Therefore, a right kind of education to remove the mass unemployment and disguised unemployment which are principal causes of mass poverty must be developed. The relevance of functional and vocational training to benefit the lower income groups is much greater in under developed countries where there is marked shortage of labour skills, the adult education should, there cater for these needs through Income Generating Programmes in continuing education centres in simple trades and occupations leading to greater employment opportunities and self-employment avenues.

STRENGTHENING OF COMMUNICATION CHANNELS

If the rural and urban poor are insufficiently linked with the modern sectors through effective communication system, the benefits of the industrial growth are unlikely to trickle down for a long time to come, the problem of ensuring access to education for lower income groups is important for reaching the economic development to lower strata of the economy thus strengthening the process of development. The adult education programme with its bias in favour of the poor and the disadvantaged instrument providing educational opportunities through equivalency programmes in continuing education centres.

AWARENESS GENERATION

The process of Economic Development makes growing demands on human resources and in a democratic set-up it calls for social values and attitudes where in education enters as an important factor. The adult education facilitates and contributes to economic development not only by skilled manpower for specific tasks of development, but, by creating the requisite attitudes and personality traits among the masses leading to a proper climate for development through the quality of Life Improvement Programmes in Continuing Education Centres.

MOBILIZATION AND CO-ORDINATION OF THE RESOURCES

Non-Government Organisations, Government Development Departments, Universities, Youth Clubs and such other agencies have been able to organize local specific programmes, according to the felt needs of the society. They help in providing infrastructure, motivating people, grass-root level planning etc. The Preraks in the CECs will make the efforts to mobilize money and material resources from these agencies to help the community.

Co-ordination is always seen inadequate in the functioning of various government and NGO's, universities, functionaries and in the implementation of various schemes and programmes. Continuing Education Centres build proper co-ordination among the government, NGOs, the community to concentrate in this aspect for maintaining the momentum.

MOTIVATION OF THE LEARNERS

The Individual Interest Promotion Programmes organizing in the CECs aims to provide opportunity for individuals to participate in and learn about their chosen social, cultural, spiritual, health, physical and artistic interests motivate these programmes will promote self-reliance, learners to attend the C.E.Cs personal development and self-actualisation interests help in the quality of human resources of the society.

To sum up Information and communication technologies today have divided people globally into two groups based on knowledge irrespective of gender, caste and region. While a small section of people in every society are ensuring developing technology, they are also the main beneficiaries of this advancement. Government and Non-Government efforts in civilized societies are directed towards ensuring that the pace of development is accelerated and the benefits accrue to large numbers in society. Adult education in the 21st century will cover education in this direction. The intellectuals, academics, the media, the men and women should show concern to arouse social conscience of mankind to build a new social order free from diseases, hatred, fear and apathy. Slogans like 'Education for all', 'Science for All' and 'Food for All' should be converted into reality.

REFERENCES

World Development Indicators database, April 2002

The Times of India, 11 September 2008.

World Development Indicators database, April 2002.

World Bank Report 2002.

'Poverty in India: A New Dimension', Meri News, 4th November 2008.

'One World South Asia News', 12th December 2008.

Sustainable Agriculture Through Biotechnology and Rural Development

8

Nazeerudin

Biotechnology has the potential to spur economic growth, reduce hungry and malnutrition and minimize environmental degradation. The new global trends made the member countries to recognize the scope and importance of biotechnology in the increase productivity in the agricultural sector. In this situation, agricultural biotechnology act as a tool on developing transparent, science based approaches, including capacity building activities and developing research on the effects of gene flow and genetically modified organisms(GMOS). Agricultural biotechnology is a collection of scientific techniques, including genetic engineering, that are used to modify and improve plants, animals and micro-organisms for human benefit. That is not a substitute for conventional plant and animal breeding but can be a powerful complement. Biotechnology has to play multi directional role to achive the inclusive growth in the country. In this backdrop, the paper made an attempt to explore what roles bio technology may play in contributing to sustainable agriculture and rural development, with particular concerns for bio safety and bio diversity .it examines the biosafety as major domain for addressing the impact of biotechnology on health and environment.

It further suggests policy issues that will need to be resolved by Governments if biotechnology is to contribute effectively to the food and lively hood security of developing countries in the next millennium.

SECTION - 1

INTRODUCTION

Biotechnology is currently a vibrating discipline in all domains of human welfare of the globe. It has the potential to exploit the rural technology for sustainable agriculture through integrated approach, which ensures the food security, enviornmental protection,to human health etc: In this back drop, Bio techonology has to play multi directional role to achive the inclusive growth in the country. Agricultural bio technology considered to be an significant one. Agricultural biotechnology is a collection of scientific techniques, including genetic engineering, that are used to modify and improve plants, animals and micro-organisms for human benefit. It is not a substitute for conventional plant and animal breeding but can be a powerful complement.. In this context, Rural Bio technology also plays an important role through integrated use of bio technology, microbiology and engineering of the capabilities of micro organisms and cultural tissues/cells for rural development An integrated knowledge of this field is a foot to bring a potential development in the rural population in which an inter relationship is needed as an essential support between rural people and bio technologists/ industrialists and extension agencies.

Methodology: This paper is based on the report, a simple descriptive and a explorative methodology is followed.

AGRICULTURAL BIODIVERSITY

Agricultural biodiversity encompasses the variety and variability of animals (including aquatic animals), plants, forestry and micro-organisms—at the genetic, species and ecosystem levels—necessary to sustain the key functions of the agro-ecosystem and its structure, as well as processes for and in support of agricultural production and food security. The biological resources contained within agricultural biodiversity are of direct and vital importance to the food security and socio-economic development of all countries.

FAO and the Conference of Parties to the Convention have continually promoted the development of national plans and strategies for the conservation and sustainable use of agricultural biodiversity. Because modern agricultural biotechnologies offer ways to improve and expand the sustainable use of genetic resources, they should be considered in any national planning regarding the sustainable use of agricultural biological resources in order to meet sustainable agriculture and rural development objectives.

SCOPE OF BIOTECHNOLOGY FOR SUSTAINABLE AGRICULTURE AND RURAL DEVELOPMENT

Agricultural biotechnologies have major potential for facilitating and promoting sustainable agriculture and rural development. They could also generate environmental benefits, especially where renewable genetic inputs can be effectively used to substitute for dependency on externally provided agrochemical inputs. The fact that genes or genotypes (e.g., varieties, breeds) can constitute locally renewable resources is of profound significance to the further development of sustainable agriculture and rural development. However, the power of modern biotechnologies to generate useful genotypes has not yet been harnessed for poorer farmers.

Nevertheless, the extent to which modern biotechnology will contribute to the achievement of food security for all is still an open question.[1] *Science alone is unlikely to provide a complete solution to the problems of rural development. There are many processes, factors and socio-economic structures underlying poverty in rural areas, such as lack of access to land and other productive resources, low purchasing power, political powerlessness, fragile environments and distance from markets.* Agricultural (or indeed plant biotechnology) research is but one factor which could impact on rural poverty; it is not a panacea for sustainable agriculture and rural development.

Comparative reviews of the state of agricultural biotechnologies in some developing countries have been carried out by the International Service for National Agricultural Research – Intermediary Biotechnology Service, a Consultative Group on International Agricultural Research (CGIAR) centre, and the Organisation for Economic Cooperation and Development (OECD), which concluded that the majority of developing countries have limited practical access to the tools and germplasm necessary to apply more sophisticated biotechnology research to their national needs. The barriers to such access are many and include lack of financial, scientific and infrastructural resources.

Biotechnology research has not been closely integrated with the problems and constraints confronting low-income farmers in the agricultural sector of developing countries. Biotechnology needs to be focused on some key problems within sustainable agriculture and rural development that historically have not been effectively addressed by conventional technologies.

Governments, scientists, non-governmental organizations, donors and CGIAR will have to consider the development of innovative mechanisms for the transfer of biotechnologies in developing country agriculture. Long-term public-sector funding will be necessary if the dissemination of agricultural biotechnology research is to benefit the poorer strata of society.

Over the longer term, there is little doubt that some biotechnological approaches to agricultural improvement could generate social, economic and environmental benefits if specifically targeted at the specific needs of poorer groups. While a vast range of approaches for the biotechnological improvement of such agronomic traits are either under study or in early development phases, given the current lack of focused public sector support for pro-poor agricultural biotechnology it is unlikely that poorer farmers will have economic access to such improvements in the short term.

A search through the scientific literature on biotechnology reveals a range of agricultural biotechnological research that could impact favourably on all of the priority areas. However, the relevance of uncritically listing all biotechnology research which is under way and might meet sustainable agriculture and rural development objectives should be questioned. The development of a technology does not guarantee its widespread dissemination—especially to poorer social groups. When it comes to food security, it is the practical application of the research that matters, rather than the promise of the "pipeline" research orientation. The agricultural biotechnology research community lacks concrete examples of pro-poor applications of molecular-level biotechnology being put to use in farmers' fields on a scale necessary to have an impact on rural poverty.

Very few public-sector institutions or organizations are involved in the transfer of appropriate biotechnologies to the crops and farming systems of rural groups in developing countries, reflecting the current bias in agricultural biotechnology research to commercial markets. Internationally, there are only a handful of underfunded agricultural biotechnology initiatives (public or private sector) with an explicit focus on poorer farmers as their primary clients/ markets. Some examples are the Center for the Application of Molecular Biology to International Agriculture; the FAO-facilitated Technical Cooperation Network on Plant Biotechnology for Latin America; the International Centre for Tropical Agriculture Cassava Biotechnology Network; and other biotechnology networks created and managed by the CGIAR international centres. Several national Governments of developing countries have good programmes on agricultural biotechnologies, such as Mexico, Argentina, Brazil, China, India and Egypt.

SECTION - 2

ASSESSING IMPACTS OF BIOTECHNOLOGY ON HEALTH AND THE ENVIRONMENT

There are concerns about potential risks posed by some aspects of biotechnology. These risks fall into two basic categories: the effects on human and animal health, and the environmental consequences. Caution must be exercised in order to reduce the risk of transferring toxins from one life form to another, of creating new toxins or of transferring allergenic compounds from one species to another, that could result in unexpected allergic reactions. Risks to the environment include the possibility of out-crossing, leading, for example, to the development of more aggressive weeds or wild relatives with increased resistance to diseases or environmental stresses, upsetting ecosystem balance. There is also the potential loss of biodiversity, for example, resulting from the displacement of traditional cultivars by a small number of genetically modified cultivars, and the potential for increased crop vulnerability resulting from the possible widespread adoption of varieties with simple, monogeneic, disease resistance mechanisms. However, in principle, these latter effects are no different from those that may result from many conventional approaches to plant breeding.

Policy decisions taken in regard to biosafety regulations will have long-term implications for the sustainability of agriculture and food security. Many genetic engineering approaches to crop improvement arise from a lack of suitable conventional approaches to dealing with a particular agronomic problem or need. It appears that long-term negative implications for agriculture and food security can arise equally from having biosafety regulations that are either too lax or too stringent.

Genetic engineering approaches have considerably broadened the range of gene pools which are now accessible for crop improvement purposes. If countries expect to benefit from modern biotechnologies in their agriculture and food sectors, they will have to give serious consideration to the drafting of biosafety regulations that are tailored to meet their socio-economic needs. Biosafety regulations and standards for risk assessment need to be harmonized within eco-regions since environments are common across political boundaries.

In the context of biotechnology risk assessment, there is a widely held scientific consensus that risk is primarily a function of the characteristics of a product—whether it is a purified chemical or a living organism to be field tested—and is not per se a function of the method of genetic modification. However, the current legal definitions of genetically modified organisms upon which most biosafety legislation is being constructed are largely process- rather than product-oriented. The scientific consensus emerging from the vast range of biosafety studies of transgenic plants is that each case should be evaluated on its own merits and hazards. Hence, biosafety decisions might differ according to the particular type of transgene, crop, environment and end use involved.

There is no evidence to suggest that transgenic crops or biotechnology per se would either decrease or increase biodiversity in agricultural or in "natural" ecosystems. Within agricultural systems, plant biotechnology research could be applied to either increasing or decreasing genetic diversity, depending on research objectives. With modern biotechnological methods, the use of the genetic resources from wild crop relatives may actually increase. The selective advantage that a particular genetically modified organism will confer in the agro-ecological niche in which it is applied should be considered in risk assessment.

In general, any risks of transgenic crops to biodiversity should be assessed relative to other non-transgenic options. Most risk assessment studies regarding genetically modified organisms fail to do comparative studies to assess each particular risk relative to the levels of risk to health and environment from other options.

CONCLUSION

Today how can India ensure sustainable food security for a population of more than a billion through agriculture biotechnology? In this context,expenditure on food consumption of poor considered to be significant aspect of the food security.

Expenditures on food staples typically absorb half the income of people below the poverty line. Food staples are their main source of nutrients. There is little doubt that if plant biotechnology research were applied to well-defined social or economic objectives, such as improving the food staples of the poor, it could benefit poorer rural and urban groups.

There remains the valid concern that the needs of poorer farmers or nations are unlikely to be a factor which favourably steers the research objectives of biotechnology research, which is dependent on private investment. At the governmental level, there are currently no policy instruments which promote the type of biotechnological research that could contribute to food and livelihood security in resource-poor situations, especially in developing countries. Long-term public-sector investment in agricultural research will be essential to address the needs of poorer farmers and consumers, who do not constitute a significant commercial market for private-sector biotechnology research and development. Increased participation by farmers and other key actors in the overall sustainable agriculture and rural development process is of vital concern. It is important to strengthen the communication among public-sector agricultural biotech research, on-farm research and farmer groups to facilitate the realization of sustainable agriculture and rural development.

There is a need to adopt a holistic and integrated approach in the application and evaluation of the impacts of agricultural biotechnology. Evaluation of newly engineered crops must consider biodiversity as a value; monitoring bio-indicators can help in reaching decisions about their environmental impacts. Many actions in several fields need to be developed by Governments and by international organizations to make sure that the pro-poor potentialities of agricultural biotechnologies are realized. Care should be taken that the current gap between developing and developed countries does not increase as a result of their lack of appropriate action concerning those key issues.

REFERENCES

Asian Development Bank and Winrock International Institute for Agricultural Development (1992), proceedings of the regional work shop 15-19 June.

FAO of United States Report of the Conference Rome 1993.

Per Pinstrup-Andersen et al., *World Food Prospects: Critical Issues for the Early Twenty-First Century*, 2020 Vision Food Policy Report

(Washington, D.C., International Food Policy Research Institute (IFPRI), 1999); IFPRI, a member of the Consultative Group on International Agricultural Research,

G.J. Persley, ed. (1999), *Biotechnology for Developing Country Agriculture: Problems and Opportunities*, 2020 Vision Focus 2 (Washington, D.C., IFPRI).

For background information papers on the Committee, visit: http://www.fao.org/ag/cgrfa/docs.htm .

Dalit Empowerment in Nepal: Achievements and Challenges

9

Ved Raj Acharya

INTRODUCTION

Although cast discrimination had begun in Nepal about 2500 years ago, but untouchability got its root only about 1500 years ago. In fact Dalits were forced to be Dalits. They had their own identity in the beginning. History says that caste system did not exist in early time in Nepal. Later on castes were divided according to the works performed by them. This kind of division of works led to untouchability. People were divided into four major castes- Brahmin, Khetri, Baisya and Sdra, Sudras were called to lowest caste and regarded unholy. It happened so in Nepal during the Lichchhabi King Man Dev. Untouchability existed in India at the same time and it deeply influenced the then Lichhabi King Man Dev. He started caste system in Nepal, two. In 1416 A.D., during the rule of Jayasthithi Malla, occupations being practiced by the people were divided according to their castes in Kathmandu valley. Sudras were penalized if they did not follow the prescribed occupation. They were also prohibited from reading, writing, living in beg house, wearing better quality clothes and ornaments and taking part in state affairs. Dalits were penalized more than non-Dalits for the same kind of crime. Written low of caste division based on theology was formulated. This practice and tradition was followed at the time of Ram Shah, too. After the unification of Nepal by, Prithivi Narayan Shah, a new structure of 'Hindu Kingdom' was built based on caste system and untouchability. Rais and Limbus of Eastern Nepal used to make their own clothes, tools and shoes in the past. They gave up these works due to fear of untouchability. During the reign of King Surendra Bir Bikram Shah, Jung Bahadur introduced Muluki Ain in 1854 A.D. and it enforced recognition of social discrimination and untouchabiity in Nepal. Upper caste people were demoted to lower caste if they married to lower caste. Similarly, upper caste people could not eat or drink anything touched by lower caste. People who did such things were socially boycotted and compelled to leave their places. During the time of Ranas, such types of people could purify themselves by giving cows to Brahmins and by organizing feasts for the people. This tradition was called patiya.

The state of destitute from own caste is a situation were a person cannot use his religious and economic rights. People are socially and psychologically demoralized when they are restituted from their caste. There is similarity regarding language, religion and celebration of social festivals among and between Dalits and non-Dalits in the hilly regions. But they were discriminated in various ways socially, religiously, economically and politically.

PRESENT CONDITION OF DALIT COMMUNITY

According to Brihat Nepali Shbdakosh, Dalit are define as "the community deprived of social rights, prestige and recognition or the people who are socially backward, exploited and discriminated." Similarly, Nepali Sabda Sagar defines Dalits "as the people backward or under-developed because of irrational social system and beliefs." In-fact, the word 'Dalits' represents extreme economic exploitation and social discrimination. In other word, "Dalits belong to the community which is economically exploited, socially unrecognized, politically voiceless and psychologically suppressed."

All Dalits are not deprived and restituted. Dalits of valleys and HIls are socially and economically in a better position in comparison to Terai. Similarly, social discrimination, untouchability and economic exploitation are very high in Western Nepal than in Eastern Nepal. Social discrimination and untouchbility are practiced by Dalits themselves, too. Some castes of Dalits regard themselves superior to other and behave accordingly. A kind of inferiority complex exits among Dalits, they themselves regard 'We are untouchables." Some Dalits belong to socially, politically and economically privileged class, while other fall to socially, politically and economically under privileged class (ERPAN, 2000). According to the national census of 2001, the population of Dalits in Nepal is around 4 million (CBS, 2002).

The current constitution of Nepal has ban on all sorts of discrimination on the grounds of religion, race, gender, caste, etc (The Interim constitution of Nepal, 2006). It has further stated that persons denied access to public places or deprived of public utilities on the basis of caste and per4ceeived as untouchable will be subjected to legal sanctions. However, such discrimination in different forms still prevails in the name of so called low or untouchable castes.

The constitution of Nepal, 2006 not only bans discrimination on the grounds of religion, race, gender, caste, etc but goes further the extent that persons denied access to public places or deprived of public utilities on the basis of cast received as untouchable will be subjected to legal sanctions. Legal acts, such as the civil liberty Act 1999, explicitly seek to redress the destructive social and economic implications of the caste system and refer to special provisions for the development of such vulnerable groups categorized as Dalit.

National policies over the years have focus Dalit concerns both in strategies of national importance and legal provisions. Ninth plan (1996- 2001) created a separate chapter on Dalits. The Chapter outlined objectives, policies, strategies, and programmes for Dalits and other disadvantaged groups (NPC, 1996). More specific strategies to achieve effective participation of Dalits in national development were developed through the

Tenth Plan (2002 - 2007), which emphasizes pro-poor policies, working through a decentralized framework, and partnership with civil society (NPC, 2002).

In line with Tenth Plan, Government of Nepal formed the National Dalit Commission with the aim of promoting and protecting, through a holistic approach, the rights and welfare of Dalit Commission with the aim of promoting and protecting, through a holistic approach, the rights and werfare of Dalit. Dalit Commission formed in 2002 recorded a segment of population as dalits. These groups have been placed in three categories i. e. Hill, Never and Tarai Communities. Hill Dalits are Kami, Sarki, Damai, Lohar, Sunar and others, Kusule, Kasai, Chyame, Pode and Dyala are Newar dalits and Tatma, Paswan, Dushad, Dowe, Mushahar and others belongs to Tarai dalits. The comprehensive strategy suggested by the commission encompasses economic, educational, and social empowerment to cultural awareness and political participation. Activities centre on inter alias information dissemination, awareness - raising, research and provision of legal sanction.

Similarly, in recent year, many non-governmental organizations have emerged to represent voice of marginalized communities. This institutionalization process is gaining momentum due to wider acceptance by the people whose voice was never heard by the main stream government before (NLF, 2008).

But in practice, Dalits are still lacking free access to tea stalls, temples, educational institutions and other public places. They are restricted from studying in various Sanskrit Educational Institutions including Bankali Bed Bidyashram. Most of Dalits are landless and without resources. Their major occupation is to work in farmland as laboures. Their traditional occupation regarded as respect less. They earn very scanty money. Discrimination is found in terms of wages between men and women for the same nature of work. Being regarded as untouchable, they cannot work in notes, own shop of trading consumer goods and milk. It is difficult for them to get agricultural credit and employment. Due to malnutrition, illiteracy, hard work and giving birth to children every year, women are living with bad health. Their average age is 50 years. They are also suffering from unwanted social discrimination, family violence, social and economic exploitation and rape.

Accesses of Dalits to higher executive posts have not been able to occupy them post as a Judge, Secretary, Director General, CDO, Genera Manager, Chairman etc (ERPAN, 2002).

Similarly, Madhesi Dalits are also suffering from vicious circle of poverty. These people are always found as poor. Though the people of other communities have raised their income level and living standard but Madhesi Dalits are at the bottom line of the poverty.

Lack of education, unskilledness, social discriminatioin, ignored, low level of income, sickness, low saving, low investment on Dalits, upliftment, low number of landownership and low level of economic development are the causes of poverty of Madhesi Dalits (Jha, 2003)

Nobody is born as a Dalit or lower caste. Prevailing situation has compelled to become a Dalits. Present social, political and religious conviction and tradition is present social, political and religious conviction and tradition is responsible for it. Nobody should be discriminated as untouchable on the bass of caste. Practice of untouchability and social discrimination are the result of existing feudal system. Unless this system is totally abolished, Dalits cannot be free from malpractices. They should work in organized way and united for total social changes. (ERPAN, 2002)

At present, 260 million Dalits people are in all over the world. In India there are 251.4 million, in Nepal 4 millions, in Pakistan 1.2 millions, in Sri Lanka 65 thousands and in Indonesia 7 thousand Dalits are living. These people are converted into before 5000 years. Even now the voice is not heard even in UNO (Aahuti, 2003).

To change the status of Dalits women, first of all they should be made self-dependent. Economically self - dependency is the prime factors to change the lifestyle on the whole. Literacy, awareness and skill development are the process of economic development. Especially, the Dalits women are in need of such things. If they are made trained and some facilities are provided to them, they can certainly do much better in their field and the practice discrimination between Dalits and non-Dalits world be made narrow (Jha, 2003). According to Nepal living standard survey almost half of all Dalits live beloved the poverty line (The World Bank & DFID, 2006). Income earning local white-collar jobs is largely unavailable to the Dalits. Educational participation of Dalits is also low (Gurung, 2001)

DALIT MOVEMENT

Dalit movement is an continuous process for the social and economic betterment of their community. First of all, the Dalit movement was started by 'Shahles in Mithila area before 600 years. Now days he is known as the god 'Shahles'. Temples of Shahles are made and statues are erected in various parts of Nepal. Actually he was a Dalit and he started the movement against untouchability and discrimination behaviour of upper caste people (Aahuti, 2000).

The next remarkable movement was held in 1947. two Dalit person traied to enter into the Pashupatinath temple. At that time, the entrance in temple by Dalits was not permitted (EARPAN, 2002). Similarly, the next effective movement was held during the period of March 20, 1998 to Feb. 13, 2001. In this movement, Dalits decided to avoid throwing carcass considered as an un-respectful work. Social and economic blockade was imposed upon Dalits by non Dalits when they refused throwing carcass. Dalits were compelled to start the movement. Later on this movement expanded to various districts to national level. As they said "Movement was not their desire, but consequence of social and economic exploitation for a long time.

ACHIEVEMENT OF THE DALITS

The movement has enhanced Dalits communities to be unite, organized and active. They have established themselves as an organized strength after the movement. Dalits have realized that women should be literate and basic education should be provided to children.

- Women have become conscious and active socially and economically. Now they are actively participating in the activities like basic health service, sanitation, education, group saving mobilization and income generating activities.
- They have started to raise their voice against existing unequal wage system and struggling for equal wages for both men and women for the same nature of work.
- Dalit women have started to participate in various other activities.
- Playing leading roles to beloved even non- Dalit problems.
- Have established their own organization.
- They are trying to findout problems actively. Participating to solve these problems by conducting health, education, skill development, savings, income generating activities.
- Organized strength of Dalits has significantly contributed to reduction in untouchability practices in public places. They have strengthened campaign to their land rights, right to citizenship and their leadership in decision-making processes at all levels.
- Dalit rights has come out as a key agenda in the present political and development discourage as a result of national wide mobilization of Dalit people's organizations and Dalit activities (AAN, 2006.

PROBLEMS OF DALITS

The Dalits of Nepal are facing a number of problems in their every day life. Some of them are as follows:

- Education as an essential element of better quality of life is not internalize by the majority of Dalit population.

- The formal, informal, vocational, technical and other kind of higher education is largely out of reach to majority of Dalit population because of social discrimination and poverty.
- Dalits have poor health due to their poor living conditions, unhygienic food habits and poor living conditions, unhygienic food habits and poor sanitation within their communities.
- Absence of knowledge on nutritious food and balanced diet, resulting mal nutritious food and balanced diet, resulting malnutrition among children and women.
- Access to safe drinking water is problematic for Dalit in most parts of the country.
- Through poverty of people is the major problem in Nepal as a whole, poverty is more rampant among Dalits than other groups in Nepal.
- Unemployment and disguised unemployment are more prevalent among Dalits than other.
- A number of Dalits families are landless for generations and generations.
- Credit facilities to Dalits are not easily available from a banks and financial institutions because of illiteracy and lack of collateral.
- Dalits have less access to foreign employment services through various manpower agencies because of lack of capital initially and appropriate people to support them in the process.
- A higher rate of drinking and gambling in various groups of Dalits resulting poverty and domestic violence within the family members and community at large (NDSF, 2002)

DALIT UPLIFTMENT AND DEVELOPMENT IN INTEPIM PLAN 2007/08–2009/10

The condition o Dalits is comparatively lower than other communities. Dalit community is lacking the economic and social services and even access of political opportunities. The bad habit of practicing untouchability is existed till now. They are victimized by the non-respectful behaviour by so-called upper-casts people in public place. Though the country is declared as free-touchable but the view on looking the Dalits is remained traditional and negative.

Out of the total number of population. Dalits consist is percent. When the nation could not bring the Dalits in mainstream of development, the socio-economic development of the country is not possible. Thus, this plan has aimed to mainstreaming the Dalits.

The overall condition of Dalits is as follows:

Particulars	*National Average*	*Dalit*
Average life expectancy		50.8
Child mortality rate (below 5 years) per '000'		171.2
Infant mortality rate per '000'		116.5
Fertility rate of per women		4.7
Literacy rate (%_		32.8
SLC & above		3.8
Graduation & above		0.4
Poverty (%)		47
Representation in constituent Assembly (Elected)		5
Total	601	43

Source: The Interim Plan, 2007 and Maharjan, 2009

The long term perspective of the plan is to make the costless, discrimination less & equitable society.

OBJECTIVE

To increase the access of Dalits in Social and economic resources of the country in accordence with the proportion of population and to improve the effectiveness

- Quantitative targets.
- To increase the HDI and HEI of Dalits by 10%,
- To increase the participation of Dalits in central and local authority as per the proportion of population.

- The feeeling of Dalits will be reduced by not expressing the castes in written form.
- The GDI of Dalits female will be increased by 10%.

STRATEGIES

- The structural and policy level barriers of Dalit empowerment will be alleviated by changing the rules and regulations.
- The organizations of Dalits will be made more effective for their empowerment,
- Targeted programmes for marginalized Dalits will be conducted,
- The positive discrimination, reservation and provision of special rights will be followed for their social improvement, and
- The abolition of untuchability will be transformed into practice.

In constitutional Assembly 2007

The number of Dalits numbers are increased. In the parliamentory action of 1991 the number of parliament was in 1994 it was nil, in 1999 and in 2007 the numbers have increased to 44. This change can be taken as a major achievement in political sector (Manandhar, 2009)

CONCLUSIONS

The Dalits are in the process of their betterment on the society. However, the Dalit movements of the most could be taken as a milestones for bringing them from deprived position to the way of respectful and humanitarian condition. The efforts of the government and other stakeholders are inadequate and ineffective. The focus is needed to be given in education, sanitation, health and gainful economic activities which can change their living standard and improved out look of so called upper castes people.

REFERENCE

Aahuti (2003), *Our Movement is Dalit Mukti, Oct.-Dec. 2003.* Lahan: Dali8t Studies Group.

Action Aid, CARE, Nepal, Save the Children (2002), National Dalit Strategy Report: Kathmandu Action, Aid, CARE Nepal and SCF.

Action Aid, Nepal (2006), *Reflecting and Learning 2006*: Kathmandu: Action Aid, Nepal,

Central Burean of Statistics (2002), *Population Census o Nepal: National Report*, Kathmandu: CBS

ERPAN (2002), *Steps of Social Transformation, Birtuagn ERPAN and Action Aid, Nepal.*

Jha, Hari Bansa (2003), *Dalit of Tarai and Dalit women:* Kathmandu: Centre for Economic and Technical Studies. And Fredic Ebert stiftungtical Movement

Jit Gurung (2001), *Promotion of Socio-cultural; Economic and Political Participation of Dalits and Other Disadvantaged Groups:* A Strategic Approach Kathmandu, Nepal.

Mandhar, Pancha Narayan (2009), *Seminar Paper on Inclusive Election System in Federal Nepal*, Paper presented in Sept.5, 2009 programme organized by society for constitutional and parliamentary exercise.

National Planning Commission (1996), *Ninth Plan 1996–2001*

National Planning Commission (2002), *Tenth Plan 2002-2007*, Kathmandu: NPC

National Planning Commission (2007), *Interim Plan 2007/07–2009/10*

Nepal Labour Foundation (2008), *A Situation Analysis Workers of Nepal:*. Kathmandu: NLF

The World Bank and DFID (2006), *Unequal Citizens:* Kathmandu: The World Bank and DFID.

Economic Reforms and Rural Poverty Scenario in India

10

J. Mohan Raj, M. Perumal

INTRODUCTION

The significance of agriculture and rural development in India, has rightly been stressed by the new Prime Minister Dr. ManMohan Singh. The crux of the matter is; whether antipoverty programmes have had much dent in to the rural areas and during the post globalization era? After 1991, is there any perceptible breakthrough in poverty eradication and employment generation?

No doubt, antipoverty programmes have been implemented. But, it is equally true that, rural poverty and unemployment still haunt the rulers. So, a multi-pronged attack on reduction of poverty and increasing rural employment, by a massive increase in public sector in vestment, is the need of the hour. Keeping in mind the above facts, this Doctoral Dissertation tries to examine not only the causative factors of rural poverty but also makes an impact study of anti-poverty programmes, globalization and food security. In order to undertake a comprehensive on rural poverty, a brief discussion about rural economic status in the context of globalization deserve due attention on the part of this study.

RURAL ECONOMY AND GLOBALIZATION

Rural development, uplift of rural people and more specifically, the alleviation of rural poverty continue to be the central concern of development planning in India. It could be noted that in India nearly 60 per cent of the population depend on agriculture and its allied activities for their livelihood either directly or indirectly. However, there is a growing concern on rural development in India in consequence of the implementation of New Economic Policy since 1991. There is a growing concern the deleterious impact of **GATT** on Indian agriculture and rural development. Borrowing from International Monetary Fund and acceptance of **GATT** treaties of **WTO** has imposed a check on agricultural subsidies. The new economic reforms introduced in India in consequence of **GATT** and **WTO** agreement and treaties have created worries among people. This thesis analyzes the impact of new economic reforms in rural development.

ECONOMIC REFORMS AND AGRICULTURE

The state intervention in agriculture could be analyzed carefully. The structural adjustment measures and government economic interventions have some influence over the others. It includes providing non-marketable facilities, marketable facilities, price distortions and regulations to subsidies and levies. Adjustment towards true price system i.e., a price system that correctly reflects the scarcities in the economy, the necessity of providing market facilities and removing price inhibition or regulations is far less evident. It could be noted that in developed countries, also while a vital role is played by private sector in production and of marketing agricultural products, the role of the state in determining floor and ceiling prices for agricultural commodities, stock piling of excess quantities and providing a legal framework for all transactions, especially relating to land ownership. In these countries, a sort of division of labour between state and private enterprise has been put into operation. Developing countries should draw lessons from this particular division of labour.

The rapid growth of agricultural and non-agricultural segment of the rural economy would require a larger flow of institutional credit than in the past. The banking and cooperative credit agencies have to gear themselves up to meet this difficult challenge.

ECONOMIC REFORMS AND PRICE POLICY

It is evident that the government has liberalized international trade in food grains allowing domestic prices adjust to international levels. Currently, prices of wheat, coarse grains and pulses in India are roughly 10 per cent more than the international prices and rice prices 30 per cent less. However, the agreed **GATT** Agreement is likely to push up relatively the prices of wheat and coarse cereals by 5 per cent while bringing down the rice prices. Hence the liberalization of agricultural trade in the post **GATT** scenario may involve a rise in the domestic relative prices of food grains by about 15 to 20 per cent. The effect of such a price rise, as measured by calculation of price elasticity, would be the reduction of consumption of the poor while leaving that of relatively affluent unaffected. Export surpluses of food grains could be at the cost of the poor consuming significantly less than even the inadequate amounts they consume today. It should be noted that while the effect of exporting food grains upon domestic prices and availability is direct and, therefore, more obvious. Similar results would occur even if other non-food cash crop exports are encouraged, in so far as these imply acreage shifts away from food grains rather than substantially increasing total supply.

The outcomes of price policy depend upon a number of factors, viz., (i) the exporters of a product, whether they are self-employed small peasants or capitalists, (ii) the commodity exported, (iii) proportion of the poor in different sectors, (iv) weight accorded to the poor in overall policies, and (v) effects of contraction in expenditure. If the exporters are poor and small peasants then, adjustment through devaluation will benefit the poor. When the commodity exported is staple food of the poor, prices will rise and the poor will be the suffers.

The contractionary effects of adjustment will hurt the poor as a consequence of contraction of public investment associated with further contraction of private investment. When the effects fall on social expenditure, the poor are the victims of a decline in health and education services.[9]

EFFECTS OF ECONOMIC REFORMS AND RURAL EMPLOYMENT

New Economic Policy (NEP) has effects on rural employment. These effects occur in the form (i) withdrawal of subsidies on inputs in agriculture, and (ii) liberalization of industrial and trade policy.

Many studies have mentioned the well known fact that within agriculture, there are heavy subsidies for fertilizers, power and irrigation. These subsidies contribute to huge fiscal deficit and, therefore, it is proposed to withdraw these under NEP. These subsidies create inequality between regions and distort the allocation of resources; even then, they have a role to play in increased employment and output within agriculture. The cost of inputs to the farmers is reduced, which in turn contributes to intensive use of land. This has got direct and indirect benefits on employment. Larger input-use leads to generation of employment, which is a direct benefit. However, indirect benefit is achieved through employment generated by additional output.

Hence withdrawal of subsidies for inputs in agriculture would reduce employment in agriculture sector, It happens in the form of (i) price elasticity of input use, (ii) elasticity of employment to yield and (iii) elasticity of crop yield to input use.

Fertilizer is one of the most important inputs and the subsidies are most prominent in this respect. It has been found that in many states of India, elasticity of crop yield to fertilizer use is positive and the price elasticity of fertilizer use is negative. a relative rise in the price of fertilizer may induce substitution by organic manure, which is good for sustainable agriculture development; and has to be deliberately promoted. A rise in produce price along with a rise in fertilizer price could arrest the increase in the relative price of fertilizer and work against disincentives to use. But the rise in produce price is not less inequitable than subsidy on fertilizers. The non-price factors such as improved access to credit and improved fertilizer prices may act as a cushion. As a result of reduction of fertilizer subsidy, there can be some employment uses. However, there is need for a phased withdrawal of subsidies in agriculture.

The internal and international competition improves efficiency because of liberalization and the domestic gross capital formation is also increased due to **Foreign Direct Investment (FDI)**, which in turn is expected to step up growth rates and also employment, depending upon the changes in technology and their effects on elasticity of employment to output. The multi-national corporations have displacement effects on employment. It is observed that i the **MNCs** employ techniques which are more capital-intensive than domestic enterprises, and ii) the chance that a local project would have emerged in the absence of direct foreign investment. It is evident that the techniques employed by **MNCs** are more capital-intensive than those employed by local enterprises. In the case of second issue, this is least likely in areas where local firms do not have access to knowledge.

The more capital-using techniques of **MNCs** will have some adverse effect on employment. The adverse effect of technology, consequent on entry of MNCs, could be compensated only by additions to investments and rate of growth far higher than what could be obtained without such investment. Such compensatory benefits are likely to be realized in short and medium terms. Therefore, one would expect the rate of labour absorption in the sector to decline.

Liberalization of trade is unlikely to expand agricultural and rural exports in the absence of development of infrastructural facilities for export markets. The short-term effects on employment are unlikely to be favourable even if exports are stepped up through promotion of agro-processing, since the employment intensity of modern processing is likely to be less than the corresponding intensity of traditional industry. Modern processing develops a whole range of new industries, resulting in addition to aggregate employment. Then the modernization of agro-processing should result in more efficient use of raw material and also contribute to utilization of by-products, which remain unutilized. Both these effects are likely to be observed in the long run, but in the short run one should expect a reduction in employment as traditional processing is replaced by modern processing.

ECONOMIC REFORMS AND RURAL POOR

The effects of structural adjustment could fall on the rural poor in the following ways: (i) some people are direct victims of structural adjustments such as employees of rural health and school teachers in village retrenched as a consequence of cut back in public expenditure in the areas of health and education. They may be called new poor (ii) some individuals and families whose income are so low that price increases by structural adjustments may push these people below the poverty line. The concern here is with all the categories of rural poor not just the newly poor or the border-line poor pushed into the poverty net.

Adam Smith, the founder of the English Classical Economics School, outlined policies, for rapid industrialization, in his magnum opus, "An Enquiry into the Nature and Causes of the wealth of Nations" (1776) Even Kard Marx, in his "DAS CAPITAL" discussed about exploitation of the proletariats. But, it was Gunnar Myrdal who voiced the pitiable conditions of the poor in Asian region. His book " Asian Drama" - set the trend for a deep insight into Poverty Eradication, John K.Kennedy, the late U.S. President rightly observed "That Poverty any where is a threat to prosperity every where". Amartya Sen, the Nobel Laureate in Economics, has called for a multi-pronged attack on Poverty in India, through Education, Adequate Nutrition and Proper health benefits, to the rural poor. The world development Report (1999) has stressed the need to harness global forces, for the upliftment of the poor.

The business line dated November 15, 2005 in its editorial rightly observed that "GOING BY THE Dhaka Declarations- issued at the end of the 13th SAARC, summit, it would appear that the fo-cus of the meeting was on regional economic cooperation. A good part of the document dealt with this subject. However, the thrust was on poverty allevia-tion, with the heads of state laying emphasis on the continuation of efforts "to free South Asia from poverty, hunger and other forms of deprivation and social injustice which present a daunting challenge". In fact, the Summit took some specific action towards this end: it declared 2006-2015 as the SAARC Decade of Poverty Alleviation and also set up a SAARC Poverty Alleviation Fund."

The idea of freedom from want expresses an aspiration as old as mankind.... But in this generation freedom from want has been taken out of the realm of utopian ideas. The conviction has spread that it can be achieved; indeed it is held by hard - headed businessmen and skeptical scientists no less than by the dreamers and idealists. Freedom from want means the conquest of hunger and the attainment of the ordinary needs of a decent, self respecting life if this can be done within and among nations by their separate and collective action, some of the world's worst economic ills, including hunger and extreme poverty will be on the way to extinction".

CONCLUSION

This challenge is not lifted, as it may sound, from a report on the Millennium Development Goals or the recently discussed proposal on U.N. Reform in Larger Freedom. It comes rather from the June 1945 General Report on the Work of FAO made to the United Nations Interim Commission of Food and Agriculture. As the United Nations and the Food and Agriculture Organization mark their 60th anniversaries this month, it is work re-examining. How far have we come and how differently we see our current challenges.

REFERENCE

Myrdal, Gunnar, (1970), The Challenge of World Poverty, New York, Pantheon Books.

Gahguli B.N. and (1976), "A Historical Genetic Perspective of the Levels of Living Delhi, Sultan Chand and Company, pp. 63-190.

Desai (1986), Rural Development, Mumbai, Himalaya Publications House.

Yadav (1980), "Eradication of Rural Poverty in China-A Lesson to India," Bangalore, Indian Institute of Management, p.3.

Appu, P.S. (1977), Inadequacies of Politices and Programmes Kurukshetra, 27(8): 16.

Thimmaiah, G. (1985), "Inequality and Poverty," Mumbai, Himalaya Publishing House, p. 34.

Dasgupta, R. (1981), A Cross Sectinal Analysis of Poverty and Undernutrition in Rural India, Working Paper No. 126 Trivandrum, Centre for Development Studies, p.1.

Pant (1980), Poverty, Unemployment and Food for Work, Agricultural Situation in India, 35(2): B4.

Varadarajan and Aiyasamy (1983), "The Structural Content of Rural Poverty in Tamil Nadu," Paper Presented at the Fourth Annual Conference of Association of Economists of Tamilnadu and Pondicherry, at Tirupathur.

Ahluwalia, M.S. (1978), "Rural Poverty and Agricultural Performance in India," Journal of Development Studies, No. 14.

Subramaniam (1986), "Poverty and Inequality in Tamilnadu Working Papers Madras Institute of Development Studies, No. 74.

Bandyopadhyaya (1988), "The Poverty of Nations, New Delhi Allied Publishers, pp. 4-9.

Dandekar and Rath, Nilakantha (1971), Poverty in India, Poona: Indian School of Political Economy.

Bardhan (1973), On the Incidence of Poverty in Rural India in the Sixties Economic and Political Weekly, Vol. 8, Annual No. Feb.1974

Minhas (1986), "Planning and the Poor," New Delhi, Sultan Chand and Company.

Ojha, P.D. (1970), "A Configuration of Indian Poverty: Inequality and Levels of Living," Reserve Bank of India Bulletin, (January).

Panikar, P.G.K. (1972), "Economics of Nutrition," Indian Journal of Agricultural Economics, 32:4 (October-December), pp. 35-36.

Mundel (1983), "Agricultural Production and Pros on Indicence of Rural Poverty. Economic and Political Weekly 18(26), p. 257.

Thakurtha Guha, B.K. (1980), "Poverty in Calcutta, 1950-1972" Arthavijnana, Vol. 22, No. 4, December, pp. 565-575.

Kurien, C.T. (1978), Poverty, Planning and Social Transformation," New Delhi, Allied Publishers.

Daniel Gustafson (2005), Agriculture, Development, and Freedom from want, THE HINDU, October 28.

Economic and Political Weekly Vol XXXVIII No. 4, January 25-31, 2003. pp.25-26.3

Sharma and Haque, T. (1987), "Impact of Fertilizer Subsidy on Growth and Equity," Highlights of Agricultural Research, IASRI.

Ibid, p. 322

EBW p. 385

Srinivasan, T.M. (1991), Cited in References Susan Horton and Others, Labour Markets in an Era of Adjustment, International Labour Review, Vol. 30, No. 56.

Efforts for Promoting Decent Work in Nepal

11

Ved Raj Acharya

WORKERS IN DEMOCRATIC MOVEMENT

Nepalese workers have developed a strong believe that only democracy can protect their rights. As such once again workers involved themselves in democratic movement. The historical people's movement of 2006 succeeded with a huge participation of Nepali workers and marginalized people. In April 23 and 24, 2006, more than 6 million people took to the streets. Among them more than 60% were workers. This was a successful people's movement, which is said to be another milestone for the overall development, peace, security and rapid socio-economic change, but till date no significant achievements have been observed except for the wider peace agreement between the Government and the Maoists. Economic position has not improved. Law and order situation is worst than before. Although Maoists are in government their cadres are attacking the working people, general public and government officials. They are still collecting donations using physical threats.

There is diverse opinion across the stakeholders as regards to the autonomy, independency in workings and affiliation of Trade Unions to political parties. Except ANTUF other three

Trade Union federations namely, DECONT, NTUC, and GEFONT are mainly guided by welfare and rights of laborers. Party and political lines do not directly intervene in their workings, they say. NTUC the legendary organization that created the history of TU in Nepal and DECONT another federation formed by a group of NTUC leaders pleading freedom from political intervention and internal democracy are guided by democratic thinking and human rights in their core values and show their attachment to Congress Party. GEFONT with largest networks is build around left wing political thinking and is inclined towards CPN-UML. However, hardly less than 1% members belong to UML party structure, GEFONT claims. Even then the government officials and employers at times look at TUs from political angles(NLF,2008).

To conclude there are four trade unions registered in Labour Department as confederations to take care of the rights and welfare of Nepali workers. These trade unions are engaged and are involved in promoting trade union movements to reduce vulnerability, hunger, and poverty and improve socio-economic condition of the workers' families by educating them about their rights and organizing workers and management for the decent work

1990s and then after witnessed several noticeable developments in the area of improving labour market situation. Several Acts and Rules like Labour Act, 1992, Labour Rules 1992, Transportation Act, 1992, Child Labour Act, 1992, Trade Union Act 1992, Working Journalist Act 1994 and Labour Court Regulation Act 1995 were promulgated. A tripartite National Advisory Board was established in 1994, Labour Relations Committees have been constituted and a Labour Court was established in 1996 to settle industrial disputes.

DECENT WORK

The International Labor Organization (ILO), the first specialized agency of UNO formed in 1946, has been contributing to reducing vulnerability, hunger and poverty and in the promotion of well-being of workers by providing employment protection, ensuring quality of working condition and prescribing international labor standards (ILS).

Unlike in any other countries of the region, ILO's main focus in Nepal has been to promote decent work in the labour market. Decent work by definition is related to the type of work, conditions at work, and feeling of value and satisfaction It is a universal aspiration.

ILO with its following four strategic objectives is supporting Nepal to promote opportunities for women and men, in particular from poorer sections of the population, to obtain decent and productive work in conditions of freedom, equity, security, and human dignity. It is not just about quantity but also about quality.

- Rights at work–conditions in the workplace;
- Employment–developing capacities; accessing sufficient opportunities; earning adequate income to move from subsistence to existence;
- Social protection–protection against and addressing vulnerabilities and contingencies (e.g. old age, sickness, redundancies, loss of livelihood, etc.) that take people out of work; and,
- Social dialogue–freedom of association; ability to participate; promotion of conflict resolution, social equity, and effective policy implementation; means through which rights are defended, employment is promoted, and work is secured.

ILO has linked these objectives to the elimination of underlining factors that cause and/or perpetuate poverty, in particular inadequate income-generating opportunities, social and economic exclusion through discrimination, lack of safety nets, and absence of voice. Decent work is inherently pro-poor and is an input, not an output, to securing less poverty. ILO has been mainstreaming gender and development into all of its activities to realizing the Organization's objectives.

ILO's goal of achieving decent work for all is supported by activities related, inter alia, to awareness raising and advocacy efforts, capacity building, and reducing gaps in policies, legislation, and strategies(ILO, 2000).

There are four main components of the functions of decent work. They are: 1) work and employment itself; 2) right at work; 3) security, and 4) representation and dialogue.

The first component is related to work itself. It means to achieve adequate opportunities for productive and meaningful work in decent conditions by the job seekers. It includes working time and work intensity, the need for a living income, the possibilities for personal development and the opportunities to use one's capabilities. Decent work covers formal and informal work, in the home, in the factory, or in the street. It includes women and men- much work by women especially in the home. Decent work may also mean, not working too much or the possibility of retirement.

The second component is concerned to basic rights at work. These have been expressed in the ILO's core labor standards: freedom of association, freedom from discrimination, freedom from forced labor and freedom from child labor.

The third component is concerned to security. Much work is insecure, either because it is irregular or temporary, or because income varies, or because it is physically risky or generates vulnerability to disease, or in other ways. Security is very important aspect especially for the workers. It can be gained in a variety of ways- through (a) formal social insurance systems which provide for contingencies such as illness, unemployment or old age; (b) informal mechanisms of solidarity and sharing; (c) investment in workplace safety, and (d) labor market institutions and polices which protect workers against fluctuations in employment. It can be managed by legislation or collective agreements to discourage layoffs or training systems which offer routes back into the labor market.

The fourth component is concerned to representation and dialogues. The way in which people voices are heard is a crucial aspect of decent work.

Decent Work in Nepal

Nepal as a member country of ILO has been trying to fulfill conditions laid down under various conventions, recommendations and standard in its constitution, laws, policies and practices since 1966. Out of 181 ILO conventions, Nepal has so far ratified following eight recommendations.

Convention Year	*Conventions*	*Year of Ratification*
14(1921)	Weekly rest (industry)	Dec.1986
98(1949)	Right to organize and collective bargaining	Oct.1976
100(1951)	Equal remuneration	Oct.1976
111(1958)	Discrimination (Employment and occupation)	
131(1970)	Minimum wages	Sept.1974
138(1973)	Minimum age of employment	Oct.1996
144(1976)	Tripartite consultation	March1995
182	Worst form of child labor	Nov. 2000

These labor standards are important in formulating national polices legislation and practices on diverse social and labor aspects. It is binding obligation of the every ILO member state to install the spirit of the provisions of the ratified conventions, recommendations and standards of ILO into their constitutions, polices, legislations and practices. These provisions of several conventions, recommendation and standard prescribed by ILO need to be included in policy, programmes and legislations prior to formal ratification

Most of workers who are in the formal sector are also less aware of the decent work ILO is promoting. Informal sector is far behind from this exposure. Nepalese Trade Unions are trying to implement the recommendations and various ILO conventions.

In the case of work and employment, the alarming situation of unemployment and underemployment hardly make it possible to implement in practice in a underdeveloped situation of country like Nepal.

About the basic rights at work, organized sector, especially some multinational companies working in Nepal have accommodated to some extent in their working situation. Nevertheless, in the informal sector it is not in practice.

The third dimension is security. Few organizations are providing some security facilities at work place. The state has not been able to provide job security to its citizens.

The fourth dimension is about representation and dialogue. In Nepal labour market, few formal sector organizations practice ways and means of representation and dialogue. To some extent the voice of workers are heard by the management especially in collective bargaining and local level decisions. But in the informal sector there is no such culture of representation and dialogue.

Employment Categories

The Labour Act, 1992 has made workers' classification in following categories. This classification is applied in any industry, firm, business or institution of the formal sector. They are:

- Permanent basis
- Probation period
- Temporary basis
- Daily wage basis
- Trainee
- Contract Basis

Job Safety

After the issuance of appointment letter for employment in the mentioned position any worker who completes one year of uninterrupted services (240 days) his/her name is registered in the attendance register and is considered become a permanent employee. The Labour Act, 1992 has protected permanent labours from loosing jobs without reason other than mentioned in the regulations.

In response to job security asked to formal sector workers 47% feel that their job is safe. Among those who do not feel safe 48% feel that they can be terminated at any time from employment without any notice. Hardly few (9%) identified lack of skills as reason for job termination. 63% and 78% even know about the provision of issuing of identity card and appointment letter respectively, survey shows (Mo L,J& PA,1992).

In response to how safe women are at work, 37% formal and 42% informal sector workers feel that women workers face sexual harassment at the work place. 53% formal and 68% informal sector workers have in mind that woman workers face such harassments from employers, coworkers and customers. Among these, they said women are at high risk from coworkers (30% formal and 16% informal) (NLF, 2008).

MINIMUM WAGE TO WORKERS

In January 2000, Nepal government fixed minimum wage for agricultural workers. Accordingly, a worker is paid Nrs. 60 per day (Nrs. 7.50 per hour). District Development Committees have been given free hand to increase the amount of minimum wage to adjust it to the local condition. On April 25, the government, in accordance with the Labor Act, 1992 and with the recommendations of the committee formed to fix the minimum wages, fixed the minimum wages for workers and employees working in institutions other than the tea industries where the act is yet to be enforced. The Labor Ministry fixed minimum wages Rs. 1,450, Rs. 1,500, and Rs. 1,610 per month for unskilled, semi-skilled, and highly skilled respectively. Rs. 1,144 was fixed for child workers. The above-mentioned minimum wage also includes an additional dearness allowance of Rs. 666 for adults and Rs. 500 for children. Likewise, adult workers working on a daily wage basis are entitled to receive Rs. 74 per day while children receive Rs. 60 per day. But in April, 2009, the government fixed minimum wages for the labours Nrs. 190 per day. Even today labours are living in pitiable and demorlising condition to fulfill their basic needs while industrialization of the country is a pre-condition for the profession of the labour(Ramaswamy & Ramaswamy,1981).

In respect to the minimum wage 85% formal sector and 80% of informal sector workers are aware of minimum wage and 78% workers of formal and 49% of informal sector are paid accordingly, survey shows.

As regards to the equal treatment of women and men in wage rate, working hour and fringe benefits 66%, 72% and 51% respondents of formal sector workers have found treated equally to women and men in wage, working hour and fringe benefits respectively.

Similarly, 21%, 43% and 19% workers of informal sector have also found women and men receiving equal treatments in wage, working hour and fringe benefits respectively.

The survey shows that wage income of the formal sector worker (21%) is sufficient to support family for the whole year compared to informal sector (12%). 69% of the respondents of formal sector support their families out of wage income for up to nine months.

WORK SAFETY IN FORMAL AND INFORMAL ECONOMY

Unhealthy and hazards work and working conditions produce distress and suffering among workers and their families. This will be a big loss to the enterprise and the society. Hence, it becomes the prime responsibility of every management to take care of health and promote safer working environment.

Protection of health and safety-related provision made in the present The Labour Act, 1992 is much in line with the ILO recommendation number 23(1919) concerning the prevention of industrial accidents, recommendations number 97 (1953) concerning the protection of workers health and ILO convention number155(1981) which is concerned with the occupational safety and health and working environment.

The need for health and safety measures for factory workers in Nepal is necessitated by factors like the structure of workforce, poverty and its consequent effect on health of workers, nature of production process and poor health delivery system of the country.

Poverty has greater impact on health of Nepalese workers. Most people in Nepal are poor. The productivity of the worker is low due to the poor quality educational system (MOI,C&S).The annual per capita income is only US$ 484(MoF,2009). In the case of human development Nepal ranked last among five South Asian Countries, Bangladesh, India, Pakistan, Nepal and Sri Lanka (UNDP, 2009). They do not get enough nutrients to eat, and live in unsanitary situations. In the basic needs ILO includes first of all, certain minimum requirements of a family for private consumption; adequate food, shelter and clothing, secondly, the report included essential services provided by and for the community at large, such as safe drinking water, sanitation, public transport, health and educational facilities. Within fulfill the basic human rights which are not only ends but also goals.ILO states that in reality, many labourers are working in demoralizing, undignified, inconvenient and even dangerous condition. So, in the issue of basic needs the quality of employment or condition of work should be another objective (ILO, 1976). These could lead to intermittent or prolong illness. This might cause absenteeism from work which ultimately affects adversely in production. Similarly, the chances of being exposed to occupational hazards among under- developed countries is high because most of the installations and capital equipments are mostly out- model, worn-out and dangerous imported from the developed countries at a very low price. In developing countries, workers are facing the problem of poor working condition. They have to face hazards in working. The workers themselves have little interest in safety and working conditions (ILO,1983). Because the demand for any other commodity (Krishnan, 1996). Most of the Nepalese entrepreneurs import machinery and equipment without paying much attention to the quality. Machines in textile mills, iron and steel industries, pharmaceuticals and chemicals industries, soap, food and beverage factories may be cited as examples. No one makes it a point to see it whether the machines are compatible to local conditions where the skill of workers is questionable. Likewise, adequate safety and pollution control equipments are not installed. The contractors are rarely concerned with the health of contract workers since they do not form the part of the firms' workforce. Their plight is not even recorded. The use of obsolete machinery and use of untrained workers have led to a rising cases of accidents resulting in loss of limbs is another problem of Nepalese industrial sector.

The health services facilities in Nepal are not symmetrically distributed. People walk for several hours to get health services. The poor are denied access to health services because of the cost. The health and nutrition status of the Nepalese people can only be described as extremely poor. It can be said without exaggeration that at any given time almost every one in Nepal is either ill or imminently at risk of major health problem. The limited access to health facilities, very low level of quality nutrition, acute problem of sanitation are the common attributes of Nepalese health status.

BARRIERS IN PROMOTING DECENT WORK

Gender Based Violence: Prevalent forms of sexual and gender based violence (SGBV) in Nepal include but are not limited to domestic violence, trafficking, child and forced marriage, sex selection, dowry and witchcraft-related violence, discrimination against sexual minorities, sexual harassment, rape, harmful traditional practices such as *Chaupadi*, *Deuki* and other customs affecting women and girls of disadvantaged communities such as the *Badis*.

Gender based Violence Defined

Article 1 and article 2 of Violence Against Women (VAW) defines Gender Based violence. Article 1 states that any act of gender-based violence that results in, or is likely to result in, physical, sexual or psychological harm or suffering to women, including threats of such acts, coercion or arbitrary deprivations of liberty, whether occurring in public or in private life.

Article 2 of VAW states that the definition should encompass, but not be limited to, acts of physical, sexual, and psychological violence in the family, community, or perpetrated or condoned by the State, wherever is occurs. These acts include: spousal battery; sexual abuse, including of female children; dowry related violence; rape, including marital rape; female genital mutilation/cutting and other traditional practices harmful to women; non-spousal violence; sexual violence related to exploitation; sexual harassment and intimidation at work, in school and elsewhere; trafficking in women; and forced prostitution.

UNFPA also recognizes the expanded VAW definition of the 1995 Beijing Plan of action, which was more specific about sexual violence, stating: violations of the rights of women in situations of armed conflict, including systematic rape, sexual slavery and forced pregnancy; forced sterilization, forced abortion, coerced or forced use of contraceptives; prenatal sex selection and female infanticide. It further recognized the particular vulnerabilities of women belonging to minorities: the elderly and the displaced; indigenous, refugee and migrant communities; women living in impoverished rural or remote areas, or in detention.

Child Labour: Nearly one in every three children in Nepal is a child labourer. An estimated 1 million children are engaged in hazardous and exploitative activities. As a result of caste-based discrimination and extreme poverty, children of *Dalit* households are especially vulnerable to this sort of exploitation. They are over-represented in the number of child labourers involved in bonded labour, commercial sex, and activities similar to slavery.

Facts about Child Labour

- According to ILO-IPEC (Child Labour Situation in Nepal, 1996), of all children ages 5 to 14:
- 41.7% (2.6 million) regularly work
- 36.7% work and go to school
- 15% do nothing (are idle)
- 15% do non-economic work, such as household chores.
- Of all working children, 55% are girls.
- Of economically active children, 94.7% (1.58 million) are involved in agricultural work.
- 0.9 million work in the non-economic sector
- 1.6% work as service workers
- 1.6% works in construction, transportation, and communications
- 0.8% work as general technical workers
- 0.8% works in production sector

- 0.4% work as sales worker
- 5000 children are working and living on the streets
- Of working children in Nepal: 64% go to school, 36% do not go to school. 26% of male children do not go to school; 49% of female children do not attend school.
- About 1.7 million children in Nepal are engaged in economic activity. 1.4 million are involved in unpaid activities, and 278, 000 in paid.
- More than 4 out of 10 children work. Child work participation is 41.7%. For every 80 boys who work, 100 girls work.
- Girls work longer hours than boys. 88% of economically active girls work 14 hours or more per day, compared to 80% of boys. 35% of economically active girls worked 42 hours or more per week; 22% of boys did the same.
- More children work in the mountains than in the Tarai. Work participation rate is 52.3% in the mountain region, 45.4% in the hilly region and 36.3% in the Tarai region.
- 1.4 million Worked 14 hours or more during the last week of the survey, i.e. 83.3% of economically active children.
- According to ILO-IPEC, some 127,000 are involved in most hazardous and worst forms of child labour.
- The recent Rapid Assessment conducted by the ILO, 2001 on worst forms of child labour estimates:
- 4,000 rag pickers in Nepal which 88%boys and 12% girls. The rag pickers work 6 hours on average and the average earning is NRs. 87 per day
- 55,000 domestic workers
- 46,029 child porters
- 57,000 bonded child labourers between age group 5-18.
- 12,000 girls are trafficked every year and 20% of the sex workers in Nepal are under age of 16
- Ongoing conflict situation in Nepal has adverse effects not only in general but also in the increase in number of children working in exploitative conditions.

Forms of Child Labour

Many different forms of child labour are present in Nepal. Fifteen main areas of work have been identified, as follows (source; Ending Child Labour, A Briefing Kit on Child Labour in Nepal, (CWIN).

1. *Factory/industry:* Carpet- mostly child migrants work in this area. The children work an average of 15 hours a day, with only one hours' break, 7 days a weeks. The conditions in which the children work are usually poor. Damage to health and injuries are commonplace. Trafficking of children to work in carpet factories in India also occurs. Other forms in this category include: garments/textiles, handicrafts, printing press, welding, confectionery, bread making, making matches, pottery and brick kilns.
2. *Mines and Quarry:* This includes children working in stone quarries and coal mines, as well as in the mining of magnetite.
3. *Plantation:* Children are involved planting a variety of different substances, such as sugar cane, tea, tobacco, millet, maize and rice.
4. *Domestic Service:* Children do various domestic tasks, including; fetching water, collecting fuels and fodder, caring for younger siblings, working in the kitchen and cleaning. Other tasks include washing the dishes and doing the laundry. Domestic service, being invisible compared to other works makes children more vulnerable to abuse.
5. *Shop keeper/service:* This includes the selling of sweets, working in teashops and in restaurants and bars.
6. *Transportation:* Work such as conductors, ticket collectors on buses and tempos, as well as rickshaw drivers. Children from outskirts of urban areas are attracted to becoming conductors in tempos or micro buses.
7. *Porters:* Including street porters, tourist or trekking porters, and domestic porters. There are generally 2

types of porters, as identified by IPEC; long-distance porters who carry loads rurally, and short-distance porters who work mainly in urban areas such as in bus parks.

8. *Construction Work:* Children work to build roads, houses, bridges, and sewerage systems.
9. *Street Work:* Street vendors of newspapers and other items, rag pickers, beggars, street singers, shoe shiners/makers. Street children are more prone to becoming drug addicts, to contracting HIV/AIDS, as well as to becoming exposed to a world of crime.
10. *Commercial Sexual Exploitation:* This includes child prostitution, middlemen or contractors/pimps, work in massage parlors, cabin restaurants and dance bars. Many children are trafficked from Nepal to India, to work in the commercial sex industry.
11. *Bonded labour:* However the Kamaiya system, is abolished in July 2000, the bonded labour continues to influence many children's lives. There are also many debt-bonded labourers, who tend to work in places like carpet factories, households, restaurants, brick kilns, and so on.
12. *Migrant Child Labour:* Often, children migrate from rural to urban centres such as Kathmandu, Biratnagar or Narayanghat with the aim of finding employment. Children sometimes migrate from India to work in Nepal.
13. *Refugee Children:* Children of Tibetan refugees often work in carpet factories, frequently in Tibetan areas of the country or capital city, such as in Katmandu's Bouddha and Lalitpur's Ekantakuna. Many Bhutanese refugee children try to find work in Eastern Nepal.
14. *Circuses/music Industry:* Many children work in circuses. A new phenomenon is the trafficking of children to work in circuses in India. Children also work in puppet or magic shows, or in commercial music programmemes (NLF, 2008)

SOCIAL PROTECTION AND DECENT WORK

In March 2002, in Monterrey, Mexico, President George W. Bush announced his goal to increase U.S. development assistance to foreign nations by 50 percent in the next three years - a $5 billion annual boost over current levels of funding - and to improve the effectiveness of this assistance. Because sound policies are an essential condition of development, the new funds will be held in a Millennium Challenge Account (MCA) and distributed to nations that, in the President's words, "govern justly, invest in their people, and encourage economic freedom." To decide which nations meet these standards, a new Millennium Challenge Corporation will use specific indicators of performance.

Considering the key role of Human Capital in economic growth social protection has gained focus in labour market development programmes. Social protection is the set of policies and programmes designed to reduce poverty and vulnerability by promoting efficient labour markets, diminishing people's exposure to risks, and enhancing their capacity to protect themselves against hazards and interruption/loss of income.

Social protection includes five major components. They are:

- labour markets
- social insurance
- social assistance and welfare service programmes
- micro-and area-based schemes
- child protection

Why Social Protection is required in Nepal?

Several rationales can be advanced in favor of social protection in Nepal. Some of them are mentioned below.

(a) Poverty and income inequality: Poverty and income inequality has placed Nepal in 138th position in the list of the poorest countries of the world.

Poverty and Income Inequality

Year 2006	HDI Rank	Share of income or consumption (%) poorest 20%	Share of income or consumption (%) richest 20%	Inequality measures- ratio of richest 20% to poorest 20%	Inequality measures -gini index
Sri Lanka	93	8.3	42.2	5.1	33.2
Maldives	98	..	..	..	..
India	126	8.9	43.3	4.9	32.5
Pakistan	134	9.3	40.3	4.3	30.6
Bhutan	135	..	..	..	..
Bangladesh	137	9	41.3	4.6	31.8
Nepal	138	6	54.6	9.1	47.2

Source: Online HDI statistical database

Social Exclusion: Several exclusions have contributed towards increasing poverty in Nepal. Some of the known exclusion causes are:

- Income
- Caste/clan
- Ethnicity
- Religion
- Language
- Health condition
- Ability/disability
- Geographic location/"distance"
- Citizenship and migration status
- Age
- Recurrent emergency situations
- Conflict situation

Government's Efforts in Nepal: The government of Nepal with poor coffer has introduced several social protection measures. They are:

Old-age Pension: Old-age pension scheme known as *Jestha Nagarik Bhatta* was introduced for the first time in 1995. The qualifying age for the scheme is age 75 (1.1% of the total population - 2007 estimate). The older people receive NRS 200 each month. The benefit reaches 83% of eligible population and meets daily needs at 40% (according to 2003 survey).

- Widow allowance: NRS 150 per month is paid as widow allowance. The qualifying age for this protection is age 60.
- Disability Pension: Disability Pension of NRS 200 a month is given to
- those who are fully incapacitated
- Scholarships for girls and disadvantaged groups
- Free health care services in all health posts and sub-health posts
- Targeted free health services- anta natal and post natal services
- Free prescribed drugs for all at health posts and sub-health posts
- "One Family One Employee" scheme launched in Karnali
- The Birthing grant

Donors' Efforts in Nepal: The following section provides list of activities by which donors are involved in social protection by implementing cash and kind transfers in Nepal.

- WFP- food Assistance for conflict effected populations: Country programme (Food for work and food for education).
- ADB- Reaching the most disadvantaged groups in mainstream rural development (conditional cash transfers for the ultra-poor)

  – Strengthening decentralized support for vulnerable and conflict-affected families and children
- DIFD- Maternity scheme
- ILO- Old-age pension and employment benefit
- UNICEF- Child grant
- WB–Community block grant

Due to the absence of proper information updating mechanism, various protection schemes which are underway, as for example *ghardailoma Bisweswore* (Bisweswore at every door step for giving employment to one from every family program), through different civil society organizations, left unrecorded and unrecognized making it difficult to assess observed impacts. However, Out of 81 workers' families that receive one or more social transfers from both formal and informal sectors 35% receive old age pension and 28% widow allowance. Few other transfers are also taking place in some workers families. Other transfers taking place are public work programme, school fee for underprivileged children, disability allowance, and incentives for girls' education.

UNIONISM AND DECENT WORK

Trade Union

In a country of rule of law, Acts are framed to regulate and define roles and relationship between parties concerned. Labour Act, 1992; Trade Union Act; 1992; Labour Regulations, 1993; Trade Union Regulations, 1993; and subsequent other acts provide broad frame of regulations that specifies rights and duties and responsibilities of all concerned parties including TUs, workers and employers. Labor Act, 1992 and Trade Union Act, 1992 are second to the *magna karta* in the field of Nepalese industrial relation. These acts and regulations soothe relationship between labourers and management and protect rights of marginalized children, women, and workers at risks. The Labour Act, 1992 and Labour Regulations, 1992 operate and are applicable not only to workers in productive sector but the provisions thereof are applicable to all workers who are involved in economic activities. However, except for the minimum wage the provisions do not cover agriculture and other workers in informal sector. As such it has made difficult for TUs to take care of welfare and rights of workers in unorganized sector (NLF, 2008).

CONCLUSION

Nepal is at the cross road of challenges and development in many aspects. After the successful movement of 2006, it has achieved many things in political sector like republic, inclusive, secular and federal state. But the achievements are limited within the peripheries of political aspect. The economic sector, which can improve the living standard of the people, opens the door for the advancement and reduced proverty in the country, has been remained. Constant without changting the economic condition of the people and the gainful employment opportunities of credating of self-employment opportunities the country can not be developed. Economic development it self is the solution of so many problems like reducing the vulnerability and creating decent works in practice. The real achievement is to transform the theoretical aspect into practice. Only the perception of theory is to throw dust in the eyes of the people.

REFERENCES

Department of Labour(2007), An Introduction of the Department.

ILO (1976), The Impact of International Labour Conventions and recommendations, Geneva: ILO.

ILO (1985), Introduction to Working Conditions and Environment. Geneva: ILO.

ILO (200), The ILO What it is? What is does? Geneva. ILO.

Krishnan, T.N. (1996), Health, Poverty & Labour. The Indian Journal of Labour Economis, Vol. 39. 1.

Ministry of Industry, Commerce & Supplies (2004), Nepal: Trade and Competitiveness Study. Kathmandu: MoI,C&S.

Ministry of Law, Justice & Parliamentary Affars (1998), Labour Act 1992. Kathmandu: MoL, J &PA.

Ministry of Finance (2009), Economic Survey 2008-2009. Kathmandu: MoF.

Nepal Labour Foundation (2008), Workers in Nepal: A Situation Analysis. Kathmandu: NLF.

Ramaswamy, EA and Ramaswamy, Uma (1981), Industry and Labour: An Introduction. Delhi: Oxford University Press.

UNDP (2009), Nepal Human Development Report 2009. Kathmandu: UNDP.

Impact of the Employment Programme on Rural Women

12

D. Kumar, M. Anandan

INTRODUCTION

The first generation of women decision makers in India was the product of the independence movement. The preamble stated that the conference was held at a defining moment in the history of International cooperation and provided an overview of the main issues covered in the ICPD programme of action and the context for action in the field of population and development. It stressed that the ICPD is not an isolated event and that the programmes of action builds on the considerable international consensus that had developed since the 1974 World Population conference in Bucharest and the 1984 Mexico City International conference on population. The ICPD's broader mendate on development issues reflected the growing awarness that population, poverty, patterns of production and consumption, and other threads to the environment are so closely inter connected that none of them can be considered in isolation. The conference followed and build on other resent International activities and the programme of action was expected to make significant contributions to upcoming conferences (e.g., The world summit for Social Development, the Fourth World UN conference on Human

Settlement). It was anticipated that these conferences will highlight further the call of the conference for greater investment in people and for a new action agenda for the empowerment of women to ensure their full participation at all levels in the Social Economic and Political lives of their communities.

EMPLOYMENT GENERATING PROGRAMME IN INDIA

Self-Employment Generation Programmes

These programms offer self-employment to the poor by way of providing subsidized loan to purchase asset for augmenting their income. Integrated Rural Development Programme (IRDP). Training of Rural Youthfor Self-Employment (TRYSEM), Development of women and Children in Rural Areas (DWCRA) are some of the self-employment generation Programme.

Wage-Employment Generation Programme

Under these wage employment is offered to the poor on various public works. Jawahar Rozgar Yojana (JRY) which came into being after merging the erstwhile National Rural Employment Programme (NREP) and Rural landless Employment assurance Scheme (EAS) and MPs Local Development Scheme.

Special Area Development Programme

These programmes are aimed at development of infrastructure in the backward areas which also give employment to the under privileged Drought Prone Area Programme (DPAP), Desert Development Programme (DDP), Hill Area Development Programme (HADP), Command Area Development Programme (CADP) and Integrated Tribal Development Programme (ITRP).

Minimum Needs Programme

These are programmes to develop infrastructural Facilities in rural areas and to cater to the basic needs of the rural people.

Elementary and Adult Education, Rural health Water Supply, Rural Roads, Rural Electrification, Rural Housing, Environment, Nutrition, Rural Domestic Cooking Energy, Rural Sanitation, Public Distribution System(PDS).

Institutional Reforms

This stream of programmes are aimed at reforming and revitalization of the grass roots institutions such as the Panchayat Raj Institutions(PRIs) to provide viable and effective plot form for people's participation and decision making. Revitalization of PRIs Land Reforms and supporting the activities of Non-Governmental Organizations (NGOs) constitute such programmed. Thus a multipronged strategy has been adopted to accelerate rural development.

WOMEN IN THE FIVE YEAR PLAN

Women Received attention of the government right from the beginning of Indian planning however, the shift from "Welfare" to "development" of women took place in the Sixth Five year plan (1980-85).

The Eight Plan (1992-97) promised to ensure that benefits of development from different sectors do not bypass women. The Rashtriya Mahilakosh was set up 1993 to meet to credit needs of poor and asset less women.

The ninth plan (1997-2002)made two significant changes in the strategy of planning for women, Firstly "Empowerment of women" become a primary objective and secondly the plan attempted" convergence of existing services" available in both women-specific and women related sectors.

The Tenth plan (2002-2007) has made a major commitment towards "Empowering Women as the agent of Socio-Economic change and development" based on the recommendation of National Policy for Empowerment of Women, The Tenth plan suggest a three-fold strategy for empowering women, through social empowerment, economic empowerment and gender justice.

The government has constituted a committee of "feminist" economist to ensure gender sensitive allocation of public resources in the 11th five year plan,wijn a view to promote gender equality and more inclusive growth.

NEED OF THE EMPLOYMENT PROGRAMMES IN INDIA

In India, Self-Help Groups (SHGs) have been in operation for a long time many fields such as environment dairying etc., Mutual help in agriculture or household matters is an important characteristic of the rural women in India. The rural poor with the intermediation of voluntary organization also join together for self group to secure better economic growth.. this has resulted in the formation of a large number of self help groups in the country, which mobilize savings and recycle the resources generated among members. Most SHGs have come up due to the dynamic leadership of certain individuals within a group or through the catalytic role played by the NGOs in developing such groups. Self Help Groups operations have become to be recognized as a possible and practical alternative for reaching credit to the weaker sections particularly to the poor women in the informal sector. The success of these SHGs is crucially dependent on their efforts constructively through motivated and inspired field workers. This is especially true for SHGs running savings and credit programmes due to the added responsibility of handling funds. In most cases, although the field workers have latent talents and skills, it takes time to evoke these due to their lack exposure and illiteracy. Thus need of the employment programmes of Self-Help Group savings and credit groups becomes complex and external agency is required to provide impetus for its proper re-orientation.

Rural Women Work Paricipation Rate in India States Per 1000 Female

States	*1993-94*	*1999-2000*
Andha Pradesh	462	443
Assam	86	87
Bihar	131	132
Gujarat	254	311
Haryana	56	33

Contd.

States	*1993-94*	*1999-2000*
Himachal Pradesh	363	281
Karnataka	326	354
Kerala	152	159
Madhya Pradesh	301	331
Maharastra	404	393
Orrisa	210	203
Punjab	37	40
Rajasthan	299	272
Tamilnadu	405	401
Utterpradesh	131	122
West Bengal	84	116
INDIA	238	231

Source: NSSO. Govt of India.

EMPLOYMENT OF WOMEN

The 1991 census showed the Work Participation Rate (WPR) of women as 23 percent for the rural women the WPR is 27 percent and for the urban women it is 10 percent comparing the 1971 and 1981 census, this rise in WPR is considerable.

Year	*Female Work Participation Rate (WPR)*
1901	31.7
1911	33.73
1961	27.96
1971	11.86
1981	14.44
1991	22.69

Source: Census of India 1991.

WOMEN AND RURAL INDIA: KEY FACTS & FIGURES

1. Indian population comprise of 48.1% women & 51.9% men.
2. Rural population 71% of India's population. Farm production: 55.66% of total lab our.
3. Male-based sex ratio: Rural areas: 9.4%;urban areas:8.9% work 1064h, a man 1212h and a women.
4. 70% of the population earn their livelihood from agriculture

5. Work force participation rate of women: 22.7 (male 51.6%) Rural areas: 27.2%, Urban areas: 9.7%.
6. Agriculture & allied sectors employ 89.5% of total female in rural India.
7. Female literacy: 38% as compared to male literacy rate of 66% Rural areas: 30.4%; Urban areas: 63.9%.
8. Rural poverty: 39%; Urban poverty: 30%.
9. Proportion of pregnant women with anemia: 88%
10. Human Development Index rank and gender-related index rank: Same 105 out of 146 countries-indicating low life expectancy at birth, low educational attainment, low income and gender disparities.
11. Women have heavy work load with dual responsibility for farm and household production.
12. Women's average contribution in overall farm production: 55.66% of total labour. In the Indian Himalayas a pair of bullocks work 1064h, a man 1212h and women work 3485h in a year on a one-ha farm.
13. Taking the economy as a whole, women perform two-thirds of the work, but earn only one-tenth of the income.
14. Inter-state and intra-state variations in gender roles in agriculture, environment & rural production.
15. Unequal access to land & property rights.
16. 90% women in forest & tribal belts earn their livelihood by carrying heavy loads on their heads.
17. In dairying 75 million women are engaged as against 15 million men, while in animal husbandry the ratio is 25 million to 1.5 million.
18. Country is loosing 1.5mha of forest cover annually, whereas a fuel-wood contribution to 84% of the total household energy consumption in rural India- contributes to hardship for women.
19. A Hula-user inhales 40mg of carbon monoxide (CO) per Kg of woods as against 17mg/kg & 43mg/kg of CO inhaled by active and passive smokes respectively: injuries to health.

Source: Census of India, 1991; ESCAP, 1997: UNDP Human Development Report, 2002.

IMPACT OF THE EMPLOYMENT PROGRAMME ON RURAL WOMEN

Culture and Rural Women

A rural woman are encouraged culture exchange language courses, festival celebration keeping into consideration global media coverage and global market. Careful projection of women Singers, Dancers, Painters, Actresses, Poet, Writers, Journalist, art-critiques, film makers and educationist has a hidden agenda of promoting India's multi-cultural heritage, their invdvement in building new educational institutions and cultural centers has been fruitful. These women are self made intellectually independent, conversant with foreign languages, life-styles and fit into a norm of "Global Citizens".

Media and Rural Women

Construction of new gender relations based on egalitarians principles as portrayed in some of the advertisement must be encouraged even the chat shows projecting new and realistic images of self-confident career women, caring father, efficient male cooks (who are not comic characters) male beauticians, male fashions designers with professional touch are gender-sensitive. Interview with women entrepreneurs, women industrialists, women managers convey that both, the interviewers and the interviewees know their profession well.

House Work and Rural Women

Rural women has definitely changed attitude towards housework of 50 percent of India's population, which has purchasing power. Thousands of home appliances shown in the advertisement and through door-to-door sale have made men interested in house work. Introduction of modern equipments in housework has on encornged male members of the house to share housework, Men's participation in the food and fashion Industry has challenged patriarchal stereotyping of women's place among the educated middle class Variety of processed and semi-cooked food has increased men's interest in working.

CONCLUSION

Rural women has made civil society inward looking caste, religious and kingship networks are activated within the community. All networks are executing development projects, which would benefit their stake groups. In this situation, women's rights activists with multicultural perspective can play an important role as catalysts for women's empowerment without ensuring women's rights. Female headed households are the poorest of the poor households. Public investment should be made in technologies for poor people especially in the rural areas of medical and agriculture research.

REFERENCES

Kurukshetra May-2003 Vol-51

Yojana May-2004 Vol-48

Yojana Jan-2005 Vol-49

Yojana May-2007 Vol-51

Reforms and female Employment in Rural India

UNFPA In corporating women into population and development knowing why and knowing how, New York, UNFPO-1992.

Diariam. S., The Other Half's Rights: Universal,Indivisible: Interdependent, Interrelated, and in Peril. Populi 22(7), 1995 (18-21)

The Urban Poverty in India

13

G. Paramasivan, J. Sacratees

NTRODUCTION

People must not be allowed to become so poor that they offend or are hurtful to society. It is not so much the misery and plight of the poor but the discomfort and cost to the community which is crucial to this view of poverty. We have a problem of poverty to the extent that low income creates problems for those who are not poor. The first requirement of the concept of poverty is of a criterion as to who should be the focus of our concern. The specification of certain consumption norms or of a poverty line may do part of the job: the poor are those people whose consumption standards fall short of the norms, or whose incomes lie below that line. A famous study of poverty in York, Seebohm Rowntree (1901) defined families as being in 'primary poverty' if their 'total earnings are insufficient to obtain the minimum necessities for the maintenance of merely physical efficiency'. It is not surprising that biological considerations related to be requirements of survival or work efficiency have been often used in defining the poverty line.

Many cities, today, have become global cities, shaping the world's economy, as these cities facilitate flow of international trade, capital, information, and services across borders. Urbanization has been continuing unabated in many parts of the world, and the majority of the world's population is now living in urban areas. However, in most developing countries, the process of urbanization, which is accompanied by incessant movement of rural people towards the cities in search of means of livelihood, is not supported by judicious planning, efficient management and good governance. Urbanization in developing countries has created an unprecedented challenge to urban planners and managers due to its massive scale and complex nature. Metropolitan cities in these countries have serious shortages of power, water supply, sewerage, developed land, housing, transportation, communications, and other facilities, and the provision of urban infrastructure and services to support large concentrations of population and related activities is lagging far behind the pace of urbanization. Large proportions of urban populations, in cities in developing countries, live below poverty line, resulting in proliferation of slums, growth of the informal sector, and deteriorating health levels of urban inhabitants.

Urbanization is considered to be sine-qua-non of economic development. In recent years, most of the developing countries, in a bid to have fast economic development, have also experienced galloping urbanization and their pace of urban growth has been truly dramatic. This spectacular growth rate of urban population along with the urban bias in the development strategies has brought in its wake multifaceted problems viz. over crowding, slum formation and above all urban poverty, which till recently was considered as fallout of the rural phenomenon. But now since growing urbanization is making urban poverty increasingly an urban phenomenon, an understanding of the former becomes indispensable in order to have a thorough insight into the complex dynamism of the latter.

In the economic analysis of poverty, it is measured in terms of the percentage of people who do not have a minimum level of per capita consumption expenditure required for a specific amount of energy intake. Estimates of poverty are derived from the National Sample Surveys on consumption expenditure carried out by the National Sample Survey Organization, Govt. of India. Since the definition of poverty is based on the basic human need of food, the urban population living below the minimum consumption expenditure required for the intake of 2100 calories per capital per day is living in absolute poverty. Hence, the present study seeks to deal with the problem or urban poverty in the context of urbanization in India. Urban poverty still persists there and achievement of the desired objective requires an in depth understanding of both the phenomena. There are so many related issues which have been taken up by different scholars form time to time. Consequently, the present paper would scan some of the necessary background for the concerned study.

GLOBAL PICTURE OF POVERTY

The World Bank has long used the income of $ 1 per day per person, measured at purchasing power parity to determine the numbers of extreme poor in the world. Income of $ 1 per day to $ 2 per day to measure moderate poverty. The overwhelming share of the worlds extreme poor, 93 percent in 2001, live in three regions: East Asia, South Asia and Sub-Saharan Africa, but have taken in East Asia and South Asia. Therefore, one can say, one sixth of the world's population achieved high-income status through consistent economic growth. Another two thirds have risen to middle income status with more modest rates of economic growth. One sixth is stuck in extreme poverty, with very low rates of economic growth during the whole period. Conservative estimates from the World Bank indicate that 30% of poor people live in urban areas, a figure estimated to 40% by 2020 and 50% by 2035. According to United Nations projections, 40 percent of the population in developing countries was to live in urban areas by the turn of the century. In the less developed regions, the percentage of population living in urban areas will reach 50 percent only by 2015 by the year 2025, about 4 billion urban residents are projected to live in less developed regions and by the year 2030, two-thirds of population in developing countries will live in urban areas (UN 1993)

URBAN POVERTY

According to Singh (1993), Though the increase in urban population may result from growth in existing urban population, rural to urban transfer, numerical proliferation of urban centers and spatial expansions of existing urban areas, however, rural-urban transfer has been the moving force behind the rapid pace of urbanization of the Third world countries. Since growing urbanization and an inexorable growth rate of urban population has made the phenomenon of poverty more pronounced, an understanding of the former becomes indispensable in order to have through insight into the complex dynamism of the latter. In words of Pernia (1994) "In an analysis or urban poverty, issues of urbanization and its spatial development form an essential part for a number of reasons." Urban poverty which is a cruel reality, is considered to be the most demanding urban challenge and number one urban problem because it us poverty which leads to many other problems in the urban areas. Taking various dimension of urban poverty into consideration.

The phenomenon of urban poverty has altered the landscape, the social fabric and overall character of the Indian cities. Measurement of absolute poverty in urban areas, normally, employs a nutrition-based poverty line, which includes the urban cost of a minimum healthy diet and a factor of housing cost and clothing. Based on the definition of poverty and quality of data, though various countries might have different estimates of urban poverty and quality of data, though various countries might have different estimates of urban poverty, yet there is no denying the fact that it has emerged to be a formidable challenge in most of the developing countries and it is expected to remain there, regardless of the economic growth performance of these countries.

URBANIZATION IN INDIA

India's urban population is the second largest in the world, with China occupying the top position. Both, natural increase and rural to urban migration, have contributed towards the urban growth. While natural growth was dominant in 1960s and 1980s rural - urban migration along with natural growth played significant role in 1970s. The concern for 'urban poverty' in India, like any where else in the world, is comparatively new. The few programmes, that were undertaken in the country to uplift 55-60 million people estimated to be living below the official poverty line, have essentially been the outcome of expediency and the need to respond to the most immediate and visible forms of deprivation rather than the result of a comprehensive analysis of poverty issues, problems and perspectives.

The fallout of urbanization has been analyzed by some social scientists. A picture of urban living conditions in general has been painted by Bhattacharya (1975). The problems of urbanization in general like shortage of housing, critical inadequacies in public utilities viz. power, water, etc., deteriorating urban environment, urban unemployment, congestion, etc. have been discussed by Mullick (1981) and Raju and Reddy (1986). Singh and Steinberg (1995) describe the problems like deteriorating quality of life, environmental crisis and increasing urban poverty which are putting all development efforts and economic liberalization at risk. In fact, urban poverty is considered to be the biggest problems of urban areas because it is poverty which leads to many other urban problems.

Table 1
Population Census and Growth of Urbanization in India

Year	*Population (million)*			*Decennial Growth Rate (%)*	*Rate of Urbani-zation*	*Density (Persons per Sq. Km.)*
	Total	*Male*	*Female*			
1951	361.1	186	175.6	13.3	17.3	117
1961	439.2	226	212.9	21.5	18.0	142
1971	548.2	284	264.1	24.5	19.9	177
1981	683.3	353	330	24.7	23.3	216
1991	846.3	439	407.1	23.9	25.7	267
2001	1027	531	495.7	21.34	27.8	324

Source: Director of Census Operations, Tamil Nadu, Chennai.

From the above table there has been growing awareness of the scope of rapid urbanization and associated industrial growth in many developing countries. Increasing life-spans and lower death rates, coupled with a steady migration form rural areas, have fuelled urban growth and are predicated to double the world's urban population in the next 25 years. Most of this expansion will occur in the developing world. Already, cities in the developing world are absorbing two-thirds of the total population increase. The number and size of cities in the developing world have dramatically increased over recent decades. Cities of more than five million people can presently be found in every continent.

Table: 2
Projection of Urbanisation in India and Major States

State	Level of Urbanization 2001	2011	2021	2031
A.P.	28.94	32.65	36.84	41.56
Bihar	15.31	17.81	20.85	24.33
Gujarat	34.35	36.44	38.65	41.00
M.P.	24.57	28.13	32.12	36.89
Maharashtra	43.19	48.07	53.51	59.55
Orissa	14.84	18.40	22.80	28.25
Punjab	34.26	38.35	42.94	48.07
Rajasthan	22.09	23.25	24.47	25.75
Tamil Nadu	40.16	44.80	49.98	55.76
Uttar Pradesh	18.94	20.26	21.68	23.19

Source: Reena Bhasin (2001), Urban Poverty and Urbanization, p.95. (A.P.- Andhra Pradesh, M.P. Madhya Pradesh.)

Rural-Urban migration, and thus urbanization, is considered to be a consequence of the push factor and pull factors. Unemployment, rural poverty, unavailability of socio-economic facilities and services are commonly the economic pressures of plush in the countryside, which compel the people to move to the cities in search of employment and livelihood. Improvement in medical technology and, consequently, the reduction in rates of mortality have resulted in demographic expansion which gets manifested in high density of population in rural areas and this factor also works as a push factor. It is also argued that since only a small dent is made by the development programmes and given the mass poverty, and landless poor small farmers continue to migrate to urban areas.

URBAN POVERTY IN INDIA

The problem of poverty has continued to remain the central challenge of development at the global level. Nevertheless, growth–poverty relationship has remained obscure even after three decades of empirical research on development–region-wise, status-wise, and for all categories of countries. The experience with the poverty in India, as in the entire developing world, is rapidly acquiring an urban face and is destined to become a huge issue in the course of India's urbanization. It is a phenomenon, now universally acknowledged, as the urbanization of poverty. While this has been partly on account of international population growth that has suffered deprivation, it is accepted that there has been urbanization of poverty in cities and towns. Rural poverty strategies have largely been unable to stem this exodus, not primarily because of a failure of rural intervention, but because of the inevitability of urban dynamics, so emphatically surfacing across the entire developing world and already fully manifested in the developed world.

The urbanisation of poverty has altered India's urban face by imposing two distinct dimensions upon cities: Deprived of a proper urban habitat, the poor have had to find residential foothold in slums. And in their search for employment and enterprise, they have been forced to find survival in the informal sector. Urbanisation of Poverty has thereby been accompanied with the informalisation of poverty.

It would not be inaccurate to state that nationally, success in tackling urban poverty has been limited. Figures stated in the Tenth Five Year Plan document reveal that whereas 56.4% of rural and 49% of urban population were poor in 1973-74, in 1999-00 these came down to 27.1 % and 23.6% respectively. However, what is alarming is that while the rural poor population dropped from 261.3 million to 193.2 million during the cited period, the numbers of urban poor rose from 60 million to 67 million in the same period, despite a drop in percentage terms. These numbers highlight the rapid rise in the migration of the rural poor to urban locations.

Table 3
Percent below Poverty Line in India

	Poverty %		*Number of Poor (Millions)*		
Year	*Rural*	*Urban*	*Rural*	*Urban*	*Total*
1956-57	54.1	NA	182	NA	182
1957-58	50.2	NA	172	NA	172
1958-59	46.5	NA	162	NA	162
1959-60	44.4	NA	158	NA	158
1960-61	38.9	40.4	141	32	173
1961-62	39.4	39.4	145	32	177
1963-64	44.5	42.5	171	37	208
1964-65	46.8	45.7	184	42	226
1965-66	47.4	46.4	190	44	234
1966-67	56.6	48.4	231	47	278
1967-68	56.5	48.3	236	49	285
1968-69	51	45.5	217	47	264
1969-70	49.2	44.4	214	48	262
1970-71	47.5	41.5	210	46	256
1972-73	49.4	44.6	227	53	280
1973-74	56.4	49.6	261	60	321
1977-78	53.1	45.2	264	65	329
1982-83	45.6	40.8	252	71	323
1987-88	39.1	38.2	232	75	307
1993-94	37.3	32.4	244	76.3	320
1999-00	27.1	23.4	193	67	260
2007*	21.1	15.1	19.3	170	49

Source: Planning Commission, 2000
* Poverty projection for 2007(source: Tenth Five Year plan, Vol1, Planning Commission

In the urban context, what is further important to note is that the traditional manner of looking poverty, largely in income or calorific terms does not do justice to the complex nature of urban poverty. While the rural settlement does not impose overwhelming legal and institutional constraints on a poor person's shelter or employment or services, the urban settlement almost completely throttles the lives of poor women and men through informalisation and legal and institutional bias. Even as the rural poor are starved of opportunities and alternatives but yet are an integral part of the village, the urban poor are treated as aliens who cannot legitimately find a place in the city.

At state level, among the major states, Orissa, Bihar, West Bengal and Tamil Nadu had more than 50 percent of their population below the poverty line in 1983. By 1999-2000, while Tamil Nadu and West Bengal had reduced their poverty ration by states with poverty ratio of 47 and 43 per cent respectively. Among other Jammu and Kashmir, Haryana, Gujarat, Punjab, Andhra Pradesh, Maharashtra, Karnataka have also succeeded in significantly reducing the incidence of poverty. Rural Orissa, rural Bihar and Jharkhand continued to be the poorest among rural areas in 1983, as well as in 1999-2000. In urban areas, the poorest three states in 1983 were Mahya Pradesh, Uttar Pradesh and Orissa whereas in 1993 it was Orissa followed by Madhya Pradesh and Bihar."

CONCLUSION

Shelter for all to be an agenda for the Government, affordable land and low cost housing finance is essential for urban poor. Through a participative process, every city should undertake a citywide poverty situational analysis to promote a better understanding among all the stakeholders concerning the multiple dimensions of poverty in their city. Since the majority of UN member states including India has agreed to reduce urban poverty and support a campaign of cities without slums, Central and State Government should formulate and actively disseminate their policy on the provision of basic services for the poor, clearly specifying the implementation responsibilities of local Government and other agencies and stakeholders. Each State should formulate its policy and action plan on land tenure adequate to safeguard poor people's shelter needs and rights, along with security from forced eviction and priority for in-situ upgradation and effective convergence of all pro-poor programmes and resources. Each State should ensure the necessary amendments to the statutory planning processes to incorporate pro-poor participatory city planning. Each city must draw up a city-wide action plan to target integration of the poor and marginalized population into the city with special attention to land tenure, basic services, housing and employment needs, including support for informal enterprise of the poor, particularly women. Local Government should work in partnership with non-government and community-based organization to support the organization and mobilization of the poor, particularly women, to promote constructive dialogue and shared decision-making. State and Local Governments should actively facilitate the social and economic empowerment of the poor through, among other actions, ensuring access to education, health and other social services, the promotion of self-managed thrift and credit societies linking the poor to formal credit, knowledge sharing and awareness rises. Central, State and other institutions should identify successful initiatives and encourage sharing of these experiences between cities by promoting visits and other innovative activities.

REFERENCE

Edwin S. and Becker (1986), Studies in Indian Urban Development, Oxford University Press, New York, p.17.

Firdausly, C.M. (1994), "Urban Poverty in Indonesia: Trends, Issues and Policies," Asian Development Review, 12(1) pp. 68-89

Jain M.K., "Data on Urbanization in Indian Censuses", Journal of Development Studies, special issue on censuses in India; Retrospect and Prospect, Vol.1 No.1, April–June 1992, 99.73-92

Jones, R. and K. Sen (2001), "On India's Poverty Puzzles and Statistics of Poverty", Economic and Political Weekly (Jan. 20) pp. 211-217

National Steering Committee (1996), India–Draft Final National Report, Jan.

Pernia Ernesto M. (1994), Issues of Urban and Spatial Development in Ernesto M. Pernia (Ed), Urban Poverty in Asia–A Survey of Critical Issues, Oxford University Press, New York.

Rowntree, S. (1901), Poverty: A Study of Town life, London: Macmillan.

Sen, A. (2005), Poverty and Famines: An Essay on Entitlement and Deprivation, Oxford University Press.

Singh, Ram Bali (1993), "Process of Urbanization in the Third World" in Jaymala Diddee and Vimala Rangaswamy, urbanization-Trends, Perspectives and Challenges, Rawat Publications, Jaipur.

Turner, Roy (1962), India's Urban Future, Oxford University Press: California.

United Nations (1993), World Urbanization Prospects–Revised as of 1992, New York.

World Bank (1990), Poverty–World Development Indicators, World Development Report.

Impact of National Rural Employment Guarantee Scheme (NREGS) in Tamil Nadu

14

T. Sivasakthi Devi, R. Balasubramanian

INTRODUCTION

Development oriented strategies for poverty reduction are growing interest to government, non-governmental organizations, development assistance and other agencies. Such strategies function both by creating asserts that benefit to the poor and by raising the productivity of the poor through education, public health and other human resources. Poverty has many dimensions changing from place to place and across time. There are two inter-related aspects of poverty-Urban and Rural poverty. The main causes of urban poverty are migration of villagers to near by towns for seeking subsistence living. In this process, they even lose the habitats and basic needs. In the case of rural poverty, over-dependence on monsoon with non-availability of irrigational facilities which result in crop-failure and low agricultural productivity (Ray, 2000). Government of India estimates, in 2007 there were nearly 220.1 million people living below the poverty line. Nearly 21.1per cent of the entire rural population and 15 per cent of the urban population couldn't able to meet their physical and financial requirements (Deaton and Dreze, 2009). For that the government of India has implemented more anti-poverty programmes to eradicate the poverty and also it has been integrating elements of India's development strategy. It includes the efforts for the welfare of backward areas, backward classes, weaker sections, women and children. The poverty alleviation programmes continue to get priority since the beginning of the fourth five year plan. The objective of the Government has been to reach to the poorest of the poor through programmes of asset building, income generation and wage employment. Integrated Rural Development Programme (IRDP), Development of Women and Children of Rural Areas (DWCRA), National Social Assistance programme and Training Rural Youth for Self Employment Programme (TRYSEM) Public Distribution System (PDS) and some other wage employment programmes ,Rural Manpower (RMP) [1960-61], Crash Scheme for Rural Employment (CRSE) [1971-72], Pilot Intensive Rural Employment Programme (PIREP) [1972], Small Farmers Development Agency (SFDA), Marginal Farmers & Agricultural Labour Scheme (MFAL), National Rural Employment Programme (NREP) and Rural Landless Employment Guarantee Programme (RLEGP). Jawahar Rozgar Yojana (JRY) [1993-94], Employment Assurance Scheme (EAS), Employment Assurance Scheme (EAS) and National Food for Work (NFFWP) [2005] and the recently implemented scheme namely National Rural Employment Guarantee Scheme (NREGS) [2006] is an important programmes for poverty alleviation in rural areas (Government of India, 2009).

OVERVIEW OF NREGS IN TAMIL NADU

NREGA (National Rural Employment Guarantee Act) was amended on 2005 and NREGS has been implemented during February, 2006. The programme was implemented in three phases *viz.*, Phase I, Phase II and Phase III in Tamil nadu. Phase I was started in February, 2006 in six districts, *viz.* Cuddalore, Dindigul, Nagapattinam, Sivagangai, Thiruvannamalai and Villupuram. Based on the success of the scheme, it was extended to Phase II in April, 2007, to cover four major districts namely, Thanjavur, Thiruvarur, Thirunelveli and Karur. Based on the success of the scheme on poverty alleviation it was extended to Phase III and implemented in all the remaining 20 districts of Tamil Nadu in April, 2008, (TN-FORCES, 2006). The present study was undertaken to analyze the impact of NREGS on rural households *i.e.*, the consumption expenditure and inequalities in assets and migration of participants and non-participants of NREGS in Tamil Nadu (Government of Tamil Nadu, 2009).

CRITERIA FOR CLASSIFICATION OF STUDY AREA

In our study, three districts were selected from phase I and II namely, Cuddalore, Thiruvarur and Thirunelveli, based on the poverty level of rural people. The study area was located in North, Middle and Southern part of the State. Hence, it is expected to give an overall picture of consumption expenditure, inequalities in assets and migration of participants and non-participants of NREGS for the whole state. Number and percentage of families under Below Poverty Level (BPL) in major districts were given in below Table 1.

Table 1
Number of Families Below Poverty Level (BPL)

Name of the District	*Family Under BPL (2006)*	*Percentage BPL (2006) Families*
Cuddalore	145583	32.00
Dindigul	107182	30.93
Sivagangai	90277	32.58
Thiruvannamalai	145463	30.19
Villupuram	196449	34.99
Nagapattinam	67405	35.01
Karur	63192	32.85
Thanjavur	147977	34.73
Thirunelveli	141251	31.80
Thiruvarur	87036	43.12

Source: District Profile -2007-2009

Multistage sampling design was applied for the selection of study area. Primary data were collected from 360 households of which 180 households were NREGS participants and 180 households were non-participants of the NREGS in Tamil

Nadu. Based on the objectives, Tobit model was used to study the participants and non- participants of the NREGS.

PARTICIPATION OF NREGS PROGRAMME

Tobit analysis was used to assess the participation and duration of participation in NREGS. The dependent variable, duration of participation of NREGS would denoted as Y=1 or more than 1, and 0 otherwise. Income is the major determining factor to participate the scheme for that the variables included occupation, farm size, family size, age of the head , education and number of persons migrated to other place. X, explained the household's participation status (participating status in NREGS or not).

Algebraically, a general specification is in terms of an index function (d*),

$$d^*_i = X'_i\beta + \varepsilon_i$$

$$d_i = 0 \ if \ d^*_i < 0$$

$$d_i = d^*_i if \ d^*_i > 0$$

Where d (denoting days worked in NREG) takes a value >0 for the participants and 0 for non-participants, and X is a vector of household characteristics. For our purpose, since d^*_I is unobserved, and d_i is, the following result is useful

$$\frac{\partial E[d_i / X_i]}{\partial X_i} = \beta\theta \ (\frac{\beta' X_i}{\sigma})$$

It was estimated using maximum likelihood (Raghbendra, Raghav and Shylashri, 2008).

$$Y = a_0 + a_1 OCPH + a_2 FSIZE + a_3 AGEH + a_{54} EDU + a_5 NMIG + a_6 FS + U_i$$

Y	-	Family head participation in the NREGS (Number of days)
OCPH	-	Occupation of the head (labour-1, Non-labour-0)
FSIZE	-	Family size

AGEH - Age of the head

EDU - Educational status (Number of years)

NMIG - Number of person migrated to other place

FSIZE - Farm size (ha)

Ui - Error term.

RESULTS AND DISCUSSION

Education of Rural Households

Education is significant tool to create awareness among the rural poor to participate in the NREGS. The education details of the households were given in the following table.

Table 2
Education Details of the Rural Households

Particulars	*NREGS Participants*	*NREGS Non-participants*	*Total*
Illiterate	88.00(48.89)	111.00(61.67)	199.00(55.28)
Primary	34.00(18.89)	36.00(20.00)	70.00(19.44)
Secondary	52.00(28.89)	31.00(17.22)	83.00(23.89)
Higher secondary	6.00(3.33)	2.00(1.11)	8.00(2.22)
College	0.00(0.00)	0.00(0.00)	0.00(0.00)
Total	180.00(100.00)	180.00(100.00)	360.00(100.00)

It could be seen from the Table 2 that more than 50 per cent of the NREGS participants were literate when compared to non participants of NREGS (38.33 per cent). It indicated that the education level was important tool to create awareness among the households.

OCCUPATIONAL DETAILS

Employment is one of the major factors influencing the food and nutritional security of the rural households. The occupational details of the household members of the study area were given below.

It could be revealed from the Table 3 that the earnings of the family were highly depends on the agriculture. The results were indicated that more than 80 per cents of NREGS participants were agricultural labourers followed by farmers (11.11 per cent) and non-agricultural labourers (7.78 per cent). In the case of non-participants of NREGS 76.11 per cent of the households were agricultural labourers followed by 16.67 and 7.22 per cent of households were farmers and non-agricultural labourers respectively.

Table 3
Occupation Details of the Rural Households

Classification	*NREGS Participants*	*NREGS Non-participants*	*Total*
Agricultural labour	146.00(81.11)	137.00(76.11)	283.00(78.61)
Non- agricultural labour	14.00(7.78)	13.00(7.22)	27.00(7.50)
Farmers	20.00(11.11)	30.00(16.67)	50.00(13.89)
Total	180.00(100.00)	180.00(100.00)	360.00(100.00)

It could be concluded from the statistics that the agricultural labourers and marginal and small farmers were highly depend on NREGS in off seasons and dry areas due to non availability of work.

INCOME OF RURAL HOUSEHOLDS

The household Income was key element to determine food and nutritional security of the rural poor. The following table has shown the income of the households.

Table 4
Income Details of the Participants and Non Participants

Classification of Income	*NREGS Participants*	*NREGS Non-participants*	*Total*
< 10000	0.00(0.00)	40.00(22.22)	40.00(11.11)
10000-20000	82.00(45.56)	53.00(29.44)	135.00(37.50)
20000-30000	54.00(30.00)	31.00(17.22)	85.00(23.61)
30000-40000	22.00(12.22)	32.00(9.44)	54.00(15.00)
40000-50000	19.00(10.56)	17.00(9.44)	36.00(10.00)
>50000	3.00(1.67)	7.00(3.89)	10.00(2.78)
Total	180.00(100.00)	180.00(100.00)	360.00(100.00)

From the above Table 4 it is clear that in 22.22 per cent of NREGS non-participants were earning less than Rs.10000 whereas it was reverse in NREGS participants *i.e.*, all participants were earning more than Rs.10000. And also more than 50 per cent of the NREGS participants were earning more than Rs.20000 when compared non-participants. About 3.89 and 1.67 per cent of NREGS non-participants and participants were earning more than Rs. 50000. This variation due to cultivation of crops and non-farm activities are available throughout the year.

MIGRATION DETAILS

Migration of the rural households is stressing the essential of NREGS to the rural poor. The migration details of the study area was given below

Table 5
Migration Details of the Rural Households

Classification	*NREGS Participants*	*NREGS Non-participants*	*Total*
Off-Season	44.00(24.44)	66.00(36.67)	110.00(30.56)
Throughout the year	23.00(12.78)	102.00(56.67)	125.00(34.72)
Non migrant	113.00(62.78)	12.00(6.67)	125.00(34.72)
Total	180.00(100.00)	180.00(100.00)	360.00(100.00)

It could be seen from the Table 5 that 67.78 and 6.67 per cent of the households were non-migrants in NREGS participants and non-participants respectively. Throughout the year (56.67) and off season migration (36.67) were more in non-participants of NREGS when compared to NREGS participants. It was clearly indicated that NREGS was reducing the migration of the rural households. It has a good sign to prevent the urban poverty.

LIVESTOCK DETAILS OF THE RURAL HOUSEHOLDS

It is an important productive asset and could ensure food security to rural households by yielding milk, meat and egg. Besides, it is providing supplementary income throughout the year by sale of milk products. The following table has shown the livestock population.

Table 6
Livestock Population

Livestock	*NREGS Participants*	*NREGS Non-participants*	*Total*
Cow	39.00(33.91)	44.00(44.90)	83.00(38.97)
Buffaloes	20.00(17.39)	17.00(17.35)	37.00(17.37)
Goat & Sheep	52.00(45.22)	32.00(32.65)	84.00(39.44)
Poultry	4.00(3.48)	5.00(5.10)	9.00(4.23)
Total	115.00(100.00)	98.00(100.00)	213.00(100.00)

It could be seen from the Table 6 that cow and buffaloes population were high in NREGS non-participants when compared to NREGS participants. But it was reverse in the case of goat and sheep, where population was high (45.22 per cent) in NREGS non- participants. It clearly indicated that dependency of the NREGS was high in dry areas.

CONSUMPTION EXPENDITURE PATTERN

The consumption expenditure of households which is basically the budget share of each food and non food item, relies on the income of households. The expenditure pattern also reflects the food demand pattern, food habits and living conditions of households. The fallowing table was shown the expenditure of food items

Table 7
Expenditure Pattern of Food and Non-food Expenditure

(Rs/ per capita/ month)

Particulars	*NREGS participants*	*NREGS Non-participants*	*Total*
Rice	818.22(28.03)	613.76(29.15)	1431.97(28.50)
Other cereals	71.35(2.44)	47.81(2.27)	119.16(2.37)
Sugar	69.15(2.37)	50.73(2.41)	119.88(2.38)
Oil	394.57(13.52)	282.24(13.41)	676.81(13.47)
Pulses	164.29(5.63)	136.60(6.49)	300.89(5.99)
Others	285.06(9.77)	220.25(10.49)	505.30(10.06)
Fruits & vegetables	228.56(7.83)	183.53(8.72)	412.09(8.20)
Meat & egg	302.56(10.37)	169.45(8.05)	472.01(9.36)
Milk	345.86(11.85)	264.38(12.56)	610.23(12.15)
Fish	239.40(8.20)	136.60(6.49)	376.00(7.48)
Total	2919.01(100.00)	2105.33(100.00)	5024.34(100.00)

It could be inferred from the Table 7 for the NREGS participants and NREGS non-participants, the average expenditure on food items of rural households worked out to Rs. 2919.01 and Rs.2105.33 per capita/year respectively. Invariably in both groups cereals took major share ranging from 30.47 per cent to 31.42 percent of total food expenditure. It indicated that more cereals were consumed to meet their calorific requirement of NREGS participants and non-participants, followed by Pulses, others fruits and vegetables.

In total food expenditure rice was occupying the major share, average expenditure share on rice was Rs.818.22 and Rs.613.76 per capita/year in NREGS participants and NREGS non-participants respectively. The expenditure of meat and egg (Rs. 302.56 and Rs.169.45 per capita/year) and fish (Rs. 239.40 and 136.60 per capita/year) was higher in NREGS participants when compared to NREGS non-participants.

Comparing the overall expenditure on food expenditure of two groups, the following inferences can be made. In the case of NREGS participants there was a shift in expenditure on cereals, in general, to non-cereal quantity foods like meat and egg, fish and milk as these food items showed a significant proportion of the overall expenditure when compared NREGS non-participants.

PARTICIPATION OF NREGS PROGRAMME

In this section, the participation of rural households in NREGS was examined by fitting a Tobit model. The results obtained by applying this model are furnished in table

Table 8
Participation of NREGS

Variables	*Coefficient*	*'t' value*
Occupation of the head	-9.750	-0.783
Family size	4.683	1.902**
Age of the head	-0.131	-0.378
Educational status	4.486	4.450*
Number of person migrated to other place	-38.919	-7.687*
Farm size	-24.172	-2.874*

It could be seen from the Table 8 above that all variables had significantly influenced by the participation of NREGS except occupation of the head and age of the head. Among the variables, educational status was positive and highly significant, number of person migrated to other place and farm size had been negative and highly significant. It shows that the NREGS has reduced the migration of rural people and also prevent the urban poverty. The marginal and small farmers are highly depending on the scheme.

CONCLUSION

The study showed that the education was an important to create the awareness among the rural households. The tobit analysis indicated that educational status was positive and highly significant, number of person migrated to other place and farm size had been negative and highly significant. It shows that the NREGS has reduced the migration of rural people and also prevent the urban poverty. The most of the marginal and small farmers and agricultural laborers were highly depending on the NREGS due to non availability of employment during the lean season in dry areas.

In consumption pattern, the expenditure on food item had significantly increasing in the NREGS participants. The results showed that there was a shift in expenditure on cereals, to high value foods like meat and egg, fish and milk items in NREGS participants when compared NREGS non-participants. Over all, the NREGS was improved the food and nutritional status rural poor and also increasing the standard of living of the rural households.

REFERENCE

Deaton, A and J. Dreze (2009), "Food and Nutrition in India: Facts and Interpretations", *Economic Political Weekly*, Vol.XLIV, No.7, pp.42-63.

Government of India (2009), "National Rural Employment Guarantee Act (NREGA)-Two Years 2006-08", Ministry of Rural Development, Government of India, New Delhi.

Government of Tamil Nadu (2009), National Rural Employment Guarantee Scheme (NREGS), DRDA, Cuddalore district Tamil Nadu.

Ray. R. (2000), "Poverty, Household Size and Child Welfare in India", *Economic Political Weekly*, September 23, pp. 3511-3520.

Impact of NREGP on the Rural Hands of India

15

Krishna Moorthy Kn

INTRODUCTION

Poverty and unemployment, the two major problems facing countries all over the globe abinitio of the 21st century. Not only developing countries but also some of the developed countries of the world are struggling with the above said problems as result of recent economic crisis. But compared to developed countries the situations of most of the developing countries are too worse. An in-depth analysis of such problems in those countries exhibits the need of a national employment programme .India one of the country among them recognize earlier the need of such a programme and speed up the steps to its implementation in the early period of 2005.In India the UPA coalition government supported by the left parties brought about an employment guarantee act instead of a scheme because the previous record of the performance of such schemes are not so credible. The act was enacted with an aim of improving the purchasing power of rural people by providing a legal guarantee of one hundred days of employment in every financial year to adult members of any rural household willing to do public work-related unskilled manual work at the statutory minimum wage of Rs.100 per day.The success of the programme tends the UPA government to change its name as Mahatma Gandhi Rural Employment Programme

ABOUT THE PROGRAMME

The national rural employment guarantee act 2005 was passed unanimously in the lok sabha on 23 august 2005.The scheme started from February 2,2006 in 200 districts, was expanded to cover another 130 districts in 2007-2008 and eventually covered all 593 districts in India in 2008. The outlay was Rs. 11,000 crores in 2006-2007, and has been rising steeply, to Rs. 39,100 crores in 2009-2010. This act was introduced with an aim of improving the purchasing power of the rural people, primarily semi or un-skilled work to people living in rural India, whether or not they are below the poverty line

The act was brought about by the UPA coalition government supported by the left parties. The promise and achievement of this project was one of the major factors that gained UPA victory in the Indian general elections 2004.Dr. Jean Dreze a Belgian born economist, at the Delhi School of economics. Delhi School of Economics, has been a major influence on this project.

The NREGA is an act and can be amended only by Parliament. The act directs state governments to implement NREG "schemes". Under the NREGA the Central Government meets the cost towards the payment of wage, 3/4 of material cost and some percentage of administrative cost. State Governments meet the cost of unemployment allowance, 1/4 of material cost and administrative cost of State council. Since the State Governments pay the unemployment allowance, they are heavily incentivized to offer employment to workers. The State Government to decide the amount of unemployment allowance, subject to the stipulation that it not be less than 1/4th the minimum wage for the first 30 days, and not less than 1/2 the minimum wage thereafter. However 100 days of employment (or unemployment allowance) per household must be provided to able and willing workers every financial year.

The Comptroller and Auditor General (CAG) of India, in its performance audit of the implementation of NREGA found that the around 4,49,40,870 rural households were provided jobs under NREGA during 2008-09, with an national average of 48 working days per household. NREGA is the first programme having been implemented with full IT support.

OBJECTIVES OF THE PROGRAMME

- To protect rural households from poverty and hunger
- Empowerment of women in rural areas by providing employment
- To create useful assets in rural areas through labour intensive methods
- To change power equations in rural society and to foster more equitable social order
- Strengthening the bargaining power of unorganized workers
- A substantial reduction of rural-urban migration
- Generating employment through the development of rural areas

FUNCTIONING OF THE PROGRAMME

Adult members of rural households submit their name, age and address with a photo to the Gram Panchayat. The Panchayat registers households after verification and issues a job card. The job card contains the details of the adult member enrolled and his/her photo. A registered person can submit an application for work in writing (for at least fourteen days of continuous work) either to the Panchayat or to Programme Officer.

The Panchayat/programme officer accepts the valid application and issue a dated receipt of application. A letter providing employment will be sent to the applicant and also displayed at the Panchayat office. Employment will be provided if possible within a radius of 5 km; if it is above 5 km, transport allowance and 10% extra living allowance will be paid. New public works can be started when at least 50 workers become available who cannot be absorbed under existing schemes. If employment under the scheme is not provided within fifteen days of receipt of the application daily unemployment allowance will be paid to the applicants. The employment allowance is to be fixed by the state government. However it must be 'not less than one-fourth of the wage rate' for the first thirty days and 'not less than one-half of the wage rate after that .No discrimination between men and women is allowed under the act. Therefore, men and women must be paid the same wage. All adults can apply for employment, not just those below the poverty line.

The NREGA achieves twin objectives of rural development and employment. The NREGA stipulates that works must be targeted towards a set of specific rural development activities such as: water conservation and harvesting, afforestation, rural connectivity, flood control and protection such as construction and repair of embankments, digging of new tanks/ponds, percolation tanks and construction of small check dams are also carried out under this scheme. Micro irrigation work such as construction of small canals is also carried out. The scheme provides irrigation facilities to land owned by people coming under SC/STs, beneficiaries of land reforms, Indra Awas Yojana, etc. Renovation of traditional water bodies is also carried out. This involves desilting of tanks/ponds, old canals, open wells, etc. Land development is also given importance. The employed are given work such as land leveling, tree plantation, etc.

The paper tries to examine the impacts of NREGP in the rural areas of India .The paper also tries to analyse the benefits given by the NREGP to rural areas of the state Kerala with special reference to the districts Palakkad, and Vayanad

The following are the benefits received by the rural areas of India from the implementation of NREGP

- *Massive creation of Employment in Rural Areas:* NREGP could provide employment to vast number peoples in the rural areas and there by created dramatic changes in their lives by providing better purchasing power. The increased level of income enabled them to acquire a better standard of living and to lead a quality life. Employment also made a positive growth in the weaker sections of the society.

– *Increased Assets Creation in Rural Areas:* As the programme insist on creating employment through development, helps to create useful assets in the rural areas. Enormous number useful assets were created in the rural areas of India by the labourers of NREGP.Such creations are more useful in accelerating the development of rural areas. The work is mostly concentrated on activities such as water harvesting, Water conservation, Drought proofing (Afforestation), Irrigation canals, Provision of irrigation facility, Renovation of traditional water bodies,Desilting of tanks, Land development, Flood control and protection works including drainage in water logged areas, Rural connectivity to provide all weather access enhances the development agriculture in rural region

– *Reduced Rate of Poverty:* Poverty one of the major problem of India could reduced to a great extent by the implementation of NREGP.Poverty can eradicate only by replacing employment and the present scheme did such a work credibly. The increased employment rate shows that poverty in majority of the rural areas were vanished and still happening so in other areas. A reasonable amount of wages provided by the government helps the rural people to find money for buying food articles.

– *Income Generation in the Hands of Household:* As the programme provide employment and thereby a reasonable amount of wages for their work generated incomes and savings in the hands of rural households. Which make them to invest in productive areas and to earn an additional income. Moreover it creates purchasing power and provide ample opportunities for small business establishments. Thus another way it is creating employment opportunities

- *Reduced Rate of Migration:* One of the major achievement of NREGP is that it reduced the rate of migration in rural areas. As employment were provided in their places the rurals are ceases to going urban areas in search of employment. Which is beneficial to both urban and rural. The survey reports shows that after the implementation of NREGP the migration status of rural areas were reduced to a large extent.
- *Enhances Women Empowerment:* The programme provides employment to all without gender discrimination enhances the women participation in it. The survey reports of various states exhibits the fact that majority of women got employment and there by created a substantial development in their lives.
- *Create Social Equitable Society:* As the work is provided on the basis of registration the people of different caste ,religion and sections of the society can work together and which creates a harmonious relationship among them. People of different groups in the society working together in harmonious way shows the social equality generated among them

The above conclusions were derived from the survey reports of the state and central government which are illustrated below

Table 1
NREGA at Nutshell: 2007-8
(till December 2007)

No of households demanded jobs	2.48crore
No of households provided jobs	2.43crore
Total Number of persondays generated	78.03crore
Average persondays per family	28.75
Total works taken up	11.68lakhs
Completed works	3.36lakhs
Ongoing or Incomplete works	8.31akhs

Source: www.nrega.nic.in

Employment Generated during the Year 2009-2010 up to the Month of October 2009

(*Source: www.nrega.nic.in*)

States	*No. of Registered*			*Employment Demanded*		*Employment Offered*	
	House Hold	*Persons*	*Job Card Issued*	*House Hold*	*Persons*	*House Hold*	*Persons*
Orissa	5400457	14330012	5311613	589925	1058758	586676	1053722
Rajasthan	9070315	22646677	9070270	4043609	5781565	4052792	5792040
Chhattisgarh	3629672	10969057	3629362	1137153	2235607	1131134	2220440
Jharkhand	3538355	7468599	3527810	790053	1227537	766416	1185315
Madhya pradesh	10756935	32569247	10701017	1663857	3208789	1659054	3197023
Tripura	618516	1343490	605549	527453	769956	527454	769967
Maharashtra	5777854	14241707	4825648	178215	361636	176641	358363
Gujarat	2686753	6643995	2537923	334901	774368	332053	767832
West bengal	9451214	19792830	9450938	2005043	2671590	1997346	2658549
Kerala	2286817	4375863	2258229	442135	483470	441540	482474
Karnataka	4636095	11199623	4580467	1410961	3340805	1407381	3331427
Bihar	8337461	12319409	8337459	85817	111773	85647	111572
Mizoram	188426	464580	187553	57945	58036	56637	56724
Haryana	413571	819905	412973	67814	99461	67617	99223
Himachal pradesh	853223	1671953	853224	165938	188457	164522	186901
Uttar pradesh	6333438	8196006	6176558	1223305	1480344	1221175	1477722
Nagaland	284763	505202	284763	242784	294455	242731	293640
Assam	2877629	4122814	2755057	262371	288712	258883	285153
Uttarakhand	760167	1317171	749427	13522	14908	13317	14655
Meghalaya	353397	760259	348554	23312	26507	22831	26007

Contd.

Employment Provided					
House Hold	Persons	Person Days	No. of Filled Muster Roll	No. of Families Completed 100 days	On going Works
569238	1014644	17864766	218882	9118	100508
4051500	5790404	163822432	1617935	128584	297337
1137475	2234988	32056188	507612	20610	107981
791787	1230474	27126327	478363	25207	171476
1672111	3225080	47332722	488600	29869	484718
527308	769027	16725051	310151	1866	45731
167466	335546	5499257	19771	8325	49254
318169	729957	8703698	87091	6333	28134
1972867	2611556	24499260	515815	2358	95062
438076	477639	7627405	80081	298	60125
1374995	3239753	60196473	277112	83416	143789
85436	111277	1894023	37514	556	36665
59766	59855	1003245	2129	0	2727
67333	98580	1806835	16598	1266	5697
162501	184210	4239596	25363	481	38174
1223324	1479995	27423151	284743	10391	227017
242540	290972	5726616	4236	360	5836
255707	281752	4414852	52049	563	9183
11621	12845	180805	2958	9	7701
23288	26527	439388	2978	1	2922

Work Status : Completed Works

Source: www.nrega.nic.in

State	Flood Control			Rural Connectivity			Water Conservation and Water Herversting			Renovation of Traditional Water Bodies		
	GP	BP	ZP	GP	BP	ZP	GP	BP	ZP	GP	BP	ZP
Orissa	7	5	0	1303	748	0	297	506	0	633	777	0
Rajasthan	1	0	0	158	1	0	188	0	0	129	1	0
Chhattisgarh	2	0	0	102	0	0	38	0	0	15	0	0
Jharkhand	30	1	0	853	147	7	2065	96	0	522	10	0
Madhya pradesh	57	0	0	336	9	0	2377	30	0	206	3	0
Tripura	33	7	1	1012	162	1	345	41	2	68	12	0
Maharashtra	0	0	0	0	0	0	5	0	0	1	0	0
Gujarat	75	0	0	33	0	0	433	0	0	4	0	0
West bengal	730	5	0	5341	58	0	2755	12	0	1686	3	0
Kerala	1711	0	0	109	0	0	426	0	0	915	0	0
Karnataka	303	0	0	484	0	0	1753	0	0	567	0	0
Bihar	0	0	0	3	1	0	1	0	0	0	2	0

Contd.

Drought Proofing			Irrigation Canals			Irrigation Facilities to SC/ST/IAY/LR			Land Development			Other Works			
GP	BP	ZP	GP	BP	ZP	GP	BP	ZP	GP	BP	ZP	GP	BP	ZP	Total
16	6	0	14	18	0	76	158	0	11	1	0	38	146	0	4760
9	0	0	2	0	0	243	0	0	695	0	0	64	0	0	1491
4	0	0	2	0	0	96	0	0	24	0	0	3	0	0	286
428	0	0	39	10	0	292	4	0	1532	24	0	949	44	0	7053

521	1	0	44	0	0	412	9	0	559	2	0	45	0	0	4611
50	14	0	600	75	5	8	1	0	760	113	7	115	31	3	3466
0	0	0	0	0	0	0	0	0	0	0	0	0	0	0	6
139	0	0	17	0	0	4	0	0	4	0	0	3	0	0	712
965	5	0	662	7	0	200	0	0	792	16	0	166	0	0	13403
227	0	0	511	0	0	178	0	0	289	0	0	50	0	0	4416
227	0	0	465	0	0	772	0	0	1181	0	0	95	0	0	5847
0	0	0	1	0	0	0	0	0	0	0	0	0	0	0	8

From the above discussions it is quite obvious that NREGP plays an important role in rural development and it can be further viewed by analysing the fruits received by the rural areas of Kerala.

Kerala has one of the highest unemployment rates in the country. But most of the unemployed are educated. Thus NREGA has only limited application in tackling the problem of unemployment among the poor of Kerala. Yet it has a niche ideal for about 4 to 5 lakh people who are willing to do physical labour and for whom an addtitional annual income of Rs.12,500/- obtained from the Employment Guarantee Scheme would be a substantial boost in income and purchasing power.

Therefore right at the beginning a political decision was taken to target the eligible families, visualising NREGS as the nucleus of a concerted and convergent anti-poverty initiative.

As the National Rural Employee Guarantee Programme (NREGP), which is believed to have aided Congress victory in rural India, dominates post-election discussions, a study by a Thrissur-based economist has found that it has effectively reduced poverty at Vadakkanchery panchayat in Palakkad district.

According to the study, conducted by economist E. M.Thomas, NREGP has helped 90 per cent of its beneficiaries clear debts. "Absence of gender discrimination in wages has contributed to empowerment of women in the panchayat. As wages are paid through banks, a good number of workers in the panchayat now have bank accounts. About 91 per cent of them opened bank accounts for the first time in their lives," Dr. Thomas says.

The Kerala Rural Employment Guarantee Scheme has been implemented in Palakkad and Wayanad districts since February 5, 2006. A majority of the households got 25 to 50 days of manual jobs in 2007-08.

The paper attempts t to examine the impact of NREGP in two districts of Kerala such as palakkad and wayanadu in terms of physical output and employment generation. Details of assessment by the beneficiaries are also added here along with a table showing the impact of the programme..

Physical Outputs of the Programme

- 6,052 works completed during 2006-07 in the State - 3324 works in Palakkad and 2726 works in Wayanad.
- 1,571 works completed during 2006-07 in the State in the sector of 'Flood control and protection' - 917 works in Palakkad and 654 works in Wayanad.
- 1,360 works completed in the State in the sector of 'Renovation of traditional water bodies' - 915 works in Palakkad and 445 works in Wayanad.
- 1,214 works completed in the State in the sector of 'Micro irrigation' -1,012 works in Palakkad and 202 works in Wayanad.
- 1,112 works completed in the State in the sector of 'Water conservation and water harvesting' - 207 works in Palakkad and 905 works in Wayanad.
- 295 works completed in the State in the sector of 'Land Development'-56 works in Palakkad and 239 works in Wayanad.
- 248 works completed in the State in the sector of 'Provision of irrigation facility to SC/ST/Beneficiaries of land reforms/IAY'-148 works in Palakkad and 100 works in Wayanad.
- 206 works completed in the State in the sector of 'Rural connectivity'-59 works in Palakkad and 147 works in Wayanad.
- 44 works completed in the State in the sector of 'Drought proofing - 10 works in Palakkad and 34 works in Wayanad.

Employment Generation Details of NREGP

- 20.5 lakh person-days generated during 2006-07 in the State - 11.57 lakhs in Palakkad and 8.93 lakhs Wayanad.
- On an average, a NREGS district in the State generated 10.25 lakh person days of employment.
- 4.12 lakh person-days generated for SCs in the State - 3.40 lakhs in Palakkad and 0.72 lakhs in Wayanad.

- On an average, a NREGS district in the State generated 2.06 lakh person days of employment for SCs.
- 2.55 lakh person-days generated for STs in the State - 0.50 lakhs in Palakkad and 2.05 lakhs in Wayanad.
- On an average, a NREGS district in the State generated 1.27 lakh person days of employment for STs.
- 13.47 lakh person-days generated for women in the State - 8.95 lakhs in Palakkad and 4.52 lakhs in Wayanad.
- On an average, a NREGS district in the State generated 6.73 lakh person days of employment for women.
- 10,016 person-days generated for beneficiaries of land reforms/IAY in the State–916 in Palakkad and 9,100 in Wayanad.
- On an average, a NREGS district in the State generated 5,008 persondays of employment for beneficiaries of land reforms/IAY.
- 34 person-days generated for disabled beneficiaries - 1 in Palakkad and 33 in Wayanad.
- On an average, a NREGS district in the State generated 17 person-days of employment for disabled beneficiaries.
- On an average, SC, ST and women beneficiaries in the State received 21, 13 and 66 percent of the total employment generated, respectively.
- On an average, SC, ST and women beneficiaries in Palakkad received 30, 4 and 77 percent of the total employment generated, respectively.
- On an average, SC, ST and women beneficiaries in Wayanad received 8, 23 and 51 percent of the total employment generated, respectively.

Assessment by the Beneficiaries

- Most of the beneficiaries (91 % in Palakkad and 74 % in Wayanad) interacted replied that the quality of work under NREGS is satisfactory.

- The assets created under the scheme were found durable by 51 and 50 percent beneficiaries from Palakkad and Wayanad respectively.
- A large segment of beneficiaries (48 % in Wayanad and 32 % in Palakkad) commented that the quality of work taken up under NREGS is 'Good/Very Good'. Only less than 1 percent of the beneficiaries in both the districts indicated that the quality of work is 'Poor'.
- 76 percent beneficiaries from Wayanad and 66 percent from Palakkad remarked that the scheme interventions resulted in generating income and employment on a sustainable basis.
- The scheme has resulted in reducing household indebtedness as revealed by 86 percent from Wayanad and 66 percent from Palakkad.
- It is interesting to note that the scheme could check migration of workers from rural to urban area or to other states, as mentioned by 20 percent beneficiaries in Wayanad and 13 percent in Palakkad.
- 58 percent beneficiaries in Palakkad and 53 percent in Wayanad mentioned that the scheme execution influenced in improving water conservation to a great extent.
- A significant segment of beneficiaries (26 percent in Wayanad and 22 percent in Palakkad) opined that the water table of the area has increased after the interventions under NREGS.
- Soil conservation activities in the area have resulted positively as shown by 37 percent beneficiaries from Wayanad and 22 percent from Palakkad.
- Several afforestation works have been taken up in both the districts, as indicated by 14 percent beneficiaries in Palakkad and 6 percent in Wayanad.
- About 29 percent of the beneficiaries from Palakkad and 20 percent from Wayanad highlighted that the scheme made a positive influence on agricultural productivity, which is an important aspect.

– The scheme resulted in achieving overall development of the village as opined by 83 percent beneficiaries in Wayanad and 69 percent in Palakkad.

The following table shows the impact of NREGP in two districts of Kerala

CONCLUSION

Majority of the people in India lives in villages, so all the efforts undertaken with the aim of development of the nation posses special emphasis to rural areas. All such efforts taken to utilize the unexplored wealth of rural areas could bring prosperity and progress in our nation and the results of NREGP programme evidenced it The promise and performance of this programme was one of the major factors that gained UPA victory in the Indian general election, 2004 and 2009.NREGP created big changes in the lives of rural people by providing employment to all .It also accelerated rural development The rural areas having potential resources for development made easy the programme to attain its objective. Almost all the rurals in India now smiling as they can lead a quality life. Besides the former it offered progress in health ,education, infrastructure,women empowerment, poverty eradication etc. And now the urbans started to demand a National Urban Employment Guarantee Programme. Compared to the previous schemes of various governments since the independence to now in India ,nothing was successful as NREGP.

Even though the programme is a good one in all ways it is not free from some drawbacks. First one among them was the programme carries the threat of inflation. Expenditure made by each state shows that there is a chance for inflation. Second one was the assets created in some areas were not justifying the expenditure incurred for it .Thirdly Educated unemployed in some states having high literacy rates shows that they are less benefited as the programme needs only unskilled workers. These are the problems encountered during the implementation of the programme .And it is to be expected that government will take necessary steps to overcome such threats and take India to prosperity and progress.

Description	Palakkad	Wayanad	Total
Number of households issued jobcards	1,39,684	74,156	2,13,840
Number of households who havedemanded wage employment	56,919	48,008	104927
Number of households providedemployment	55,150	44300	99450
Total Number of applicants providedemployment	57,038	56195	113233
No. of women provided employment	42,575	30253	72828
No. of women provided employment	11.57	8.93	20.50
Employment generated (SC)	3.40	0.72	4.12
Employment generated (ST)	0.49	2.05	2.54
Employment generated (Others)	7.67	6.16	13.83
Employment generated (Women)	8.95	4.52	13.47
Number of households which havecompleted 100 days of employment	255	282	537
Total Number of works initiated	4,860	3011	7871
Total Number of Completed Works	3,324	2726	6050
Water conservation & waterharvesting	207	905	1112
Drought proofing	10	34	44
Micro irrigation	1,012	202	1214
Provision of irrigation facility to landowned by SC/STs, land reformsbeneficiaries, IAY beneficiaries, etc.	148	100	248
Renovation of traditional waterbodies	915	445	1360
Land development	56	239	295
Flood control and protection 917	917	654	1571
Rural connectivity	59	147	206

Source: Progress reports from JPCs – Palakkad and Wayanad

REFERENCE

http://en.wikipedia.org

www.nrega.nic.in

www.idfresearch.org

www.pib.nic.in

www.crd.kerala gov.in/nrega_feature.pdf

Impact of Rural Employment Guarantee Programme and Poverty in India

16

D. Kumar, M. Anandan

"The benefit of economic development must accrue more and more to the relatively les privileged classes of society, and there should be a progressive reduction of the concentration of income, wealth and economic power"

– *Second Five Year Plan*

INTRODUCTION

The rural employment Guarantee Programmes need to improve the quality of living by promoting the accessibility of improvised households to food, housing, clothing, primary health care sanitation safe drinking water, and basic and primary education. It also needs the reinforcement of a social and community revolution directed against the monopoly of property and enduring poverty and for establishment of social justice and gender equality. In this effort they need the help of community level organization.

IMPACT OF RURAL EMPLOYMENT GUARANTEE PROGRAMME AND POVERTY IN INDIA

The National Human Development Report- 2001 prepared by the planning Commission has rightly envisaged that the "development processes has to be ultimately assessed to impact Rural Employment Guarantee Programme and human

Table 1

State-wise Rural Poverty Percent Poor

State	*1987-88*	*1999-00*
Andhra Pradesh	11.9	45.8
Assam	13.4	53.4
Bihar	8.6	47.9
Gujarat	16.3	41.2
Haryana	3.7	41.2
Karnataka	10.0	32.0
Kerala	8.4	65.0
Madhya Pradesh	15.2	30.8
Maharastra	19.6	41.7
Orissa	3.8	40.8
Punjab	5.9	56.7
Rajasthan	6.4	21.0
Tamil Nadu	17.9	63.4
Uttar Pradesh	4.9	34.6
West Bengal	11.6	53.4
All India	11.3	42.4

Source: National Human Development Report-2001, Planning Commission, GOI, March, 2002.

well-being". The human accessibility to basic necessities such as food, clothing and shelter and other fundamental needs such as safe drinking water primary education, primary health care, sanitation, nutrition, etc., are primary to quality of living Human right to food security is the beginning of the livelihood. Even after 54 years of Indian independence, hunger is still very much part of the social landscape of rural India-while remarking on hunger deaths, the Alternative Economic Survey 2000-01 has noted that" a large number of stat value deaths were occurring even though the government's gudowns were overflowing with food grains.

MEASUREMENT OF POVERTY

The extent of poverty in India is being worked out in terms of the poverty line. Boyd-Orr, the first Director General of FAO, was the first person to propound the notion of the starvation line in 1945 which referred to the consumption of less than 2,300 calories per person per day. This idea has been transformed into the poverty line. P.D.Ojha was the first economist to estimate the extent of poverty in terms of the per capita per day expenditure on the basis, he estimated that 44 per cent of the total population lived below the po9vertyline during 1960-66 For the country as whole, the percentage of people below the poverty line was 41 percent which remained constant between 1966-61 to 1968-69.

CATEGORIES OF PROGRAMMES IN STAGES FOR POVERTY ALLEVIATION

To adopt four broad categories of programs in stages for poverty alleviation

- Resource and income development programs for the rural poor
- Special area development Programs
- Works Programme for the creation of supplementary employment opportunities
- The minimum needs Programme (MNP)

First category, small formers Development Agencies (SFDA)

Second category Draught Prone Areas Programme (DPAP)

Third category NREP, RLEGP, TRYSM and the Food for Work Programme.

Lastly, there is a minimum need Programme which aims at improving the consumption levels of the poorer sections.

Table 2
Poverty Estimates for Different Years (%)

Year	*Rural*	*Urban*	*Combined*
1973-74	56.44	49.01	54.88
1977-78	53.07	45.24	51.32
1983-84	45.65	40.79	44.48
1987-88	39.09	38.20	38.86
1993-94	37.27	32.36	35.97
1999-00	27.09	23.62	26.10
2004-05	21.79	21.70	21.77

Source: Poverty estimates for 1999-00 & 2004-05 are based on mixed recall period (MRP), Planning Commission.

In India incidence of poverty declined gradually from 54.88% in 1973-74 to 21.77% in 2004-05 (Table-2) poverty at all India level on the basis of mixed recall period(MRP) consumption declined from 27.1%, 23.62% and 26.1% respectively for rural, urban and all area in 1999-00 to 21.8% 21.7% and 21.8% respectively for rural, urban and all area in 2004-05 resulting in the Rate of Decline of poverty (RDP) as 3.57 per cent. Poverty estimates for 1999-00 and 2004-05 are not strictly comparable with earlier poverty estimates.

India has had a number of anti poverty programmes since the early 1960s. These include among others, the National Rural Employment Programme and the rural landless Employment Guarantee Programme. The National Rural Employment Programme evolved in Five Year Plan 1980 from the earlier food for work programme to use unemployed and underemployed and underemployed workers to build productive community assets. The Rural landless Employment Guarantee Programme was instituted in Five Year 1983 to address to the plight of the hard-core rural poor by expanding employment opportunities and building the rural infrastructure as a means of encouraging rapid economic growth.

There were many problems with the implementation of these and other schemes, but objectives credit them with helping reduce poverty. To improve the effectiveness of the National Rural Employment Programme in 1989. it was combined with the Rural Landless Employment Guarantee Programme and renamed Jawahar Razgar Yajana, or Jawahar Employment Plan.

State governments are important participants in anti poverty programs. The constitution assigns. Responsibility to the states in a number of matters including ownership redistribution, improvement most Central government programs concerned with land return and the situation of small landless formers. The Central government tries to establish programs and norms among the states and Union territories but implementation has often renamed at the lower bureaucratic levels. In some matters concerning subsoil rights and irrigation projects the Central government exerts but the states sometimes modify or retard the impact of central government policies and programs.

CONCLUSION

Poverty is a scourge on humanity and is one of the greatest enemies of development. It is a multidimensional phenomenon and income and calories consumption as generally used in the estimation of 'poverty line' are a few among many. Poverty has to be identified with deficiency of total level of living. And total level of living includes not only energy requirement but also balanced diet needed for health and the other components of basic needs essential for human existence at a tolerable level".

REFERENCES

Kurukshetra, March, 2003

V.K.R.V. Rao Nutritional norm, by calorie intake and measurement of poverty Bulletin of the International Statistical Institute. Proceeding of the 41st session, Dec-1977, Vol-XI

National Nutrition Monitoring Bureau Report of NNMB surveys, 1996, *National Institute of Nutrition, Hyderabad.*

M.L.Jhingan, 33rd edition, Virinda Publishing (p) Ltd.

Expenditure Elasticity of the Rural Poors and Margenalised Sections: An Organised Initiative by Governmant

17

V.V. Kulkarni, Imran Ahmed Khan

The rural development terminology is used and applied under diverged nomenclature. During last few decades in most of the developing countries efforts have been made to develop various models of development and to correlate various developmental theories to the developmental model. These models and theories, strategies and methods of development have attracted the attention of the policy makers, planners, administrators, scientists, technologists, academicians and development functionaries for assessing its utility for the development of undeveloped areas and under developed sections of the society. For example, Kutumba Shree Model of Kerala, or Janmabhumi Model of Andhra Pradesh such models are mainly based on inculcating the principles of democratic decentralization and Gandhian Approach of Self Reliance and Conversion Community Action for all-round development of the population which is excluded from the mainstream of development. Perhaps this approach has acquired the pivotal position in development planning.

Comprehensive development is the commonly used terminology. This terminology has embodied its roots in development based on the principal of equality of development and equitable distribution of the benefits of development among the stakeholders. In this approach, adequate justice has been given perhaps emphasized on the development of neglected, excluded, underprivileged, and root level deserving population. However there has been a paradigm shift in the basic concepts of development in last decade.

The concept of exclusive development preponderantly emerging in society at global level especially since inception of the globalization process on the official agenda of the developing nations. The inclusive development, this terminology is exclusively used in Eleventh Five Year Plan in India and Millenium Development Goals of United Nation for the development of not only the urban or rural poor but the development of women with special reference to gender approach, development of differently able bodied population through developing their strength and capabilities, neglected sections of societies such as scheduled caste and scheduled tribes and other poor people those who are suffering by grave poverty through considering their participation in development process. The earlier concept of welfare, development, support, help, ect,. have been scqued towards making available the livelihood resources and strengthening their capabilities for not only the survival but for their own and their community as a whole.

In the prevalent rural development programme, there have been emphasis on exploration of various livelihood sources without compromising with exploitation of the natural resources for weaker sections of the society but their capabilities have remained unexplored even in the modern era of information technology. The sustained efforts of the government for Rural Development in terms of generation of new schemes, programme planning, programme implementation and organizational set up has resulted into achieving the goal of national development as the planners and policy makers, technocrats were expecting. However, yet we could not achive the level of absolute development. Two reasons have been advanced to explained this underachievement-more resources are needed to cover the uncovered sections of the society which is excluded from the process of development and effective system is needed to monitor and control for effiçient implementation of the programme of rural development. Thus one draw some of the lesions from these fascinating programmes of Rural Development.

CURRENT STATUS OF DEVELOPMENT

In a robust demonstration of its nascent strengths, the Indian Economy after growing at 8.5% and 7.5% in last two previous years is projected to grow at 8.1% in the current year. Growth of Gross Domestic Product (GDP) at constant prices in access of 8.0% have been achieved by the economy in only five years of recorded history and specially last two years as compared to previous three years. After dipping below 1% in 2004/2005, mostly on account of erratic rainfall, agriculture and allied sectors growth in 2005/2006 is projected at 2.3% with the good Kharif and bright Rabbi prospects. Food Grain production is expected to increase by more than 5.5 million tones in financial year of 2006/2007. According to the National Income Data released by Central Statistical Organization on February 6, the advance estimate for growth of GDP at factor cost at constant prices was 8.1%

The annual average growth rate of 8.0% envisaged in the tenth five year plan (2002/3 to 2006/7), the average rate is estimated to have been 7% in the first four years excluding the first year of plan results in an average growth rate of 8% in the remaining 4 years have succeeded to maintain 8% growth rate in 2006/7 and will yield a plan period annual average growth rate of at least 7.2%.

SOCIAL SECTOR DEVELOPMENT

The development and utilization of human resources and improvement in overall quality of life of the people are central to any development planning. Perhaps, it has acquired the pivotal position in overall planning process. When we think the economic progress, we have to consider two way linkages between human development and overall economic progress.

The sustained high income growth is a necessary condition and a significant driver of human development. On the other hand, if the people are healthy, educated, and adequately skilled, they can participate fully and contribute more to economic development process. The eleventh five year plan has recognized these linkages while laying down monetarable targets of human development for a plan.

Over the period of years, India has made substantial progress in human development. Sustained and high economic growth in post economic reform period reduced the poverty ratio significantly. There was also not worthy improvement in literacy rates over time leading to increase in absolute number of literates. However, India's overall performance on human development has been mixed in last decade. Improvements in Health Indicators like Life Expectancy, and Infant Mortality Rate have been much slower than expected. There is widespread under nutrition among woman and children and maternal and Child Health still remains areas of concern.

UNDP's Global Human Development Report for 2005 ranks India at 127th out of 177 countries of the world. In terms of composite Human Development Index, after 2000 onwards, the absolute values of HDI and Gender Development Index consistently improve still its rank remain invariant at 127th consecutively for last three years. On the other hand, some of the India's neighborers, not only improved their HDI and GDI values but also improved their relative ranks.

The progress of social development has varied across the states. While Kerala stood apart from the rest and achieved high level of human development comparable to the rich developed countries, the so called 'BIMARU STATES' (Bihar, Madhya Pradesh, Rajsthan and Uttar Pradesh) feared particularly badly. Social Sector subjects mostly fall under the state list. However, guided by the objectives laid down in the National Common Minimum Programme (NCMP), the Central Government has launched seversl initiatives for social sector .

Launching of National Rural Employment Guarantee Scheme in 2006 to provide enhanced livelihood security for the poor in rural areas by providing at least 100 days of guaranteed wage employment in every financial year to every household whose adult member volunteer to do unskilled manual work constituted the major milestone in social sector. This schemes one of the ongoing programme of Sampurna Gramin Rojgar Yojana (SGRY) and National Food for Work Programme (NFFWP) is covered almost in all districts of the nation. The National Employment Guarantee Act, 2005 has provided livelihood security of the people in rural areas by generating wage employment through work that develops the infrastructure base of respective area. The choice of work suggested overcoming the causes of Chronic Poverty like drought, deforestation and soil erosion. The main objective is to rejuvenate the natural resources of the area to stimulate the local economy enabling those who work for wage employment in creating an asset to take advantage of it to engage in productive ways of self employment and argument their income. The implementation of Act calls for the formulation of various committees by the state government and make the scheme for providing hundred days guaranteed employment in financial year to every household in rural areas covered under the scheme.

The trend on the expenditure on social sector in the recent year reflects the emphasis on various dimensions of social life. The expenditure on social sector as proportion of total expenditure is 20.9% in 2005/2006. It has been increased from 9.7% in 2003/2004 to 10.1% in 2005/2006. Similarly, in respect of the health sector, the share in total expenditure is increased from 4.4% to 4.9% in 2005/2006.

The incidence of Poverty is estimated by the planning commission on the basis of the large scale quinquennial sample surveys on household consumer expenditure conducted by the National Sample Survey Organization (OSSO). The latest such survey relates to the 55th round conducted in 1999-2000, and no official estimates of poverty are available beyond this date. Economic surveys for 2003-2004, on the basis of results of 55th round had indicated that there has been an impressive decline in the incidence of poverty in the 1990s. However, the extent of the actual decline in the proportion below the Poverty Line (BPL) between 1993-99 and 1999-2000 has been a subject of intense debate by academicians because of the change in methodology for collection of basic data in 1999-2000 and possible non-comparability with earlier rounds of the consumer expenditure surveys. The next official estimates of poverty incidence will be based on NSSO 61st round of large scale sample survey conducted in 2004-05, results of which are expected to be published in 2006.

POVERTY ALLEVIATION AND EMPLOYMENT GENERATION PROGRAMMES

Poverty reduction has been an important goal of development policy since the inception of planning in India. Various Anti-poverty, Employment Generation and Basic Services Programmes have been in operation fore decades in India. The ongoing reforms attach the great importance to removal of poverty, and addressing specifically the wide variations across states and the rural urban divide. Anti-Poverty Strategy has three broad components: promotion of economic growth; promotion of human development; and targeted programmes of poverty alleviation to address multi-dimensional nature of poverty. The various programmes targeted at poor have been streamlined and strengthened in recent years, including through NREGS.

THE INCOME AND EXPENDITURE ELASTICITY OF RURAL POOR

The current year trend of BPL families has shown there are more than 27% of the BPL families spread over in rural and urban areas. Most of them are either illiterate or less literate which cannot serve the purpose for providing livelihood opportunities. In rural areas, the employment opportunities are mainly centered on agriculture and agriculture related businesses. Since last ten years, the contribution of agriculture in overall economy has been reduced drastically. This reduction is mainly due to two reasons: one- dependency on nature and inadequacy of suitable technology. Though technology is developed, most of the technologies are not affordable, not accessible or not available at root level. At one hand there is increase in population and at other, conventional and traditional practices of agriculture has forced the rural population to find their ways and means of survival in non-agriculture sector. Perhaps, this is one of the most important push factors for migration from rural area to urban area. As a result of this one can observe that, almost all cities and town are suffering by the problems of slums. The population staying in slum area has been increased dramatically since last two decadės.

The slum population is mainly engaged in informal sector. This informal sector does not provide continuity of income and the livelihood sources. In this situation how the slum dweller who is poor or a poor person living in non-slum area are responding to the present economic crisis is the main challenge. The change in priorities to meet their basic need is very high among the urban poor and also the rural poor. Minimum level of basket of consumption of daily commodities has been suffered by inconsistency, irregular and shortage of income. This situation is for an ordinary man who does not possess either skills or education or financial support for creating self employment.

Within the limited resources how these poor people are responding to the current market prices and how they are changing their priorities of their needs is the main challenge in modern era. Though the government is trying to protect their interest of development, either economic or social, the prevalent conditions are operating in such a way that there is hardly any positive development. The Government's Scheme of Urban Employment, Pradhanmantri Gram Sadak Yojana, Indira Awash Yojana, Swarna Jayanti Rojgar Yojana, Sampurna Gramin Rojgar Yojana, National Food for World Programme, Drough Prone area Development Programme, Desert Development Programme or Integrated Wasteland Development Programme, Swarna Jayanti Shahari Rojgar Yojana and Valmiki Ambedkar Awash Yojana, these various programmes are helping rural poor by altering their daily necessities and changing the priority of their needs. However, the development approach and strategies have failed to yield the anticipatory results. Naturally, the relative poverty in India is decreasing drastically but the absolute poverty has been increased to the extent that the excluded population in earlier developmental planning has been thrown away from the mainstream of development. Naturally, one finds that there is large gap between poor and rich persons and even the severity of poverty varies to the great extent even within the BPL families.

For development planning, the model and approach developed and adopted by western communities have been implemented in India till, 8th Five Year Plan. In these models and approaches, top-to-bottom development was anticipated. However, as the globalization process is taking deep roots in Indian Society, the development of excluded sections of the society is evolving more complexities. This process has been already started and the polarization of wealth is being observed predominantly either in rural areas or in urban areas. Realizing the needs and the changes in developmental planning in Tenth and Eleventh Five Year Plan, community driven programmes were emphasized where there were plenty of rooms for providing justice to the sections who were excluded from the mainstream of development.

THE DEVELOPMENT OF SCHEDULED CASTES AND EXCLUDED CATEGORY OF THE POPULATION

The members of Scheduled Castes mostly reside in the countryside under enfeebling socio-economic condition and are assigned traditional caste specific stigmatized menial labour. In view of their perpetual socio-economic disability and deprivations concentrated efforts have been made for their overall development ever since the beginning of planning era. The economic development of scheduled castes along with the other weaker sections is treated as an integral part of Indian Planning and avowed goal of development. It has been in operation in all five year plan through which varying degree of emphasis. In early age of planning, welfare programme was drawn for their educational and economic development and emphasis was laid on effective implementation of commonly development programmes and land reforms. The Special Component Plan was formulated during 6th Five Year Plan and it has resulted to the Ear-marked Allocations for their overall development. A number of commissions, committees and study groups were appointed from time to time to look into their progress and suggest appropriate policy guidelines. Hence it is imperative to examine the extent to which these efforts have contributed to the economic development of these excluded population as it is an issue of major policy concern. Recently, an attempt made by Murdia, 1975; D'Souza, 1990; Thorat, 1997; Chakravarty, 1998; Jodhka, 2000; Pai, 2000 and Mohanty, 2001 have shown there is hardly any progress those who are staying at countryside and improvement in quality of life of these peoples or other aspects of life doesn't exist as anticipated by the planners and policy makers. The reason put forward by almost all studies have identified in the social hierarchy, the scheduled castes are subjected to the cumulative domination (Oommen, 1984).

These studies have concluded that the scheduled caste continues to be the economically disadvantaged community and there has been hardly any improvement. The perceptible changes in certain aspects in some states are not due to much to the progressive measures of planning but to the scheduled caste movement and organization. The dominant castes do not allow the benefits of economic development to percolate down. Beteille (2000) has rightly put "Where the disparity have been reduced, the reduction has not been smooth or painless process." The hierarchical society we inherited from the past may be linked to gigantic iceberg of which only a small upper portion was visible. Further, he has stated the environment created by the democratic politics has not succeeded in providing them adequate opportunities to contribute in the mainstream of development.

An empirical study conducted by Nadkarni (2001) has stated that Scheduled Castes and Scheduled Tribes are socially and economically most disadvantaged groups. In spite of Constitutional Provisions and different National Development Policies, their level of Income and share of landholding are still much below the National Average as reflected in the data. It has emerged that rural economy is based on land those who own land have substantially higher household income than the landless. About 70% of the household income comes from agriculture and allied activities. Naturally the household income varies with land size. Very low household and Per Capita Income is observed among the landless and Landless Wage earners. About 92% of the Household income comes from agriculture and non-agricultural wage work. However, the non-agricultural work opportunity in rural India is very low for females and there is a close association between income and ownership of household amenities. - Nadkarni, State of Life of Scheduled Caste and Scheduled Tribe in India, National Conference on Economic Development of Scheduled Caste, Gokhle Institute, 2001, pp. 80-83.

MEETING THE PEOPLE'S NEED

Rural Development Programmes are created and maintained for influencing people to make changes in their way of living. The existence of such programmes implies that the present situation of the excluded people is not what it should and could be that something different should prevail and what is possible through appropriate action to attain a more desirable status for them. This assumption is for identifying the nature of new condition that could and should prevail and devised the means for achieving them. Naturally, the process of planning for rural development implies the need for change. However, the question remains change from what, to what, by whom, where, and by what method. The changes that are important to the people are those that help them to meet their biological economic, social, aesthetic and moral well being. The rural development Programme exists to help underprivileged people to meet their needs. If this programme fails to do this, people will not participate in the nation's economy. The elements of the people's need, therefore becomes a central concern of planners for rural development. If the underprivileged section finds way to adjust itself, so that people meet their need to improve economic status. Therefore, the planning of exclusive development should consider what are the people's need, how these needs are identified, what are the priorities of the need, what resources are needed, how the resources are organized and directed to help, these are the concerned questions of development planning for rural development. For that, the plan should be aimed at understanding of the nature of the problem, these tasks are exclusively complex in nature and demands for systematic efforts, where emphasis should be on clarifying functions of planning, skills in identifying problems and needs, formulation of plan, ability to decide the significant objectives and goals and skills in improving people's participation.

In view of nature of poverty an magnitude of the excluded sections of the society, the development of these sections in rural population have been the primary concern of economic planning and development process. In the wake of economic liberalization, and structural adjustments, and in order to provide a safety- economic and social to the weaker and deprived sections of the society, top priority has been given for implementation of developmental activities by introduction of new programmes and reconstructing the existing programme. The government's effort for poverty alleviation and hunger, from rural India usher in all round development of rural masses. The paradigm shift in the policy and programmes as the rural poor are treated as resource that form and integral part of the development strategy. Accordingly, the government is implementing various programmes aimed at:

1. Bridging the rural-urban divide- in order to ensure the rapid development in rural areas, the budgetary support for implementing the various rural development schemes has been increased manifolds over the years.
2. Guaranteeing the wage employment and ensuring food security through National Rural Employment Guarantee Act and Sampurna Gramin Rojgar Yojana.
3. Making rural people arbitrator of their own destiny and to provide for economic upliftment by self employment for the development based on people's

wishes and aspirations. Hence the emphasis is put on participation of people as also social mobilization of rural poor through self help group and Panchayati Raj Institution. Creating rural infrastructure for better economic opportunities and growth. Connectivity is provided to all unconnected habitation through PMGSY and Village Infrastructure is also created through work undertaken under wage employment schemes.

4. Providing for dignified living- The government provides shelter, water, and clean environment through rural housing, drinking water and sanitation schemes.
5. Restoring lost of depleted productivity of land through Watershed Development Programme and initiating effective land reform measures for providing land to the landless poorer.

The approved outlay for the Ministry of Rural Development has been increased from 13,670 crores in 2002-2003 to 36,560 crores in 2007-2008. There is substantial allocation for land resources, drinking water supply and rural development. For drinking water supply 7560 crores of rupees followed by 1500 crores for land resources and 20500 crores for general rural development programme have been made available to implement various programmes.

REFERANCES

Beteille, Andre (2000), The Scheduled Caste: An Inter-regional Perspective, Journal of Indian School of Political Economy, Vol-12, No. 3 and 4, pp. 405-421.

Chakravarty, Gurupada (1998), Scheduled Caste and Scheduled Tribe in Rural India, their Income, Education and Health Status, Margin, Vol. 30, No. 4, pp. 100-130.

D'Souza, Victor S. (1990), Development Planning and Structural Inequalities, Sage Publications, New Delhi.

Jodhka, Surinder S. (2000), Prejudice without 'Pollution'?, Scheduled Castes in Contemporay Punjab, Journal of Indian School of Political Economy, Vol. 12, No. 3 and 4, pp. 381-404.

Mohanty. B.B. (2001 a), Land Distribution Among the Scheduled Castes and Tribes, Economic and Political Weekly, Vol. 36, No. 40, pp. 3857-3868.

Murdia, Ratna (1975), Land Allotment and Land Alienation Policies and Programmes for Scheduled Castes and Tribes, Economic and Political Weekly, Vol. 10, No. 32, pp. 1201-1214.

Oomen, T.K (1984), Sources of Deprivation and Styles of Protest: The Case of the Dalits in India, Contributions to Indian Sociology, Vol. 18, No. 1, pp. 45-62.

Pai, Sudha (2000), Changing Socio-economic and Political Profile of Scheduled Castes in Uttar Pradesh, Journal of Indian School of Political Economy, Vol. 12, No. 3 and 4, pp. 405-421.

Thorat S.K. (1997), New Economic Policy and its Impact on Employment and Poverty of the Scheduled Castes, Occasional Paper Series: 2, Department of Sociology, Pune University.

Ministry of Rural Development, Government of India, Annual Report 2006-7

Economic Survey Report, Government of India, 2005-2006.

Shetty, E.D. (2005), Clinical Approach to Rural Development, Amol Publication Pvt. Ltd. New Delhi, pp. 5-52.

Expanding Opportunity, Widening Inequality and Worsening Income Distribution under Economic (Market) Globalization 18

T. Lakshmanasamy

INTRODUCTION

The contemporary world is one of both accelerated growth with expanding opportunities and rising inequality under economic globalization. For many, economic integration across the world is inevitable for modern economic growth, while for some others this type global market integration implies a form of colonialism and/or imperialism. Compared to the previous globalization eras, the current form of globalization and the associated economic reforms raise more questions than it answers. The official World Bank definition of globalization is "freedom and ability of individuals and firms to initiate voluntary economic transactions with residents of other countries. Empirically, globalization translates into greater mobility of factors of production, capital and labor, and greater world integration through increased trade and foreign investments - both direct and portfolio" (Milanovic, 2002). And "globalization signifies the formation of a liberalized and integrated worldwide marketplace for goods and capital, and the emergence of a new international institutional order facilitating the expansion of production, trade and financial flows on a worldwide scale" (Kolodko, 2001). Globalization also means the "marginal impacts of an international economy relative to those of a closed economy. That is, it refers to aspects of economic change that occur because a country is part of an international community over and above those changes that will occur in a closed economy" (Levinsohn, 2000). The running theme of these definitions demonstrates that globalization is about the free and voluntary movement of the factors of production across countries and the required institutional mechanisms for such flows.

As such globalization is rapidly changing the face of the modernizing world. The productivity and technological distance between the industrialized economies and the developing nations is fast shrinking through the booming information technology and communication revolution. Globalization is opening domestic markets to international competition and privatization in developing countries has shrunk state production. The information and skill flows between the nations are vastly expanding the scope of development alternatives and many countries have embarked on structural reforms in their attempt to global integration and rapid development. Globalization in the form of increased competition from low-wage countries and technological advances in information and communication technology raises the demand for skilled workers relative to unskilled workers in developed economies. This raises inequality in market incomes. Globalization is also associated with growth in international production networks. This has contributed to increased demand for global managers, and an increase in their earnings. There is substantial evidence for global production share.

The modern technological and innovation based communications technology have been responsible for many significant achievements, but there are also more discontents. No doubt globalization has increased incomes and improved the living standards, but it has also left behind masses of population without any clue about the globalization processes. There are growing opportunities under globalization for every one to seize the opportunity, but at the same time there are increasing difficulties in terms of stiff competition and lack of access to quality information. There are many who become millionaires but, there are too many who become paupers. The proportion of individual performers becomes thinner as income levels grow, but the proportion falling poor has become thicker. There are increasing awareness among academics and policymakers that globalization puts certain populations at risk (Rodrik, 1999; Birdsall, 1999). Globalization, however measured, has been increasing over time and has affected changes in the global inequality and growth (Milanovic, 2003). The fruits of globalization have not been reaching the less developed areas and among disadvantaged peoples within the economy (Birdsall and Nellis, 2002). Both the world and within country income inequality has increased and many marginal groups have been simply left out of the mainstream process of development. No doubt economic growth has been occurring throughout the third world over fast few decades, but because if rising inequality, it is not rising the standard of living (in terms of food consumption, infant survival and life expectancy) for the masses (Firebaugh and Beck, 1994). That the economic growth yields little benefit for the masses in that "the most unforgivable sin of development planners is to become mesmerized by high growth rates in the Gross National Product and to forget the real objective of development" (Haq, 1976, p.24).

The growing discontent with globalization is evident from the recent value/quality of life studies. In most countries people are unhappy; only a few countries - five Nordic countries, Switzerland and the Netherlands - comprise the group of the happiest people in the world (Bjornskov, 2003). While there is some consensus that individual income does have some impact on happiness, neither richer countries are more happier nor there is any appreciable significant increase in average happiness over the years even when real income rises (Easterlin, 1974; 2006; Layard, 2005). Further, among countries with real GNP per capita less than $9000, happiness rises rapidly as one goes from poorer to slightly richer countries. In contrast, among countries where GNP per capita exceeds $9000, there is little improvement in happiness as affluence grows, exhibiting diminishing returns happiness pattern. In fact, in most growing countries, rich or poor, the average level of happiness tend to hover around 6-8 in a 10 point scale. Moreover, the way that most people spend their time is similar across countries and cultures; working and trying to provide for their families, which Easterlin himself has observed in his cross-section study. Further, if economic growth is not raising human happiness, the why to strive for income; what else causes human happiness. Easterlin himself argues that "most people could increase their happiness by devoting less time to making money, and more to nonpecuniary goals such as family life and health" (2006, p.16). Again, analyzing various objective (economic - consumption, geographical distribution, social, and political) indicators of material living levels, on quality of life, Easterlin and Angelescu (2008) conclude that quality of life 'economic growth, on balance, raises quality of life, but there are sometimes significant "bads" associated with this consumption, such as rising pollution and obesity'. And in terms of subjective indicators, 'in both rich and poor countries economic growth does not raise subjective well-being'. This prompts the question: 'people may have more goods and a much wider variety, but whether that means they find their lives more satisfying remains questionable'. In fact, some already started measuring Gross National Happiness and the research works have began to accept the 'subjective well-being' measures as comparable as objective measures like quality of life, just as the utility has been associated with satisfaction in economics.

Then, the question is what constitutes the exact 'economics' of growth? The almost two decades old search for the sources of economic growth and therefore the miracle policies that could solve the problem of underdevelopment has resulted in a substantial body of literature. Throughout the history of science of economics, right from Mercantilist to the present day economics, this search is enormous and pervades not only many fields of economics, but at sometimes transcends its boundaries like geography and sociology and culture. Within the mainstream growth economics, the neoclassical growth model of the Solow type and later the endogenous growth models search for growth determinants in the factor accumulation and their productivity growth. However, it was soon realized that the so-called growth determinants in the cross-country growth regressions explain too little of the variation in growth to constitute panaceas for development policy and shows the neo-classical model's factor accumulation and the endogenous growth theory's technological progress that the old growth panaceas can at best only explain a small portion of cross-country growth differences, speculated that endogenous growth forces (technological progress) might account for growth, and ultimately acknowledged that the unexplained variance of growth could also be due to randomness (Easterly, 2001). The most intensively studied factors explaining economic growth in the vast empirical literature are the initial level of income, the investment ratio, population growth, political stability, market distortions, and the development of financial markets (for an excellent review of these 'Barro-type cross-section linear regression models, see Durlauf and Quah, 1999; Temple, 1999). In a recent robustness analysis, Florax, de Groot and Heijungs (2005) identify investment in equipment and non-equipment, and human capital formation as the true economically significant policy variables that have a reasonably large impact on economic growth.

The almost two-decades of cross-country growth comparisons has given the learning to decisively reject misguided policies that have, at some point or another in the post-second world war II history of development thinking, been viewed as ideal solution to the problem of development: state planning, price controls, import substitution, aid directed at filling the so-called "financing gap" between domestic savings and "required" investment, debt forgiveness, policies that assumed benevolence on the part of developing countries' policymakers, ignoring the economic and political incentives to which they are subject". As Easterly (2001) puts it the search is an "elusive quest for growth". The "list of proposed search for panaceas for growth in per capita income has included, from time to time, high rates of physical-capital investments, rapid human-capital accumulation, low income inequality, low fertility, being located far from the equator, a low incident of tropical diseases, access to the sea, favorable weather patterns, hands-off governments, trade-policy openness, capital-market development, political freedom, economic freedom, ethnic homogeneity, British colonial origins, a common-law legal systems, the protection of property rights and the rule of law, good governance, political stability, infrastructure, market-determined prices (including exchange rate), foreign direct investment, and suitably conditioned foreign aid. This is a growing and non-exhaustive list" (Wacziarg, 2002). Durlauf, Johnson and Temple (2005) observes that there exists as many as 145 candidate potential growth determinants. Recently, the growth literature has begun to distinguish between determinants that are 'fundamental' as opposed to 'proximate' to growth. In fact, the search for the sources of economic growth and therefore the miracle policies that could solve the problem of growth is enormous and pervades not only many branches of economics, but at sometimes transcends its boundaries like geography, sociology, political science, and culture.

In recent years, the search for growth determinants has been expanded to 'economic freedom' as well – a measure of 37 components divided into 5 groups in to an index using 0-10 ordinal scale. Economic freedom means 'the degree to which a market economy is in place, where the central components are voluntary exchange, free competition, and protection of persons and property' (Gwartney and Lawson, 2002, p.5). Economic freedom provides incentives that economic actors – entrepreneurs, innovators, financiers, industrialists, and others – need for promoting economic growth, whose aspect is absent in conventional growth factors. Gwartney and Lawson (2002) find that one-fifth of the countries that have had the highest economic freedom have grown considerably faster than other countries, whereas one-fifth of countries with the lowest economic freedom have had negative growth during 1990-2000. The degree of economic freedom is highly correlated with both the level and the rate of growth of real per capita GDP and the causal results "in general show that an increase of economic freedom exerts a positive influence on the development of economic wealth" (Berggren, 2003, p.201). The empirical evidence on the effect of economic freedom on income distribution is mixed; it is plausible that economic freedom has a negative effect on Gini coefficients. However, increases in economic freedom increases quality of life, human development, and has a hampering effect on emissions of carbon dioxide. Recent studies looking at the relationship between economic freedom and economic growth, using the economic freedom indicator of Fraser Institute, find that liberalization, i.e. an increase in the economic freedom index (in terms protection of private property and freedom of its exchange) fosters economic growth (De Haan, Lundstrom and Sturm, 2006). They point towards a positive relationship between democracy (political freedom) and economic freedom, which is again a basic determinant of economic growth as well as income distribution.

THE GLOBAL INEQUALITY

In 1700, the living standard of the richest country was less than three times the poorest country (Maddison, 1995). Soon huge differences in international incomes emerged, as countries experienced large and sustained industrialization and commerce with the 20th century witnessing relatively regular income doubling every 35 years (in Western Europe) –a phenomenon Kuznets called modern economic growth. Firebaugh (1999) observed that, since industrial revolution, the income disparity is fast increasing. The average income in the richest countries, which was four times greater than those in the poorest nations at the beginning of 19th century, were 30 times larger by the end of 20th century. Cohen and Soto (2002) show that the income of the poor countries is only 30 percent of that of the rich ones, while the each of the growth determinants, viz., physical capital, human capital and technology, contributes about two thirds that of the rich countries. Milanovic (1999) estimates that the world Gini index for the richest to the poorest income groups increased 1 percent per year between 1988 and 1993 (from 0.63 to 0.66). The World Development Report finds that GDP per capita in the richest countries has grown to 37 times that of the poorest 20 economies, a gap that has doubled in the past 40 years (World Development Report, 2000/01). The population-weighted Gini coefficient for 2002 has been 53.1, which in higher than inequality in almost all countries. "Thus, if the world was a country, it would be one of the most unequal countries in the world" (Bourguignon, Levin and Rosenblatt, 2004, p.15). The inequality as measured by top quintile income share within nations has also increased during 1980s and 1990s. On average, the percent of national income accruing to the top 20 percent of the population increased by 2.4 percent (Beer and Boswell, 2002); though this figure may seem as insignificant factor, in terms of absolute amount it is quite substantial, even to the size of national income of small economies. What is worrisome is that nearly 30 percent of the nations exhibit top quintile changes of +/-10 percent, of these majority experiencing worsening inequality. The advance industrial nations tend to have lower inequality than developing countries, especially the Scandinavian social democratic countries. Even there had not been any dramatic changes in inequality among developed countries (+5-8 percent).

While Latin American and African countries experienced growing disparities due to their late starting of modern economic growth, Asian countries, with their growth miracles, experienced large increases in relative income in a relatively short period after 1950 (Parente and Prescott, 2004). Even with in the rich group, it is not the top 20 per cent, or even the top 10 per cent, who are the winners from rising inequality. The big gains have gone to a much smaller, much richer than that group. Between 1972 and 2001, in the US, the income at the 90th percentile of income distribution rose only by 34 per cent, or about 1 per cent a year; but, income at the 99th percentile rose 87 per cent, income at the 99.99th percentile rose 497 per cent (Dew-Becker and Gordon, 2005). Simiiar patterns have also been observed in India. Recently Piketty and Banerjee (2004), using individual tax returns data, shows that the 'gradual liberalization of the Indian economy did make it possible for the rich (the top 1 per cent) to substantially increase their share in national income' and the top 0.1 per cent with big gains. Many attribute this rising income inequality to increasing skill components of highly educated workers. However, the winners are not a fairly large group, in fact, the real earnings of college graduates actually fell in recent years. It seems that only a minority of elites and influential groups have appropriated the globalization proceeds. The foreign investment dependence benefits the elite segments of the income-earning population over the poor 80 percent (Beer and Boswell, 2002).

Even with the availability of advanced technology, the output per worker in developing countries is much lower than that of developed countries - there exists a 32-fold difference in output per worker between the richest and the poorest economies (Hall and Jones, 1999). Economists try to find an answer to this puzzle through the production function analysis by looking at the 'externalities' of productive resources or the much debated 'total factor productivity' (Prescott, 1998). If externalities are assumed away, differences in capital-output ratios can be shown to contribute to a factor of 2, schooling only a little more than 2, and 'effective' human capital a factor of 8 in explaining the cross-country differences in output per worker (Pikoulakis and Minoiu, 2006). The 'external effects' of human capital, which crucially depends on the laws and institutions that protects skills and promote workplace practices that enables skills to develop, explains the vast differences in living standards between the rich and poor; the richest countries are 13-fold richer than the poorest countries.

The world average annual growth of income between 1980 and 2002 has been about 1.5 percent. However, this growth has been uneven, both across countries and over time. Indeed the fast growth of China and India has been negated by the 26 poor performing countries, mostly from Africa, many of with negative growth. The evolution of global inequality has become a serious concern and has generated a lot of conflicting views and evidences (Bourguignon, Levin and Rosenblatt, 2004; Bourguignon and Morrisson, 2002). The stylized facts about global inequality are: (i) if countries are weighed by their population, then inequality across countries has declined (Firebaugh, 1999), (ii) if one countries are treated equally, then inequality has been increasing (Barro and Sala-i-Martin, 1992; Quah, 1997; Jones, 1997). Analyzing income mobility across countries, Bourguignon, Levin and Rosenblatt (2004) show that, in terms of final outcomes of income mobility, inequality declined whereas in terms of the countries that have lost, the world income distribution has worsened. In the inter-country distribution of income in 2002, the poorest 40 percent of the world population received just over 10 percent of world gross national income, while the richest 20 percent got more than 60 percent of world's wealth. However, when weighted by population, the bottom 80 percent of the countries has increased their income share; but the progress of the poorest decile reversed in the 21st century. Between 1980 and 2002, the income of those who were the poorest in 1980 grew much faster than that of richer countries. The poorest decile's income increased at an annual rate of close to 8 percent. Yet, when one compares the poorest of 2002 and the poorest of 1980, the income growth of bottom decile increased by only 1.5 percent–about the world average. This implies that a non-Pareto superiority in the distribution of world income between 1980 and 2002.

With the availability of comparable broad cross-section and panel data for a wide range of countries and the with the developments of microeconometric techniques, the new growth empirics (Durlauf, Johnson and Temple, 2005) has shown that,

(i) Over the period 1960-2000, most countries have grown richer, but vast income disparities remain and substantial heterogeneity exist across countries. While south and East Asia have unprecedented sustained growth rates, Western Europe and industrial countries either maintained or substantially improved. The weakest performers are mostly in sub-Saharan Africa, while the South and Central America produced volatile and mixed record.

(ii) The international distribution of GDP per worker shows an emerging bi-modality; while the distribution has shifted rightwards to reflect overall growth, there has been a noticeable thinning in the middle of the distribution. The poor countries from the left mode are extremely unlikely to experience 'transition' into the right mode (and vice versa).

(iii) A host of factors beyond the factor accumulation and technical change that drive the Solow model affect growth, mostly the institutional setup and externalities. In fact, the world income distribution is tending towards polarization; Anderson (2003) shows that between 1970 and 1995, the polarization between rich and poor countries increased.

(iv) On intercountry inequality, the centuries old trend of rising inequality leveled off since 1960, primarily due to different rates of population growth in rich and poor nations.

These results are corroborated by many studies; for example, Cornia and Court (2001) observe that

(i) Since the early-mid 1980s inequality has risen in most countries, and in many cases sharply.

(ii) It is the 'new causes', such as liberal economic policy regimes and the way in which economic reform policies are carried out, rather than the 'traditional causes' such as land concentration, education, urban bias, etc, that are responsible for the worsening inequality.

(iii) The higher the level of inequality, the less impact economic growth has in reducing poverty.

(iv) High levels of inequality depresses the rate of growth, with unfavourable non-economic impacts.

(v) Rising inequality is not inevitable in a world of rapid technological change and globalization; countries can maintain low inequality and still grow fast.

The rising global inequality is partly due to the failure of the past few decades to significantly reduce global poverty in an era of increasing liberalization despite robust economic growth (Milanovic, 1999). Although the percentage of individuals living in poverty has declined somewhat, the absolute number of poor people has increased (Chen and Ravallion, 2000). Most studies on intercountry inequality agree that "the level of world inequality is .... primarily due to differences in averge incomes across countries rather than to intra-country inequalty" (Berry, Bourguignon and Morrisson, 1983, p.217) and some estimate that inequality across countries accounts for over 90 percent of current world income inequality as measured by the Gini index (Korzeniewicz and Moran, 1997). By mid-late 1990s, 46 out of 73 countries, accounting for 59 percent of the population and 78 percent of the overall GDP-PPP, the Gini coefficients were higher than 0.35-0.40, the threshold beyond which growth and poverty alleviation can be perceptively affected, where as only 29 countries had such high inequality in the early 1980s (Cornia and Court, 2001).

THE POOR AND POVERTY

As the primary route to improving the lives of those in developing countries traditionally related through the integration with the world economy, the economic growth with equity in order to benefit the economic growth to the poor, depends on the existing level of inequality within nations. This is evident from the observation that inequality is a constraint on pro-poor growth (Chen and Ravallion, 2000). The agricultural sector of the poor countries is the worst affected section due to globalization. According to the FAO, some 450 million waged agricultural workers – the largest labour force in the world, accounting for 40 per cent of the 1.1 billion total workfoce in agriculture– are suffering from a high incidence of poverty and hunger. Globalization has led to less and less permanent labour and marginalized the workforce; migrant workers and women are hard hit by globalization. The agricultural workers often earn well below those earned by industrial workers, with low levels of job protection, health, safety and environmental standards and social protection. The scenario among the farm households is even worst. According to the recent NSS data as many as 48.6 per cent (an estimated 43.4 million) of farmer households are indebted. It is not surprising why so many farmers in Andhra Pradesh and Karnataka have resorted to suicide in recent years. The NSS also reports that more than 40 per cent of farm households will quit agriculture, if there is an option. Moreover, an assessment of reforms under globalization shows that most privatization programmes around the world appear to have worsened the distribution of assets and income, at least in the short run. Besides increasing economic inequality, the social and cultural changes are also so dramatic that many ethical issues have been recently raised. Given that that globalization and its associated repercussions are here to stay, more serious questions are how the spread of prosperity can be accelerated and in what ways the poor people's access to the integrated world output can be enhanced.

There has been intense debate about the possible impact of reform-driven economic growth on the incidence of poverty. Datt and Ravallion (1997) argue that while the incidence of poverty in India has increased sharply in the immediate aftermath of macroeconomic crisis of 1991, poverty declined to pre-1991 levels soon after 1991, consistent with the official figures that the incidence of poverty declined from 38.9 percent in 1988 to 26.1 percent in 1999, with the similar rate of decline for both urban and rural India. Deaton and Dreze (2002) argued that while India had traditionally witnessed lower income inequality than many other developing countries, consumption inequality had increased in the country during the 1990s. The increase in inequality might well have been on account of the rapid increase in income of households in the upper income percentiles during the 1980s and 1990s (Piketty and Banerjee, 2004). While the inequality during 1980s was driven by unequal distribution of observed skills, inequality during 1990s was a consequence of unequal returns on observed skills (Kijima, 2006).

THE MODERN GROWTH EMPIRICS

The modern growth empirics on cross-country growth differences using different growth determinants broadly demonstrates that (Durlauf, Johnson and Temple, 2005): (1) Most countries around the world have grown richer since 1960s, but vast income disparities and substantial heterogeneity exist across countries (Sala-i-Martin, 2002). While the Western world have either maintained or reasonably improved, most South and East and Southeast Asian countries have unprecedented growth rates, most African economies have barely grown, and some have even become poorer, and Latin American countries have been volatile. (2) The international distribution of GDP per worker shows an emerging bi-modality (twin-peaked), a change from unimodal shape of earlier studies; while distribution has shifted rightwards to reflect overall growth, there has been a noticeable thinning in the middle of the distribution (Quah,1997). (3) A host of economic, political, geographic, social and religious factors appear to influence growth, beyond the factor accumulation and technical progress. (4) Recently Anderson (2003), using stochastic dominance techniques, finds evidence for polarization of income; the gap between rich and poor are increasing.

The growth accounting approach estimate that the bulk of cross-country variation in per capita income levels or in growth rates is due to differences in total factor productivity; only about 10 percent or so of the variation in growth rates and only about half of the cross-country variation of output per worker reflect differences in the growth of physical and human inputs (Klenow and Rodriguez-Clare, 1997; Easterly and Levine, 2001). Among the three usual factors that contribute to growth within the Solow framework–physical capital, human capital, and total factor productivity, the former two have been almost disregarded as having no or too small externalities, while the latter stands scrutiny as the famous residual, which lends itself to the analysis of other kinds of inputs such as institutions or infrastructure as they are called in Hall and Jones (1999). The various approaches to identifying robust growth determinants conclude that at least two of the four canonical Solow variables–initial income and the rate of physical capital accumulation–are robust determinants of growth. To some extent human capital accumulation and life expectancy may be robust. Further, during 1980s and 1990s in terms of trade flows, the top ten biggest traders are rich, very small, or both, whereas the smallest traders are very large, very poor, or both. While market exchange rates estimate higher inter-country inequality (global Gini coefficients), PPP based comparisons substantially lessens the estimated amount of inter-country inequality. Assigning appropriate weightings to use for countries of differing sizes and population results estimates of decreasing international inequality. The strongest conclusion from the literature on inter-country Gini coefficients is that changes in the global distribution of income in recent years have largely been the product of inter-country trends rather than changes in the income distributions within countries (Bourguignon and Morrison, 2002).

In terms of the experiences of national growth rates between globalized and non-globalized countries, Sachs and Warner (1995) and Dollar and Kraay (2001) conclude that trade is an important driver of economic growth in developing countries. But, Sala-I-Martin (2002) and Sutcliffe (2003) argue that whereas a small group of industrialized countries at the top of the distribution have benefited from trade openness, middleincome and poor countries have been getting poor. Further, Birdsall (2002) contends that globalizers among low income countries have fared badly because they have not yet reached the minimum development threshold - in terms of human capital, physical infrastructure, political institutions, etc., to benefit from international openness. Similarly, Agenor (2003) shows that low income countries have been hurt not because globalization goes too far, but because it does not go far enough.

The vast literature across social sciences on changes in international distribution of income and the effects of globalization on them shows sufficient diversity in its methods, measures, and inferences to have given pundits ample evidence to reinforce their prejudices. Only two conclusions seem to be drawn from them: (i) two developing countries, China and India, have achieved spectacular growth rates; because of their size and wider opening to international trade. (ii) the much propagated capital account liberalization in developing countries did not have the large benefits as predicted by the Washington consensus; because of the inadequate domestic financial institutions.

INEQUALITY AND GROWTH

In terms of within country inequality, globalization seems to undercut manufacturing employment in the industrialized countries while new jobs have been created in developing countries, perhaps with high earnings. As a result of the parallel dynamics, workers around the world are losing out from globalization-increasing inequality. Although roughly one-sixth of the world's population (over a billion people) continue to live in poverty, the World Bank claims that the rate of poverty around the world declined appreciably during the 1090s - 23.7 per cent. However, the national Gini coefficients on within-country inequality show an increasing trend since 1970s, particularly in the developing world. Different studies conclude that market integration has increased inequality (Agenor, 2003; Kremer and Maskin, 2002), reduced inequality (Barro, 2000), or has had no impact in less developed countries (Dollar and Kraay, 2001).

The main conclusions on inequality within countries and the impact of globalization on it are: (i) Even if globalization in recent years induced higher growth rates, the adjustment costs of greater openness tend to be borne by the poor in developing countries. (ii) Gini coefficients differ more across countries than they do over time, in developing countries initial distributions of land and education seem to have had a marked impact on national inequality trajectories. (iii) the recent increase in inequality seem to be a result of skill-biased technological change rather than globalization as such. The rise in earnings inequality, which accounts for 60-70 percent of the total income in many countries, has been the important contributor to increases in overall income inequality. Earnings inequality is influenced by changes in returns to education and human capital, as well as labour market situations.

With regard to the ability of governments to use the policy tools to redistribute wealth and risk within countries, the two different positions share the presumption that globalization adversely affects lower socioeconomic strata in society. The compensation argument suggests that governments has expanded in order to cushion globalization's dislocations; the competition thesis contends that competitive pressures in international markets for goods and services as well as mobile capital placed downward pressure on the interventionist government policies that the markets view as inefficient. The literature on the impact of international integration on government policy, in terms of size of government or government spending, does not lend strong support to the conventional view that globalization will drive out inefficient government programmes; in fact, there is resilence of government, due to political support for the public economy and government is not so inefficient to wither away (Brune and Garrett, 2005).

INSTITUTIONS AND ECONOMIC GROWTH

Even though studies so far often conclude that market based institutions do indeed foster economic growth, as Rodrik (2004) argues, different types of triggers are needed for igniting economic growth and sustaining it. He also stresses institutions such as protection of property rights, competition, appropriate incentives, etc., do not map into unique policy packages. It is therefore important to understand in what contexts market-based institutions work–especially on the historical and cultural environment, complementary institutions and sequencing matters a lot.

The empirical relationship between long-run growth and inequality has been a much debated and controversial one. The first studies by Persson and Tabellini (1994) and Alesina and Rodrik (1994) show that higher inequality at the beginning of a longer-term period has a negative impact on the growth rate during subsequent period. Reviewing a number of studies, Benabou (1996) also conclude that initial inequality is detrimental to long-run growth. Deininger and Squire (1998) also finds that the impact of initial inequality on subsequent growth is negative in most cases, but not always significant; however, inequality in the distribution of assets (such as land) has a robust and significant negative effect on subsequent growth. Similarly, Perotti (1996) finds negative inequality-growth relationship, significant for rich but not for poor countries. But, using cross-country data Barro (2000) arrives at just the opposite. A recent reassessment of the relationship between inequality and growth by Forbes (2000) arrives at the conclusion that an increase in a country's level of income inequality has a significant negative relationship with subsequent growth.

In general, studies that emphasize the cross-sectional variability of inequality find a negative relationship, while studies that emphasize time-series variability find the opposite result. Challenging these methodologies, Forbes (2000) uses panel methods. In a recent paper, Pagano (2004) observes that inequality is positively correlated with growth in rich countries, while in poor countries it is significantly negatively correlated with growth; besides, there is also a significant negative effect of growth on inequality. There is also a non-linear relationship between inequality and growth; Banerjee and Duflo (2003) finds that there is an inverted U shape relationship between changes in growth and changes in inequality. Perhaps this accounts for the different results obtained from different specifications.

There are many causes of inequality. In order to bring changes in the structure of inequality brought about by globalization, a shift in the structural change in the capital/ labor relations, to improve the productivity of factors and the reward structure for these factors. The empirical evidences show that there has been some amount of 'skills deepening', where the accumulation of various productive skills generates income for greater proportions of the population. The education variable consistently has a robust and highly significant negative relation with change in top quintile income share. Thus, nations with a desire to reduce income inequality would do well to invest in programs that increase secondary school enrollments. Expanding human capital, especially among the poor and women, is the main way to increase labour's share of the productivity gains. Related productive steps include eliminating child labour, guaranteeing occupational and environment safety, providing workplace safety, improving public health, etc. Most importantly, the bargaining strength of the poor and weaker sections should be broadened via their involvement and participation in economic growth. Public institutions that perform the regulatory and stabilization roles as well as that protect property rights, encourage competition and innovation in the private investment initiatives, and that involve and empower people are necessary for the efficiency of civic roles. Even reforms in governance, legal systems, social and organizational capital all play crucial roles in nation building via public-private partnership.

A lot depends on the institutional structure of the economy and policies of the state. Foremost in the marketization and restructuring process are the radical changes in the role of bureaucracy of the state and its policy perspectives. The bureaucratic behaviour should be changed from one of retarding to rewarding. Going beyond the basics, international rules and standards such as enhancing credibility, harmonizing rules and standards, addressing international spillovers are some of the areas in which both the market forces and the state need to intervene. As Shleifer (1998) sums up this literature "a good government that wants to further 'social goals' would rarely own producers to meet its objectives". It should provide an enabling platform for the private sector and the market to perform. Thus, the priority should be the development of market-supporting institutions for an effective mixed economy with private (market) and public institutions. Whatever be the relative role of the market vs state in the context of ongoing economic reforms and globalization, in the long or secular period, the usual urban-rural and rich-poor imbalances may get corrected, it is hoped, since development, in terms of population, technology, education, health and so on, is the best medicine for poverty and other ills. But, this staggering gulf between the rich and poor survives the decades of global economic growth as well as the academic and intellectual endeavours. Just as the quest for growth is elusive, the miracle policy that could prove to be panacea for just income distribution and poverty alleviation is still elusive.

ECONOMIC GROWTH AND REDISTRIBUTION

The burning issue is how the spread of prosperity can be accelerated. A good place to start might be the literature on social institutions that evolved, from 1950s onward, parallel to that of the neoclassical economics. How should developing societies attract their share of globalization's bounty? The institutional view argues that capitalism has worked in West but hardly anywhere else because people in the west alone can lay easy legal claim to what they own – that they hold property rights. In the west property rights, freedom and enforceability of contracts are so well established that we tend to take them for granted. Such institutions are virtually nonexistent in much of the developing world. That state of affairs prevents poor people from gaining access to financial markets in building of capital. Thus North (1990) identified the importance of institutions and property rights for economic development. He showed how the establishment and enforcement of property rights in European history helped lead to the tremendous economic growth of the west. North's work has led to a parade of books in an integrative subfeild since known as the new institutional economics now heavily concentrated on explaining the puzzle of development. In policy agenda, two are important: increase citizens' employability and align the country's resources with its population, so that more people could eat, live free of disease, become educated and emerge from poverty. One means of accomplishing both objectives straightforward as it is profound: educate women.

Infrastructure and services are crucial for generating economic growth, alleviating poverty and increasing welfare. Recognizing these, many countries implemented far-reaching structural reforms over the pat two decades–restructuring, encouraging private participation and establishing new approaches to regulation–aiming to promote competition. The challenges involved in this massive restructuring policy redirection have many institutional impediments. A better understanding of the institutional environment to improve the performance, several issues of local in nature must be considered and conditions met for these measures to achieve their goals. There is no universal reform model; every restructuring programme must take into account the econmy's (society's) features and the countries economic, social and political institutions and their characteristics. There is a clear discrepancy between the scholarly assessments and public perception of restructuring. The alleged failure of reforms have led skeptical criticisms–concerns are increasingly being expressed about the distributional consequences of privatization and market liberalization–especially their effects on basic services for poor households and other disadvantaged groups. The critics are right in pointing out the cases where privatization was undertaken without institutional safeguards. Performance of restructuring reflect a variety of country characteristics both observable and unobservable including institutional capacity, business culture, nature of organized interest groups, patterns of social conflict and codes of conduct. It would be unrealistic to expect such features to change on a timescale comparable to that of restructuring or to think that less attractive attributes would disappear overnight. Strong institutions take long time to develop and evolve. It is difficult to create such institutions overnight in societies that do not have the constitutional, political and legal traditions required to support them. Thus, achieving the public interest objectives of restructuring will take longer time than has elapsed since such reforms were introduced. Liberalization in developing countries is often code for restructuring, downsizing and reorientation. Pot-privatization improvements in performance will be limited and probably unsustainable unless accompanied by appropriate second generation reforms.

CONCLUSION

Globalization is no doubt contributing to increasing income levels and national growth rates, but is also increasing global as well as within country income inequalities. Though there appears to be no consensus on the nexus between inequality and growth evidences seem to suggest that the relationship between inequality and growth is negative. Thus, the impact of globalization ultimately widens inequalities and dampens economic growth. As the distribution of current benefits from globalization becomes more and more unequal, the increasing role of market based institutions in effective redistribution are being questioned. In fact, with both market failure and government failure, the institutional mechanisms that govern the redistribution aspects are critical. The development experience of the 20th century exhibits no simple miracle policy that could solve the problems of growth, poverty and inequality in a convincing manner.

The dichotomy between rapid economic growth and the inadequate sharing of its benefits in the Indian context has become an eye-opener; much attention has so far been paid to the rather 'high growth rate' achieved in recent years, breaking away from 'hindu growth rate' and to its prospects of sustainability or comparing it with China's growth achievements. Time has now come to look at the real side of this achievement: the policy paradigm has to look at the alternative mechanisms to the market based institutions in dealing with the redistribution of gains from economic growth. There is no simple clue or ready made alternative available. The deeper problem is the tension between political democracy and the power of the market economy. No western principle seems to suggest a meaningful way. In this context, the pertinent question as well as answer has been: Can the eastern or traditional paradigms do? Yes, it seems if one takes eastern economic views seriously. Bhaduri (2006) argues employment is at the center of this puzzle as it is the only way to develop with dignity and reasonable economics with feasible politics. Such employment is characterized by the 'reciprocity of duty and the right for every citizen to participate and derive benefit from the process of development'. In fact, this argument goes well with the recent developments of capabilities and entitlements concepts developed by Sen in the context of poverty and inequality. The broad strategy lies in devising an operational combination of rapid expansion in the domestic market and purchasing power of the poor and rural people with their participation in building decentralized productive capacity. Such a programme for full employment has to look beyond the present National Rural Employment Guarantee Scheme, into the rural realities and the ways and means to a participatory development.

Fundamentally, poverty and inequality reduction is about bringing growth process to poor areas, as such areas benefit from technical and organizational innovational made elsewhere through globalization. The puzzle is that what helps spread such 'best practices'. In fact, all productive resources are fairly easy to obtain; but what is hard to obtain are the institutions that allow these factors to be combined and translated into productive job creation. It is the private sector competition combined with public provision of the framework in which capable firms can emerge that hold promise for creating of wealth and ending poverty. What can be done to the poor people to benefit from wealth creation? Today there are fewer alternative approaches to economic systems than at any time since Karl Mark. Some still hope for non-market solutions, and still a completely different economic system emerges, we have to function within system that makes use of markets (Klein, 2003). This leads back us to the issue of the pace of globalization, as Aisbett (2005) puts it: The question that is most concerned about globalization is not 'to Globalize or Not to Globalize?', but 'What and How Much to Globalize?'.

REFERENCES

Agenor,P. (2003), "Does Globalization Hurt the Poor?", Policy Research Working Paper no.3067, World Bank.

Aisbett,E. (2005), "Why are the Critics So Convinced that Globalization is Bad for Poor?", NBER Working Paper no.11066.

Alesina,A. and D. Rodrik (1994), "Distributive Politics and Economic Growth", *Quarterly Journal of Economics*, 109,2,465-490.

Anderson, G. (2003), "Making Inferences About the Polarization, Welfare, and Poverty of Nations: A Study of 101 Countries 1970-1995", *Journal of Applied Econometrics*, 19,5,537-550.

Banerjee,A. and E. Duflo (2003), "Inequality and Growth: What Can the Data Say?', *Journal of Economic Growth*, 8,267-299.

Banerjee,A. and T. Piketty (2004), "Top Indian Incomes, 1922-2000", *World Bank Economic Review*, 19,1,1-20.

Barro, R.J. (2000), "Inequality and Growth in a Panel of Countries", *Journal of Economic Growth*, 5,1,87-120.

Barro, R.J. and X.Sala-i-Martin (1992), "Convergence", *Journal of Political Economy*, 100,2,223-251.

Beer,L. and T. Boswell (2002), "The Resilience of Dependency Effects in Explaining Income Inequality in the Global Economy: A Cross-National Analysis, 1975-1995", *Journal of World-Systems Research*, 8,1,30-59.

Benabou, R. (1996), "Inequality and Growth", in B.S.Bernanke and J.J.Rotemberg (eds.): *NBER MacroEconomics Annual 1996*, Cambridge,MA:MIT Press, 11-74.

Berggren, N. (2003), "The Benefits of Economic Freedom: A Survey", *The Independent Review*, 8,2,193-211.

Berry,A. F. Bourguignon and C. Morrisson (1983), "Changes in the World Distribution of Income between 1950 and 1977", *Economic Journal*, 93,1,331-350.

Bhaduri, A. (2006), *Development with Dignity: A Case for Full Employment*, New Delhi: National Book Trust.

Bhagwati, J. (2001), "Growth, Poverty and Reforms", *Economic and Political Weekly*, March 10.

Birdsall, N. (1999), "Globalization and the Developing countries: The Inequality Risk", mimeo, Overseas Development Council.

Birdsall, N. (2002), "Asymmetric Globalization: Global Markets Require Good Global Politics", Working Paper No.12, Washington,DC: Center for Global Development.

Bjornskov (2003), "The Happy Few: Cross-Country Evidence on Social Capital and Life Satisfaction", *Kyklos*, 56,1,3-16.

Bourguignon, F. and C. Morrison (2002), "Inequality Among World Citizens: 1820-1992", *American Economic Review*, 92,4,727-744.

Bourguignon, F.V. Levin and D. Rosenblatt (2004), "Declining International Inequality and Economic divergence: Reviewing the Evidence through Different Lenses", *Economie Internationale*, 100,1,13-25.

Brune, N. and G. Garrett (2005), "The Globalization Rorschach Test: International Economic Integration, Inequality, and the Role of Government", *Annual Review of Political Science*.

Chen, S. and M. Ravallion (2000), "How Did the World's Poorest Fare in the 1990s?", World Bank Development Research Group Paper, World Bank, Washington,D.C.

Cohen. D. and M. Soto (2002), "Why Some Countries So Poor? Another look at the Evidence and A Message of Hope", OECD Development Centre Technical Paper No.197.

Cornia, G.A. and J. Court (2001), "Inequality, Growth and Poverty in the Era of Liberalization and Globalization", UNU-WIDER Policy Brief No.4, Helsinki.

Datt, G. and M. Ravallion (1997), "Macroeconomic Crises and Poverty Monitoring: A Case Study of India", *Review of Development Economics*, 1, 1,135-152.

Deaton, A. and J. Dreze (2005), "Poverty and Inequality in India: A Reexamination", *Economic and Political Weekly*, September 7.

De Haan, J., S. Lundstrom and J.- E. Sturm (2006), "Market Oriented Institutions and Policies and Economic Growth: A Critical Survey", *Journal of Economic Surveys*, 20,2, 157-191.

Deininger,K. and L.Squire (1998), "New Ways of Looking at Old Issues: Inequality and Growth", *Journal of Development Economics*, 57,2,259-287.

Dew-Becker, I. and R.J. Gordon (2005), "Where Did the Productivity Go?", Cam.: NBER.

Dikhanov,Y. and M. Ward (2005), "Redistributing Global Income to Benefit the Poor", Paper presented at the Gini and Lorenz

Commemorative Conference, University of Siena, May 23-26, 2005.

Dollar, D. and A. Kraay (2001a), "Trade, Growth and Poverty", Working Paper no.2615, World Bank.

Dollar, D. and A. Kraay (2001b), "Growth is Good for the Poor", *Journal of Economic Growth*, 7,3,195-225.

Durlauf, S.N. and D.T. Quah (1999), "The New Empirics of Economic Growth", in J.B.Taylor and M.Woodford (eds.): *Handbook of Macroeconomics*, Vol.1A, Amsterdam: North Holland, 235-308.

Durlauf,S., P. Johnson and J. Temple (2005), "Growth Econometrics", in P.Aghion, and S.Durlauf (2005) (eds.): *Handbook of Economic Growth*, Amsterdam: North Holland.

Durlauf, S., A. Kourtellos and C.M. Tan (2005), "Empirics of Growth and Development", in A.K.Dutt and J.Ros (eds.): *International Handbook of Development Economics*, Cheltenham,UK: Edward Elgar.

Easterlin, R.A. (1974), "Does Economic Growth Improve the Human Lot? Some Empirical Evidence", in P.A.David and M.W.Reder (eds.): *Nations and Households in Economic Growth*, New York: Academic Press, 89-125.

Easterlin, R.A. (2006), "The Economics of Happiness", mimeo. University of Southern California.

Easterlin,R.A. and L. Angelescu (2008), "Modern Economic Growth and Quality of Life: Cross Sectional and Time Series Evidence", in K.C.Land (ed.): *Handbook of Social Indicators and Quality-of-Life Research*, New york: Springer, forthcoming.

Easterly, W. (2001), *The Elusive Quest for Growth: Economists' Adventures and Misadventures in the Tropics*, Cambridge: MIT Press.

Easterly, W. and R. Levine (2001), "Africa's Growth Tragedy: Policies and Ethnic Division", *Quarterly Journal of Economics*, 112, 4, 1203-1250.

Firebaugh, G. (1999), "Empirics of World Income Inequality", *American Journal of Sociology*, 104,6,1597-1630.

Firebaugh, G. and F.D. Beck (1994), "Does Economic Growth Benefit the Masses? Growth, Dependence, and Welfare in the Third World", *American Sociological Review*, 59,3,631-653.

Florax, R.J.G.M., H.L.F.de Groot and R. Heijungs (2005), "The Empirical Growth Literature: Robustness, Significance and Size", mimeo, Free University.

Forbes, N. (2000), "A Reassessment of the Relationship between Inequality and Growth", *American Economic Review*, 90,4,869-887.

Gottschalk,P. and T. Smeeding (1997), "Cross-national Comparisons of Earnings and Income Inequality", *Journal of Economic Literature*, 35,633-687.

Gwartney,J.G. and R.A. Lawson (2002), "*Economic Freedom of the World: 2002 Annual Report*", Vancouver: Fraser Institute.

Hall, R.E. and C.I. Jones (1999), "Why Do Some Countries Produce So Much More Output per Worker than Others?", *Quarterly Journal of Economics*, 114,1,83-116.

Haq,M.ul (1976), *The Poverty Curtain*, New York: Columbia University Press.

Jones,C.I. (1997), "On the Evolution of World Income Distribution", *Journal of Economic Perspectives*, 11,3,19-36.

Kremer,M. and E. Maskin (2002), "Globalization and Inequality", Working Paper, Brookings Institute Group on Globalization and Inequality.

Kijima,Y. (2006), "Why Did Wage Inequality Increase? Evidence from Urban India, 1983-1999", *Journal of Development Economics*,

Klein,M.U. (2003), "Ways Out of Poverty: Perspectives on Policies for Poverty Reduction", World Bank Policy Research Working Paper no. 2990.

Klenow, P. and A. Rodriguez-Clare (1997), "The Neoclassical Revival in Growth Economics: Has It Gone too Far?", in B.Bernanke and J.Rotemberg (eds.): *Macroeconomics Annual 1997*, Cambridge, MIT Press.

Kolodko, G.W. (2001), *Globalization and Transformation: Illusions and Reality*, OECD Development Center Technical Papers, no.176.

Korzeniewicz, R.P. and T.P. Moran (1997), "World-Economic Trends in the Distribution of Income, 1965-1992", *American Journal of Sociology*, 102,4,1000-1039.

Layard, R. (2005), *Happiness: Lessons from a New Science*, New York: Penguin.

Levinsohn, J. (2000), *Globalization and Poverty*, mimeo, University of Michigan.

Maddison, A. (1995), *Monitoring the World Economy, 1820-1992*, Paris: OECD.

Milanovic, B. (1999), "True World Income Distribution, 1988 and 1993", Policy Research Working Paper 2244, World Bank.

Milanovic, B. (2002), *Can We Discern the Effects of Globalization on Income Distribution? Evidence from Household Budget Surveys*, World Bank.

Milanovic,B. (2003), "The Two Faces of Globalization", *World Development*, 31,4,667-683.

North,D.C. (1990), *Institutions, Institutional Change and Economic Performance*, Cambridge,MA.: Cambridge University Press.

Quah,D. (1997), "Empirics for Growth and Distribution: Stratification, Polarization, and Convergence Clubs", *Journal of Economic Growth*, 2,1,27-59.

Pagano, P. (2004), "An Empirical Investigation of the Relationship between Inequality and Growth", Discussion Paper no.536, Bank of Italy.

Parente, S.L. and E.C. Prescott (2004), "A Unified Theory of the Evolution of International Income Levels", in P.Aghion and S.Durlauf (eds.): *Handbook of Economic Growth*, Amsterdam: North Holland.

Perotti, R. (1996), "Growth, Income Distribution and Democracy: What the Data Say?", *Journal of Economic Growth*, 1,2,149-187.

Persson,T. and G. Tabellini (1994), "Is Inequality Harmful for Growth?", *American Economic Review*, 84, 600-621.

Pikoulakis, E. and C. Minoiu (2006), "Why Do Some Countries Produce So Much More Output per Worker than Others? Some Further Results", ISERP Working Paper 06-08, Columbia University, New York.

Prescott, E.C. (1998), "Needed: A Theory of Total Factor Productivity", *International Economic Review*, 39,3,525-551.

Ravellion,M. (2001), "Growth, Inequality and Poverty: Looking Beyond Averages", *World Development*, 29,11,1803-1815.

Ravellion, M. (2005), "Inequality is Bad for the Poor", world Bank Policy Research Working Paper no.3677.

Rodrik, D. (1997), *Has Globalization Gone Too Far?*". Washington,D.C: Institute for International Economics.

Rodrik,D. (2004), "Growth Strategies", in P.Aghion and S.Durlauf (2004) (Eds.), *Handbook of Economic Growth*, Amsterdam: North Holland.

Sachs,J.and A. Warner (1995), "Economic Reform and the Process of Global Integration", *Brookings Papers on Economic Activity*, 1,1-118.

Sala-i-Martin, X. (2002), "The Disturbing "Rise" of Global Income Inequality", NBER Working Paper no.8904.

Shleifer,A. (1988), "State vs Private Ownership", *Journal of Economic Perspectives*, 12, 1,133-150.

Sutcliffe, B. (2003), "A More or Less Unequal World? World Income Distribution in the 20th Century", Working Paper no.54, Economic Research Institute, University of Massachusetts.

Temple, J. (1999), "The New Growth Evidence", *Journal of Economic Literature*, 37,1,112-156.

Wacziarg, R. (2002), "Review of Easterly's *The Elusive Quest for Growth*", *Journal of Economic Literature*, XL, pp.907-918.

World Bank (2001), *World Development Report 2000/01: Attacking Poverty*, New York: Oxford University Press.

NGO's and Rural Development in India: An Overview

19

A. Abdul Raheem, H. Yasmeen Sulthana

INTRODUCTION

Social sector development and anti-poverty programmes have been integral elements of India's development strategy. Several programmes have been in operation since 1951 focusing the poor as the target groups. These include programmes for the welfare of backward classes, weaker sections, women and children and a number of special employment programmes for self and wage employment in both rural and urban areas.

The government has relied mainly on three approaches for reduction of poverty and unemployment: the first entails pursuit of higher economic growth, which will improve the levels of living of all groups of people in the society including the poor, the second involves direct anti-poverty and employment programmes: and the third had stressed high priority to government expenditure on social sectors. The reforms underway since the economic crisis of 1991 sought to strengthen these approaches.

VOLUNTARY ACTION IN SOCIO – ECONOMIC DEVELOPMENT

Voluntary organisations have played an important role in India since Independence. There is a common stereotype held by many observers and policy planners that NGOs is small, convivial, participative and innovative, demonstrates a high leadership quality, is coast-conscious and austere, locally rooted and responsive, and thus a worthwhile instrument for welfare, developmental and mobilization organisation programmes. The contribution of voluntary organisations in promoting micro-level development is universally acclaimed. Voluntarism has taken deep roots in India during the past two centuries. The voluntary organisations have certain advantages over Government agencies. They have greater freedom to adapt themselves to changing needs and ideas and can modify their methods and areas of work. They have better rapport with the people and naturally get better response from them in their activities. Since voluntary organisations are characterized by greater human touch and closer personal contact they are potent agents in mobilising community resources for welfare programmes.

The greatest advantages that the voluntary development organisations have over other development agencies are their flexibility, speed of operation, ability to respond quickly to changing circumstances. The voluntary sector has been known for her virtues for human touch, dedication, flexibility, self - reliance, and nearness to the community. Voluntary action is not limited to any particular sector of the development. Four important sectors have been selected of which need relatively more attention and where the action is intensively and effectively being carried out by the voluntary sector.

Investment in Human Capital

One of the primary reasons why economic growth has not percolated to the lives of ordinary citizens is that the less emphasis was put on investment in human capital. The number of illiterate people today exceeds the population of the country at independence. Newly available data from the fifty - third round of the National sample Survey indicates that 73 percent of males and 50 percent of females are literate in 1997. These are, however, wide variations across regions, states, castes, classes, and sexes. India continues to be among the many developing countries of the world with high level of morbidity, especially among infants, children, women, and the elderly. There is also a high incidence of communicable diseases associated with low levels of sanitation and public hygiene, poor quality of drinking water and under nutrition.

Because of varying reasons, the State and Union Governments find their own ability to deliver goods in the human capital sector very limited. The voluntary sectors through its band of dedicated professionals and volunteers have achieved significantly results. The adult literacy programme anchored by ASPBAE (Asian South pacific Bureau of Adult Education) under the auspices of International Council of adult Education has made notable impact on adult illiteracy in India and other countries of Asian - pacific. Seva Mandir in Rajasthan, Ankur in Delhi, Gram Vikas in Orissa and Deccan Development Society in A.P. have done pioneering work in adult education. Many voluntary educational societies are providing better, in accessibility as well as quality, education in the field of primary education. Eklavya in Madhya Pradesh, Lok Jumbish in Rajasthan, and MV Foundation in Andhra Pradesh have shown excellent results in universalization of elementary education in a common schooling system. Their work is not a substitute for government schools; rather it tries to support them and to ensure that deprived children are able to join the same schools as other children.

Gandhian organistions like ASSEFA (Association of Sarva Seva Farms) in Tamilnadu have empowered people from within. They have functions like promotion of community health and nutrition, education, literacy and economic development. A broader network like Voluntary Health association of India (VHAI) is spearheading primary health programmes in rural and urban areas. The voluntary development organistions like Banwasi Sewa Ashram in U.P., Streehitkarini in Mumbai, Voluntary Health Services in

Tamilnadu, Action for Welfare and Awakening in Rural Environment (AWARE), Family planning Association of India (FPAI), Catholic Relief services (CRS) CARE-India, Helpage India and Chetana, Ahmedabad are some of the examples of the organistions who have used right mix of motivation and organisational innovations in community health programme. Many NGO's in different corners of the country have been effectively able to provide safe drinking water to many villages.

Sulabh International Social Service Organisation has done pioneering works in the field of sanitation improvement and rehabilitation of scavengers.

The India Human Development Report has found that "the education and health output indicators (of a village / community) have a positive association with an NGO's presence. Literacy and enrolment, especially of females are better, as is immunization and contraceptive prevalence, and birth rates are substantially lower. Short duration morbidity and extreme under nutrition are also relatively lower in villages with NGO activity. While expenditure on food grains is lower, household expenditure on education and health is also lower suggesting considerable success of NGO programmes".

Micro–Finance Sector

Financial institutions in our country, whether public or private, have almost excluded poor-men and women, landless, small farmers, artisans, labors-from their financial credibility. Providing micro-finance (small deposits, loans and micro-credits) to the poor have been increasingly acclaimed as effective means of reducing poverty and powerlessness, whether in an absolute sense or in relation to others. The poor themselves have a better appreciation of their socio-economic situation, the micro-enterprises that can come forth and the necessary support required for the same. The voluntary sector has made successful attempts in reaching to the poorest through innovative micro-financial services like saving and credits through SHG's.

Self-Help Groups have been encouraged to practice thrifts and the small savings collected are lent to individual members to meet consumption needs. Such group formation does not only help impart credit management skills to individuals but also lead better end use of credit and prompt repayment due to group pressure. The women SHGs have helped in changing gender relations by empowering their members. The SHG movement, supported by voluntary sector, has spread across the country. However, experiences have shown that what work for poor women is not credit alone, but a credit plus strategy. SEWA in Gujarat, MYRADA in Karnataka, Cooperative Development Foundation (CDF) and BASIX in Andhra Pradesh, Shramik Bharati in Kanpur, SPARC - Mahila Milan in Mumbai, and other NGOs in other parts of the country have proved that to make credit productive, poor women and men need support in terms of skills, marketing, health care, housing finance, etc. the sustainability and up scaling of this movement need to be supported by favorable policy support and linkages with the Governmental institutions. The SHG groups should be legally recognized by the institutions like bank to establish credit linkages between the bank and the SHG groups.

Non–Farm Income Generation Activities

The voluntary development sector has been involved widely in on-farm and off-farm income generating activities for over two decades. According to 1991 census, of the 222 million rural main workers, 182.6 million were either cultivator or agricultural laborers rural NFS (Non-Farm Sector) employed 39.4 million workers, accounting for 17.7 percent of the total rural main work. The employment in this sector can be achieved by laying emphasis, among other factors, on rural industries, the decentralized and small scale sector of industry, the urban informal sector, the service sector, the expansion of rural infrastructure, housing, health and educational services, the revamping of the training system, and the streamlining of special employment programmes. The rural non-farm sector, according to one estimate, has the potential to generate between 50 and 80 million new rural jobs over a decade.

Since many rural non-farm producers, especially the smaller and poorer ones, lack any representation or effective organistions, the VDOs have often performed the role of promoting their interests. Gandhian organistions, such as Gandhigram, ASSEFA (Tamil Nadu), Sanghan kshetriya Vikas Samiti in U.P. and Tamulpur Anchalik Gramdan Sangh in Assam tend to focus on traditional artisan crafts and are often highly dependent on Governmental agencies like Khadi and Village Industries Commission (KVIC). The success of the Anand pattern of milk co-operatives has also led to similar initiatives in fruits and vegetables, oilseeds and fisheries. The various rural producers' co- operatives promoted by SEWA around Ahmedabad are a well-known example of this.

The new opportunities are being created and VDOs are developing/upgrading knowledge and skills of the people to maximize the use of existing facilities. Some professional organisations like PRADAN are working with carcass flayers and leather tanners, handloom weavers and fishermen in Uttar Pradesh. ACTIONAID India has worked with 27 villages of Jagalur taluk in Chitradurga district of Karnataka to provide them fish culture, consumer service loans, brick-making, rope-making, garments enterprise, breakfast cereal and confectionery. The Social Work and Research Center in Tilonia, near Ajmeer, Rajasthan URMUL Marusthal Bunkar Vikas Samiti (UMBVS), and Rajasthan are working with wool weavers and rural artisans. All of them have sought to sustain employment among poor and in absence of any another agency, the VDOs are only providers of external push for the people in NFS for collective action.

Policy Reforms

The VDOs in India have been trying to sensitise, organize and mobilize people at village, local community level and various other levels, and also interested groups particularly the poor to enable them to pursue self-development, fight for their rights and apply pressure on the Government where needed. The impacts of such initiatives by VDOs are easily discernible in certain specific areas.

The people's movement, such as Chipko Andolan, Save the Silent Valley Campaign, Narmada Bachao Andolan, etc. on the one hand and Center for Science and Environment's scientifically acclaimed study 'Slow murder - The Deadly Story of Vehicular Pollution in India' are some of the examples of VDOs efforts. These endeavors have certainly made a considerable impact on the Government in respect of environmental security. Similarly, All India Women's Conference, Bhartiya Gramin National Memorial Trust, Self - Employed Women's Association, Jagori have been quite active in raising women's issues and working for the upliftment of women.

Support organistions like PRIA are involved in influencing policies from the vantage point of enabling participation and empowerment of marginalised. It comprises of systematic and ongoing monitoring of existing policies, their implementation and reformulation. It also involves building networks, coalitions and alliances of like-minded individuals and organistions. It implies convening fora of such different yet commonly concerned actors. it requires establishing linkages and accountability between micro and macro - issues and actors. it entails lobbying, campaigning and public education through a variety of methods. This is citizen's advocacy not just professional advocacy. PRIA has been able to intervene at national and international levels for suitable policy reforms in the field of Tribal's access to forest resources, Right to Information, Worker's Participation in Management, Health, Monitoring World Bank's Policy on participation, and Strengthening of Panchayati Raj Institutions.

PLAN APPROACHES TO VOLUNTARY SECTOR

Eight Five Year Plan Approach to Voluntary Sector

Voluntary Organisations have worked in various areas and some have matured into fairly efficient delivery mechanisms for developmental programmes. A major step towards enlisting their support for rural development was taken while formulating the Seventh plan, wherein it was stated that serious efforts would be made to involve voluntary agencies in developmental programmes.

By its definition, voluntary action suggests doing something without looking for personal gain. The scope for voluntary action is, therefore unbounded. Its heightened dedication makes it possible for voluntary organisation to do more efficiently the work done by formal organisations. They operate over a wide range of activities including the Governments anti-poverty programmes, training of rural youth, promotion of safe drinking water, rural housing, promotion of science and technology, waste land development, health care and family welfare, education, welfare of women and children and programmes for scheduled castes and scheduled tribes. The Seventh Plan document had anticipated that voluntary effort would be forthcoming in a massive way for better implementation of anti-poverty and minimum needs programmes.

Voluntary efforts will no doubt continue to grow in the coming years but it can accelerate if the environment is more congenial to its growth. If the professional and managerial capabilities of voluntary organisations are built up in a systematic manner they can make tremendous contributions in bringing about people's participation both in financial terms and through beneficiary support. Generation of awareness, inculcation of appropriate skill and convergence of developmental programmes are essential pre-requisites for the overall development of an area. In this, the voluntary organisations can act as a catalyst and can organise beneficiary, involve people in planning and development and provide the necessary support to make developmental reality.

A group set up by the government to examine some of these issues and simplify procedures for processing grant-in-aid proposals to voluntary agencies recommended

- Greater dissemination of information about the schemes through newspaper and the media, and designation of CAPART as a clearing house for rural development information;

- Simplified procedures and time bound disposal of applications for assistance: and
- Preparation of a grant-in aid code and a manual giving details of procedures.

More recently, the Planning Commission has set up a Task-Force to study and develop appropriate self-managing institutions for integrated development at the village / block and district levels. The recommendations of the Report are being processed.

Ninth Five Year Plan Approach to Voluntary Sector

The general weakness in the programme formulation and implementation come about where different models of participation by people's institutions are being adopted. The core element that emerges from the success stories in people's participation. The people are expected to undertake initiatives of their life situation and begin to perceive the options for changing that reality.

The essential ingredients of people participation for self-development, as revealed in the success stories are: assessment of local organisation like voluntary organisation for collective actions and an umbrella support mechanisms to facilitate people's development actions. If these processes and mechanisms are to be multiplied on a wider scale, these will have to be institutionalized. The multiplication process requires a major political commitment by the state to provide the necessary political space and a policy framework for a sensitive support mechanism.

The shift of location of NGO activities from relief centers, refugee camps and hospitals to villages and slums opened the eyes of volunteers to stark realities of poverty. From apparent poverty, their attention gradually extended to its root causes. From direct development projects, they shifted their service to develop grass-root self - help groups -(SHGs). Awareness that poverty anywhere will be a threat to prosperity every where and a world-wide concern of human values increased funding opportunities and mushrooming of indigenous NGOs.

Aid to NGOs formed a part of many developed countries budget. The opposition, failure and discrepancies also increased along with the increased volume of NGO activities. However, multitude of organisations with diverse functions progressed uninterruptedly. New competencies style, allies, etc. were acquired to face the new challenges. In fact, the NGO world is full of dynamism and hopes.

By centuries of committed and selfless work with whatever amount of criticism and inadequacies, NGOs have learned many things and of course the society also at large. First lesson is that development is fundamentally taking sides and as Korten says no more innocence is possible. Secondly, in all developed countries and in majority of the developing economies, statutory provisions for conventional voluntary services are more effective and efficient than NGO provisions. Unequal distribution of NGOs can be seen in different parts of the same country. Though NGOs are insignificant in scale of development needs, the value of their unique and sporadic efforts cannot be under estimated by policy-makers and professionals. Due to NGOs activism, public policies are positively influenced and poor people's organisations have been strengthened. The massive governmental and private bureaucratization cannot replace traditional informal groups in any society. At the same time in all developing economies, new forms of association and organisational innovation are taking place more effectively among the disadvantaged for self-emancipation. Believe it or not, NGO curve is moving upwards.

Tenth Five Year Plan Approach to Voluntary Sector

The Tenth Five-Year Plan lays emphasis on alleviation of poverty, generation of adequate employment and provision of basic minimum services such as drinking water, shelter and connectivity to all in a time bound manner. Programmes for providing self employment, generating income, imparting technology and skill upgradation training (SGSY) and wage employment (SGRY), Special Area development programmes (MLACDS, WGDP,DPAP), programme for people's participation to accelerate the effort of the development process and to provide for community maintenance of public assets (Self-sufficiency Scheme) and programmes pertaining to institutional reforms for people's participation in decentralized governance, planning and development constitute the core of the Rural Development Programmes. The growth of the economy has to result in increased socio-economic standards of all the people of the State. The economic growth does not automatically result in increased socio-economic standards of all the people as the society is much larger than the economy and also most of the people do not have capabilities to participate in the economy. Thus, the planning should have explicit objectives which are consistent with the growth objective and also aim at capacity building. The plan should also spell out strategies through which the desired levels of socio-economic development to be achieved.

While improving employment opportunities is seen as the primary exit route from poverty, nevertheless some employed remain poor, and there are many socially and economically disadvantaged groups who are not in a position to benefit from jobs. The Social Net has to encompass all such groups. There are numerous local and specialised welfare programmes, but nationwide three predominate:

The Swarnajyanati Gram Swarozagar Yojana (SGSY) includes the former Integrated Rural Development Programme. In the Tenth Plan the SGSY will be an holistic self-employment programme. It will emphasis self-help, and through groups will encourage thrift, entrepreneurship and effective use of micro-credit. 50% of the groups must be formed exclusively by women and 50% of the benefits should flow to Scheduled Castes and Tribes. 75% of the costs are met by the Centre, but the subsidy element is to be limited to 30%. It mobilises a range of State and local government organisations and NGO's to support implementation.

The SGRY will offer employment in the creation of rural infrastructure, with pay in the form of food and cash. In selected backward Districts, 100 days of employment per person will be offered.

The Targeted Public Distribution System (TPDS) which will be restricted only to the distribution of rice and wheat at subsidised prices to families below the poverty line.

Other programmes are targeted at Scheduled Tribes and Scheduled Castes and Other Backward Classes – who comprise about 42% of India's population, depending on the precise definition used. They receive preferential access to many nation-wide or State-wide programmes, and also access to targeted schemes for social, economic and political empowerment. Numerous further programmes benefit other disadvantaged groups such as the aged, disabled, street children and social deviants. There are Hill Area Development Programmes covering Border Areas on the one hand, and the Western Ghats area on the other. In some respects the development programmes run by specialised Departments such as the new Department for Development of the North East Region can be regarded as largely targeted at the poor.

But if there is one primary theme which runs through most anti-poverty programmes, it is priority for girls, to counter the discrimination they face from before birth onwards. Investment in their nutrition and education, as future mothers, will bring proven widespread benefits in reducing poverty.

The order of the above objectives does not reflect the order of the priorities of the State. All are equally important, internally consistent and mutually reinforcing. The total size of the Tenth Plan is Rs. 25737.25 Cr. at current prices as against the Ninth Plan approved outlay of Rs. 20075.00 Cr. These figures are not comparable as the State of Madhya Pradesh was bifurcated on 1st November 2000. The Planning Commission indicated that the size of the Tenth Plan may be 5.5 times that of the budgetary support provided to the Annual Plan of 2001-02 in nominal terms. However, the proposed size of the Tenth is seven times that of the approved outlay of the Annual Plan 2001-02.

Agriculture being backbone of state economy its growth is vital to the growth of economy and also for employment generation. The Plan would aim at increasing the productivity through improved inputs like better irrigation, higher seed replacement, increased fertilizer consumption and better credit facilities. It is envisaged to enhance the level of food grain production to 178.50 lakh tonnes, cereals to 139.54 lakh tonnes, oilseeds to 60.40 lakh tonnes and pulses to 38.96 lakh tonnes by the end of Tenth Plan. Horticulture activities will be encouraged in the Tenth Plan as income generating measure. At present, horticulture related activities cover about 3.00 percent of total cropped area which will be doubled by the end of the Tenth Plan. For diversifying agriculture, attempts will be made to develop animal husbandry and dairy and fisheries activities which have immense employment potential, besides sources of nutrition. The plan also aims at developing agriculture infrastructure like market yards, storage, handling & transportation and food / agro parks

The Government is committed to empowering the citizens through information dissemination. It shall leverage Information Technology for this purpose. It is proposed that all districts shall use information technology to disseminate information to its citizens using the Gyandoot. The Gyandoot offers an online inter-face with the government and delivers services online to the citizens through information kiosks. This model has been successful in Dhar. Some of the services currently offered through Gyandoot are agriculture produce auction centre rates, copies of land records, online registration of applications, public grievance redressal, rural e-mail facility, online matrimonial facility, information regarding government programs and schemes and downloadable forms for applications, licenses, certificates etc. It shall be the endeavor of the government to constantly explore newer technologies to find a cost effective and user friendly solution providing access.

ENTREPRENEURSHIP DEVELOPMENT AND NGO'S

Traditionally NGOs have been concerned with social welfare and community development, but of late they have even involved in micro-entrepreneurship development activities and income generation activities targeting vulnerable sections of society. They have considered the empowerment of poor and underprivileged sections of community is urgently needed for the existence for civil society and to address certain socio-economic problems, and entrepreneurship development is one of the effective strategies to attain it. These efforts received further boost in the light of several anti–poverty programmes, the implementation of which needs the inculcation of minimum entrepreneurial qualities among the beneficiaries. In this context an assessment of activities of NGOs in enterpreneurising the society is required.

It is relevant mainly because: there is a shift in development perspective of NGOs from the traditional area of 'charity and welfare' to 'development initiatives'. Secondly, their stress on 'bottom up' mode of operation for goal compliance has enlarged the credibility and legitimacy in the Government (federal or state) circles to co–operation and collaboration them in economic growth with equitable distribution.

Development of entrepreneurship (mainly industrial entrepreneurship) among the 'conventional elite' groups of the society is the domain of the established organisations or agencies of the government and the development banks. The field is left open to NGOs to experiments, as well as to promote the spirit of enterprise and entrepreneurs among the unconventional target groups comprising of less educated youth, poor (urban and poor), women and the oppressed. These small enterprise promotion activities may not neatly fit into the classical view of 'entrepreneurship' propounded by Schumpeter or in this contest the term 'entrepreneur' may be an aberration indeed. The conceptual parameter of entrepreneurship restricted to its 'heroic' view underlining the business exploits of large companies, is too narrow to accommodate the modest experiments in development of enterprise culture. Nevertheless change in the paradigm is essential to accommodate increasing developmental needs in the socio–economic setting.

In the context of expanding conceptual horizons, the activities of NGOs to promote 'self–employment' (self-empowerment) and 'income generation' should also be considered as integral parts of entrepreneurship. They are involved in a type of social change that does not primarily concentrate on structures, but rather on the conscientisation of individuals, and equipping them to break the customs out, within the socio-cultural matrix of their society. Through a 'selective approach', NGOs have concentrated their efforts for the development of micro - entrepreneurship in the informal sector rather than the more substantial formal sector business. Yet it is not an easy task to develop micro-enterprises when they deal with:

- women and men (which is harder than working with men only);
- the poor (which is harder than working with the rich);
- people with limited enterprise culture (which is harder than working in the context of a strong enterprise culture);
- The rural population (which is harder than working with the urban population).

While analyzing the tributes of successful entrepreneurship development training programmes, Harper has identified for common characteristics; (1) None of the programmes were run by government institutions, (2) Minimal use of 'foreign' experts and maximum use of local staff, (3) The programmes stayed small and resisted the temptation to grow large, (4) The people who ran the programme shared many of the features of entrepreneurs they were trying to help. Thus the organisation engaged in development of entrepreneurs must also be entrepreneurial in culture and outlook because "one cannot imbibe in others what one does not possess oneself".

Many developing countries face not only gaps in the infrastructure but also serious city problems with the state - run organisations devote for this objective. Further when entrepreneurship development carried out in the national level by involving disadvantaged target groups, government organisations have severe limitations and suffer from some operational problems.

They can be listed as follows:

- They lack intra-agency and inter-agency co-ordination among various agencies which have strengthened the status quo of the social fabric and the benefits of development has not reached the majority.
- Their bureaucratic style with no scope for flexibility in functioning leads to frustration, de - motivation among the field level personnel.
- Quality of entrepreneurship development programme suffers due to delay in timely sanction of fluids. The skills of the training personnel are regularly not updated result in perfunctory nature of performance.
- Multiplicity of agencies performing an approximately similar task provides scope for overlapping and duplication of functions at both at the apex and operational levels.
- During the recent past, implementation of anti - poverty and self employment programmes like IRDP, TRYSEM, and PMRY have exposed the manpower shortage and deficiency in their operational reach.

Activities of NGOs engaged in entrepreneurship development can be broadly classified into three:

- Direct involvement in stimulation of entrepreneurship by conducting EDPs funded out of its own resources or sponsored by others.
- Provision of counseling and consultation services in project report preparation, feasibility study, technical advise on purchase of plant machinery, etc., to assist small entrepreneurs in promotion, growth and expansion needs of business units.
- Provision of marketing (participation in exhibitions and trade fairs, assistance), assistance in securing finance (information gaps still exist about government schemes of self-employment, subsidy, loan facilities), incubation and networking facilities.

Theses NGO efforts weighed in terms of strengths and weaknesses in the context of entrepreneurship development have revealed the following.

Strengths and Weakness of NGO's

The NGOs have gained respectability among the respective governments as well as the donor agencies mainly due to their strengths.

Strengths of NGO's

- *Grass Root Presence:* The ability of NGOs to mobilise the popular participation is virtually due to their presence among the people. The field personnel who work with the people can gauge their requirements and are available to their needs. Thus the beneficiaries have more faith on these workers rather than the civil servants who visit them occasionally.
- *Motivation:* NGOs have often been founded by individuals with strong commitment to social service. The staff, though working for salaries, are not mainly driven by the pecuniary benefits. Such a motivation can hardly be found with the government officials who are on a stint of tow or three years positing. Like wise the beneficiaries too, who lack business acumen, need constant nudging without which they can hardly surmount the hurdles posed by the support system. Even today, the performance the paid staff (though not of the stature of pure volunteers) is better than the civil servants.
- *Target Group Approach:* When benefits of development failed to 'trickled down' to the masses, these NGOs have entered into the fray to initiate 'bottom up' development efforts. Enterprise development technique is one of such efforts directed to economic enlistment of the target population. If open to everyone in the community, there is the danger of such benefits being usurped by the elite.
- *Flexibility and Responsiveness:* Freed from the bureaucratic hurdles, NGOs are usually adapted to informal system of

governance and thus they are flexible in response. The flat organisational structure adopted has assisted further to increase the adaptability.

- *Heterogeneity:* Their operations are demand / need based rather than imposed from higher - ups, thus find enough leverage to introduce a variety of EDPs. Whether it is region specific EDPs or product / process EDPs they need not stick to the stereo - typed programme modules of government agencies. Tailor made training programmes for each target group have helped these NGOs to optimize their resources.
- *Experimentation and Innovation:* Overwhelming nature of NGOs is their capacity to experiment and evolve new strategies. Availability of business opportunities differs from one area to another. Depending on the raw materials, need of the market and skills possessed by the clientele, NGOs have variety of programmes to offer.
- *Dependence on Customer Satisfaction:* The fruition of enterprise development activities directly related to the satisfied clientele (trainees) and the contented donors / sponsors for fluids. Performance of the neo - entrepreneurs, though depending upon the entrepreneurial attributes of each individual, relies heavily on the follow up and escort services offered by these agencies, and NGOs are sincere in this aspect. Surprisingly the NGOs are made more accountable for the result than their public sector counterparts, probably for their dependence on others for financial assistance.

Weakness of NGO's

The bureaucracy has checks and balances, and fear of punishment, or a career to project. However, voluntary organisation system, sometimes, depends solely on its leader, and his moral strength. In practice, the inspired leaders of yesteryears are rare to find. Political culture has corrupted these organisations as well. Following are some of the well-noted weaknesses of NGO's.

- *Role Conflict:* There is lack of real knowledge and understanding of various fundamental aspects of Voluntary Organisations such as their priorities, performances and relationship with other forces in the development of entrepreneurship. Many a time's social considerations, interest of the community receive more stress than economic gains or financial viability of the project and interest of an individual in a business venture. Some compromise between the two is needed, without which the survival of NGO's as an organisation in question.
- *Leadership and Succession:* The founders of NGO's usually are of highly talented and motivated. However, their management style is not necessarily be democratic. They can serve the community better when they build broad-based rather than individualistic organisations structure.
- *Anti-business Philosophy:* NGO's prefer the word 'project' rather than 'businesses for the entrepreneurship development activities. The donors may even object to the commercial use of the funds and collection of interest on the loans. The NGO's working in more 'traditional' NGO's fields such as health, community development or education, may strongly oppose the policies, which contradict their views.
- *Dearth of Programme Integration:* Stimulation, support and sustenance activities of entrepreneurship development are highly interacting, supplementary and crucial to each other. Lack of enough knowledge on the part of NGOs may lead to the absence / negligence of any one of the above activities may render the whole effort anfractuous.
- *Inadequate Training Opportunities:* Entrepreneurship development requires highly talented and motivated staff. However, 'human resource recruitment and development' is actually one of the neglected areas in

many NGOs. This affects the whole range of activities connected to entrepreneurship development.

- *Absence of Impact assessment:* Self-righteousness on the part of development managers has not only hindered the quantitative impact assessment, but also raised several doubts about the long-term sustainability of such programmes.

The above analysis of the strengths and weaknesses has necessitated the evolution of competent instrument to survey the NGOs endeavors, not only to increase the NGOs effectiveness but also to cater the increasing demands of fledgling entrepreneurs in a logical and coherent manner.

CONCLUSION

It is observed from the above discussion, that the voluntary sectors is playing a catalytic role in terms of enabling people to define their own development priorities, and are innovative in their willingness to experiment with new ideas. Their record in alleviating poverty is uneven, although the evidence suggests that their performance is better than that of government. But that does not mean that State has lost its relevance. It is very much relevant and significant to the citizens of India.

The voluntary agencies are genuinely interested in the uplift of rural masses, they should pool all their men and materials along with the available rural potential and chalk out a common comprehensive rural development programme to be implemented wholeheartedly and fully till the point of self-reliance of the particular rural area. This makes the particular area to gain the levers of self - developmental forces on their own way. Rural development is not only a process, a method, a programme but also a movement in our country. Therefore, the forgoing chapter examine SHG's-Banking programme.

REFERENCES

1. Dasgupta, Dipankar (1997), "Voluntary Contribution to the Public Goods: a Parable of Bad Samaritans", in Issues in Economic

Theory and Public policy, Eds. Amitava Bose et al. Oxford University Press, New Delhi.

Gandhi, Jegadish, P. (1982), "Roles of Voluntary Agencies", The Hindu, August 21.

Gandhi, Jegadish (1998), "Issues in Social Development in the Present Context; An Economist's Perspective", Seminar Paper at Social Worker's Association (SWAN), Vellore, October 2.

Abusaleh Shariff (1999), "National Council of Applied Economics Research (NCAER)", India Human Development Report, Oxford University Press, p. 195- 96

Government of India (1992), Eighth Five Year Plan (1992-97) document, Planning Commission, New Delhi.

Thomas Fisher and Vijay Mahajan with Ashok Singha (1997), "The Forgotten Sector", Intermediate Technology Publications, London, U.K.

PRIA (1999), "Enter the New Millennium", Strategic Plan of PRIA, April 1999.

Ninth Five Year Plan (2002-2007), Government of India, Vol. I, p. 238-240.

10.Tenth Five Year Plan (1997-2002), Government of India, Vol. I, p. 13-34.

Harper, Malcolm (1995), "Empowerment through Enterprise: A Training Manual for NGOs", Oxford & IBH Publishing Co., New Delhi, p. 73

Kirve, Harsha & Kanitkar, Ajith (1993), "Entrepreneurship at the Grassroots: Developing the Income-Generating Capabilities of Rural Women", Journal of Entrepreneurship, Vol. 2(2), p. 177-197.

Bogaert, M.V.D. (1975), "Training Tribal Entrepreneurs: An Experiment in Social Change", SEDME, Vol. 2 (1), p. 43 -44.

Shakuntala, B & Visa Ravindran (1998), "Changing Face of Voluntarism", The Hindu, November 29.

Mathivaanan, S.C. (1991),"Voluntary Agencies and Social Change", Manas Publications, New Delhi.

Havers, Mark (1991), "NGO's as agencies for Small Enterprise Development" Small Enterprise Development, Vol. 2(3:16 -17).

Harper, Malcolm (1987), "Small Scale Enterprise Development", Crown agents Review, Vol. 3(25).

Setty, E. Desingu (1980), "Promoting Small Entrepreneurship: Problems and Prospects", Developing Entrepreneurship, NISIET, Hyderabad, p. 26 –29.

Harper, Malcolm,(1995), "Empowerment through Enterprise: A Training Manual for NGOs", Oxford & IBH Publishing Co., New Delhi, p. 73.

National Rural Employment Guarantee Scheme (NREGS): A Show Case Anti-Poverty Programme 20

Anita Medhekar

INTRODUCTION

The world has recognised India's commitment to economic liberalisation and globalisation being pursued since 1991 economic crisis. Firstly, it was economic liberalisation and reforms, rather than controls that created a proper atmosphere for economic growth of India and secondly, India cannot afford to overlook and neglect the capacity and capability of its poor, to generate employment, reduce regional imbalance, alleviate poverty and improve the overall standard of living of the poor in the rural-regional, remote areas, hilly and mountainous regions, including the urban poor (CFPR 1983; Cassen and Joshi 1996; Lal 1999; IFAD 2001; MHDC 2000). It is important to have a diverse basket of industries supporting the employment opportunities in small and medium enterprises (SME), which is essential to harness economic benefits and multiplier effect flowing from employment generation, stimulating socio-economic development and poverty alleviation in an environmentally sustainable manner through the National Rural Employment Guarantee Act (NREGA) introduced on the 2nd of February, 2005, and has recently been renamed as

Mahatma Gandhi Rural Employment Guarantee Act (NMGREGA) on 2nd October, 2009 (Wikipedia 2009).

NEGRA is a unique showcase anti-poverty employment act, and revolutionary in its promise of inclusive growth, right to work, dignity of labour and a rational participatory relationship of the worker with the state (Roy & Dey 2009, NEGRA 2009). Apart from providing livelihood to millions of households since 2006-2007, NEGRA has become a significant vehicle for promoting good governance and for strengthening grassroots democratic processes and implementing mechanisms that strengthens transparency and accountability at every step of the delivery of program, and for the citizens to raise their voice regarding various problems such as regeneration of India's depleting natural resource base and directly engage with the state (NEGRA 2009; PC 2008, TIE 2006).

One of the overarching goal for the developing countries in the Millennium Development Goals (MDGs) is to end poverty by 2015, "international fight against under development, hunger and poverty" (DFARSA, 2005; MDGs 2009). Alleviation of Poverty (both economic and institutional) by implementing anti-poverty programmes is a long term goal of Government of India (PC 2009; IFAD 2001). Poverty alleviation has made some progress in the form of trickle down effect of the growing middle class, increasing stress on education program, reservation of seats in government jobs for the underprivileged, economically weaker members of the society and empowerment of women are some of the various factors which will contribute to alleviating poverty (MHDC 2000; Roy and Blomqvist 2004).Government of India has accelerated its pace of anti-poverty programs and strategies since the implementation of National Rural Employment Guarantee Scheme (NREGS) implemented in 200 districts by 2006. Additional 130 districts were added during the year 2007-08 (Jaffer 2009; PC 2008; NREGA 2009) in recent years by mobilising greater Central Government budget resources, creating time frames for quantifiable, deliverables and linking with Millennium Development Goals global frameworks of action, which provides a benchmark approach for addressing many development and global issues (UNDP 2009). The seriousness and urgency of these anti-poverty programs, policy and resource commitments to poverty alleviation are in a single legislative Act of NREGA which strengthens livelihood security through time bound guaranteed wage employment which is the basic right of any human being. NREGA, with its *'Rights Based'* framework, is a paradigm shift from all other past development programmes that were traditionally *supply driven*, but now the implementation of this law is supported by a Central Government budget based on *demand for employment*, and the way the citizens engage with the state in a democratic manner.

The first Millennium Development Goal (MDGs) of 'Eradicating Extreme Poverty and Hunger' aims at reducing the proportion of people whose income is less than $1 between 1990 and 2015 by half (UNDP 2009; MGD 2009; DFARSA 2005). India's 11th Five Year Plan (2007-2012), has reiterated the country's commitment to the MDGs, and has set socio-economic targets for inclusive growth and development to end poverty by 2015. These include, reducing the headcount ratio of consumption poverty by 10 percentage points, increase the real wage rate of unskilled workers by 20 percent and creating 70 million new work opportunities for 300 million Indians who are living in extreme poverty. The poor people face absence of basic capabilities and necessities to function efficiently and effectively in the society with the lack of access to public infrastructure and employment opportunities. A majority of poor earn their livelihood through unskilled, casual manual labour and exploitation of the natural resource base. This dependence makes them more vulnerable to crises such as, climate change stress, natural disaster, ill-health (e.g. swine flu virus of 2009), all of which adversely impact on their employment opportunities and reduce their ability to move out of the vicious circle of poverty trap. Indian Planning Commission designed programs under NREGS, to directly attack poverty to provide self-employment among the poor, provide wage employment during the lean agricultural season, and address minimum needs such as nutrition, health, housing, education sanitation and mortality rate (Dantwala 1985; Hirway 1985; Ravallion 1991a, 1992b; Tendulkar 1998; Allen & Thomas 1997).

This chapter is structured as follows. The first part gives an overview of poverty in India. Second part discusses the Five year plans and various anti-poverty programs implemented by the Indian Government. Part three focuses on National Rural Employment Guarantee Act (NREGA) and the National Rural Employment Guarantee Scheme (NREGS) under the acts. Part four, discusses the general overall benefits of (NREGS) with reference to states and finally some critical discussion and conclusions are provided.

POVERTY IN INDIA

Poverty can be defined as a social phenomenon in which a section of the population is unable to meet its basic necessities of life and are deprived of minimum standard of living giving rise to mass poverty in case of India and many developing countries which is of major concern. Poverty can be defined in absolute or relative terms. Absolute poverty occurs when income and expenditure is below the poverty line, which means that it is not even possible for a person to purchase minimum physical quantities of food to survive. Whereas relative poverty, takes into account the income distribution of the population in different percentile groups and a comparison is made with the top 10 percent of population with the bottom 10 percent of population's standard of living. India has the world largest number of poor people in any country after China. In 1951, population census recorded 363.2 million people living in India (Dandekar 1998; Mehta 1997). Given the population of just over one billion in 2009, approximately 350 million are living below the poverty line, of which 75 % live in rural areas and more than 40 % of population is illiterate being the main cause of poverty (Agarwal 1996; Datt & Sundharam, 1997; Ahluwalia & Little 1998; Ahluwalia 1978; PC 2009; Mehta 1997). According to Kuznets hypothesis, inequality is likely to worsen in the early stages of development before it declines, as per capital income rises gradually to reach the levels of developed countries (Solow 1994; Todaro 7 Smith 2008). In the last decade from 1998-2008, economic prosperity in terms of GDP growth rate in India has been impressive but with growing inequality (Asian Development Bank, 2003; NREGA 2009; Roy and Blomqvist 2004; UNDP 2009). Thus economic growth has not eliminated or alleviated absolute poverty in developing countries (Fields 1991; Findlay & Wellisz 1994; Squire 1993; Allen & Thomas 1997).

Elesh (1973), has given three causes of poverty a) ideology of individualism b) Culture or subculture of poverty which describes the way of life of poor people and c) Social structure as cause of poverty accepted by the liberals and sociologists. Poverty is perceived in terms of poverty line, which explains what is actually needed for health, efficiency, social and work participation, nurturing of children and maintaining dignity self respect with dignity (Becker, 1966). In India, poverty line is drawn one basis of a per capita daily intake of 2 400 calories for the rural and 2,100 calories for the urban areas. On the basis of this the monthly per capita consumption expenditure is calculated (Sagar, 1990). The planning commission in 1997 March adopted the Lakdawala Committee 1993, methodology to measure incidence of poverty in India during the Ninth Five Year Plan (1996-2000) after a period of three years.

The Tenth Five-Year Plan (2002-2007), targeted 8% annual growth, in the employment-intensive sectors, so that there is equal distribution of income to sustains the pace of reducing poverty ratio by 5 percent and by 15 percent by the end of the Eleventh -plan in 2012 (Asian Development Bank, 2003; NREGA 2009). In India 230 million were living in poverty during the eighth plan from 1991-1995. This constituted 27% of total population. In the same year the numbers of people in rural areas were estimated to be 168.6 million, which accounted for 28.2 percent of rural population, as compared to urban population of 42.2 million, which is 19.3 percent of the urban poor population living in poverty (Agarwal, 1996; Tendulkar & Jain 1995).

FIVE YEAR PLANS AND ANTI-POVERTY PROGRAMS

The Government of India has adopted a pro-poor multifaceted development strategy that promotes economic growth and also addresses the needs of the poor by ensuring their basic right to work. Indian Planning Commission was established by the Government of India in 1950 (PC 2008). The First Five Year Plan was implemented in April 1951-1956, to rectify the effects of Second World War and 1947 Partition of India and aimed to solve problems within agriculture and irrigation sectors, investing 44.6% of the total planned budget. The aim of the Second-Plan (1956-61) was to achieve industrialisation by investing in basic and heavy industries, creating jobs and promoting greater equality in income and wealth to establish socialist pattern of society. The Third-Plan (1961-66) goal was to have self sustained growth in income, agriculture sector, basic industries, (steel, power and chemicals) employment creation, and decentralisation of economic power to the states and at local/regional level. The Fourth-Plan (1969-74) aimed at increasing Gross Domestic Product by 5.5%, reducing economic instability, inequality in income distribution and achieving social justice with equity. Prime Ministers cash program and employment guarantee program was also introduced in Maharashtra (1972-73) which was effective in preventing famine and dealing with short-run income variability (Ravallion 1991a and 1992b).

By the end of the Fifth-Plan (1974-79), it was realised that the benefits of growth did not trickle down to the poorest of poor due to wars, inflation and giving rise to unemployment. The Fifth-Plan thus focussed on removal of poverty (Garibi Hatao), creating jobs, removing regional imbalance, minimum wage law was introduced, export promotion and attaining economic self-sufficiency (Ahluwalia 1978; Ahuja 1997). However, with the change in the Central Government, rolling yearly plans were introduced from 1978-80, without any significant improvement in socio-economic conditions, except increase in food production due to the success of Green Revolution. The Sixth-Plan (1980-85), was formulated taking into account the failure of the previous plans in removal of poverty besides promoting economic growth; reduce unemployment, price stability, inequality in the distribution of income and wealth, technological self sufficiency and control of population growth (Tendulkar & Jain 1995). The Seventh-Plan (1985-90) focussed on employment and the eighth plan (1991-95) on poverty reduction and 3% increase in employment each year by implementing Jawahar Rozgar Yojna (JRY). Sectors like education, health, family planning, employment, welfare got a larger slice from the Central Governments budget (Bagachee 1987; Ahuja 1997; Dutt & Sundharam 1997; Dutt & Ravallion 1998; PC 2008).

The Eight-Plan (1992-97) was implemented after the 1990 financial crisis resulting in devaluation of rupee, dismantling of the Licence Raj, and reduction in trade barriers. By the end of the plan it did not show much progress in term of the benefits of growth tricking down to the poorest of poor in the rural areas and to the weaker sections in the society, hence the Ninth-plan (1997-2000), was implemented under such circumstances and lot had to be done to restructure and liberalise the economy (PC 2009) besides public-private partnerships and private finance initiatives are essential to solve the social-economic problems of poverty, illiteracy, unemployment, child labour, and infrastructure deficit (Medhekar 2005; 3iNetwork 2002). The Tenth-Plan (2002-2007) aimed to increase the growth of Gross Domestic Product (GDP) to 10% by creating market friendly environment for private and foreign investors, improve corporate transparency and infrastructure, reduce poverty ratio by 5% and increase literacy rate by 75% by the end of 2007. The current Eleventh-Plan (2007-2012), has the key objective of increasing agriculture sectors contribution to GDP by 4% per year create 70 million new employment opportunities under NREGA schemes to alleviate poverty with an overall GDP growth of 10% by the end of the plan, which is not possible to achieve given the global financial crisis.

In 1970s and 80's various wage employment programmes were introduced such as: Food For Work Program (FWP) (1977-78) and Integrated Rural Development Programme (IRDP-1978-79) which was credit based poverty alleviation program to empower women (Roy & Blomqvist 2004), National Rural Employment Programme in 1980-88 and Training of Rural Youth for Self Employment (TRYSEM), The Rural Landless Employment Guarantee Program (RLEGP) in 1983 and Jawahar Rozgar Yojna in 1989, which were very significant for creating employment in rural areas and for urban poor (Khanna 1996; Datt & Sundharam 1997;Tendulkar & Jain 1995). Since economic liberalisation in 1991, it was realised that most of these employment programs were not backed up by sufficient resources for the poor to reap the benefits. Although Central and State Governments intervention was recognised for employment generation, under liberalisation it was critical to do away with control, regulation and licence raj, mobilising private sector investment and involvement and encouraging partial or full privatisation and competition in monopolistic markets (Sagar 1990; Agarwal 1996; Datt & Sundharam 1997; Lal 1999; MHDC 2000; Roy & Blomqvist 2004; Medhekar 2005).

The Ministry of Rural Development has a gamut of targeted programmes from providing direct employment, self employment, social security, housing, building rural infrastructure and manage land resources to alleviate poverty. The safety net systems used in the past were PDS, IRDP, JRY, and sustained form of self employment through programs like Swaranjayanti Gram Swarozgar Yojana (SGSY), Self-help Groups (SHGs), National Skills Development Mission (NSDM) under public-private partnership model for developing human capital in rural unemployed youth were, merely to compensate the poor for short-run ill-effects of liberalisation and reforms (Khanna 1996; MHDC 2000; PC 2008; Medhekar 2005; NREGA 2009).

NATIONAL RURAL EMPLOYMENT GUARANTEE ACT

Federal Government formulated the National Rural Employment Guarantee Act (NREGA) in 2005, a paradigm shift from earlier *supply side programmes* to fight poverty to *demand side schemes*. See table 1, for total employment generated under NREGS (2009). With its legal framework and human rights-based approach, NREGA provides employment to those who demand it. Announced on 7th of September 2005 NREGA aims at "enhancing livelihood and security of the household in rural areas of the country by providing at least one hundred days of guaranteed wage employment in every financial year to every household whose adult members volunteer to do unskilled manual work" (NREGA, 2009). The Act covered 200 of the country's poorest and most backward districts in its first phase. NREGS, the 'human face' of India's United Progressive Alliance (UPA) government's reform agenda, an anti-poverty programme was launched nationwide on February 2, 2006 and was extended to 330 additional districts in 2007-2008 and the remaining rural areas have been notified from April 1, 2008. See Table 1 (NREGA 2009) below, which illustrates the total employment generated under NREGA schemes since implementation.

Table 1
Total Employment Generated Under NREGS

Employment provided to households	3.34 crores
Total-person days in crores	133.32 crores
SC	40.19 = 30.15%
ST	29.1 = 21.83%
Women	68.02 = 58.02%
Others	64.02 = 48.02%
Total Works Taken up	25.98
Total Works Completed	7.08
Work in Progress	18.9 Lakhs

The NREGA, Act is also a significant vehicle for strengthening decentralisation and deepening the processes of democracy by giving a pivotal role to local governance bodies, that is, the Panchayai Raj Institutions. The Scheme is sponsored by the Ministry of Rural Development, Government of India. Unique features of the Act include, time bound employment guarantee and wage payment within 15 days, provide incentive-disincentive structure to the State Governments for providing employment as 90 per cent of the cost for employment provided is borne by the Federal Government or payment of unemployment allowance at their own cost. The Act also mandates 33 percent workplace participation for women (PC 2009; NREGA 2009).

The Central Government contributed Rupees 5,500 crores, which was funded by the merging of the two programs Sampoorna Grameen Rozgar Yojana and the Food-for-Work Programme. The law envisages coverage of all of India's 600 districts within five years. The Central Government has already pledged 90% of the funds required for the scheme's implementation. The remaining 10% is expected to come from the states' coffers. Under the scheme, if a State Government fails to provide employment—mostly development work—within 15 days of an application, the applicant will have to be paid an unemployment allowance. As some states have their own Minimum Wage Acts, the NREGS Act 2005, enables the Central Government to fix a minimum wage of no less than Rupees 60 per day (TIE 2006; Jaffer 2008; NREGA 2009; PC 2009). Through short term employment, these programmes provide income transfers to poor households during critical times such as lean agricultural seasons and enable consumption smoothening. Over time, this will facilitate the transition of the village economy from subsistence to self-sustenance by increasing agricultural productivity and creating durable assets for regeneration of the natural resource base. The infrastructure will not only lead to market and supply chain linkages and but also create further employment opportunities generated under NREG Scheme. See Table 2 (NREGA 2009) which provides an example of NREGA employment schemes statistics for various vulnerable groups in 2009 in the selected states of Jammu and Kashmir in the north to Maharashtra in the west, Assam in the east and Kerala in the south west of India.

BENEFITS FROM NREGS

Benefits of NREGS under the NREG Act are numerous and not just limited to enhancing economic and social, potential of supplementing income through wage earnings, savings and investments, financial inclusion, providing employment on demand to households, but also has many multiplier effects

Table 2
NREGA State-Wise Statistics

State	*Jammu & Kashmir*	*Maharashtra*	*Assam*	*Kerala*
Employment provided to households	1,08348	13.16021 lakhs	11, 42992 lakhs	4,74909 lakhs
Total-person days in lakhs	33.76	219.35	303.82	81.41
SCs	1.91(5.685)	47.35 (21.59%)	32.01(10.54%)	15.93 (19.57%)
STs	6.26 (18.53%)	82.62 (37.66%)	102.9 (33.875)	5.89 (7.24%)
Women	1.19(3.53%)	87.13 (39.72%)	91.5 (30.12%)	67.99 (83.51%)
Others	25.58(75.79%)	89.38 (40.75%)	168.91(55.6%)	59.59 (73.19%)
Total Fund	107.14 crores	546.85 crores	711.53	314.16 crores
Expenditure	38.44	216.39 crores	403.48	118.94 crores
Total Works Taken up	9090	17365	12691	34120
Total Works Completed	2646	4658	2920	23407
Work in Progress	6444	12707	9771	10713

which are now visible in terms of building social and physical capital, democratic process which is transparent and accountable, augmenting household income, savings and investment, pro-poor climate change policy and sustainable development meeting the numerous MDGs. See Table 3 (NREGA 2009) at the end of discussion and conclusion section, which illustrates the NREGA Implementation Status Report 2009-2010, in terms of job cards issued, employment demanded by households, jobs provided for various vulnerable groups, funds for projects and expenditure in the 34 States of India.

Firstly, *Social Capital* is built under NREGS, and the most vulnerable group can help build capabilities and articulate and demand employment needs and negotiate their rights to escape the poverty trap. Nearly 33.9 million households were provided employment in 2007-08, and nearly 26 million households have worked under NREGA for 952.7 million work days. The legislation has also had a positive impact on the socio-economic empowerment of women mandating at least 33 percent participation for women. These efforts are extremely wide ranging. They include the creation of a digitised monitoring system, on site roll verification, proactive disclosure of all records and conducting regular social audits.

Secondly, NREGA projects have built *Physical Capital* and have enhanced productivity of land and regeneration of natural resources and food security in most states, through water harvesting, ground water recharging, improve moisture content, soil erosion, micro irrigation and increased access to markets and services, reducing distressed migration to urban areas, supplementing household incomes with increased women workforce participation ratio through rural connectivity.

Thirdly, it has strengthened *Democratic Processes*, and built local capacity at grassroots level for planning and decision making and encouraged transparency and accountability in grass root democratic process. NREGA has effectively used technology Management Information System (MIS), which is one of the largest data bases of rural households in the world, through their engagement in NREGA job cards. MIS makes

Table 3
NREGA Implementation Status Report 2009-2010

States	Cumulative No. of HH Issued Job Cards	No.of Households who have Demanded Employment	No. of Households Provided Employment	Person days in Lakhs				
				Total	SCs	STs	Women	Others
1	2	3	4	5	6	7	8	9
Andhra Pradesh	11899200	5182313	5182313	2372.2	602.5	316.5	1390.6	1453.2
Arunachal Pradesh	42475	23788	12718	1.56	0	1.56	0.29	0
Assam	3364342	1223120	1142992	303.82	32.01	102.9	91.5	168.91
Bihar	12145164	2353279	2353279	552.37	268.68	12.24	155.27	271.45
Gujarat	3165928	891571	891367	257.99	49.44	86.67	102.33	121.87
Haryana	405279	82541	82395	25.47	15.03	0	8.97	10.44
Himachal Pradesh	904218	291623	290200	111.21	36.17	10.52	44.92	64.52
Jammu and Kashmir	494382	269961	108348	33.76	1.92	6.26	1.19	25.58
Karnataka	4298599	1039757	1015411	417.59	85.43	42.89	190.32	289.26
Kerala	2092504	478488	474909	81.41	15.93	5.89	67.99	59.59
Madhya Pradesh	10584770	2650855	2620892	1165.54	200.34	542.47	515.08	422.73
Maharashtra	5388825	1475039	1316021	219.35	47.35	82.62	87.13	89.38
Punjab	626880	112151	112151	24.71	19.1	0	7.29	5.61
Rajasthan	9429061	5715470	5438179	3118.9	831.63	732.28	2101.93	1554.99
Sikkim	73272	43403	42875	16.39	1.38	7.25	6.51	7.75
Tamil Nadu	5842985	2512157	2512157	1283.5	751	26.86	1001.98	505.64
Tripura	602670	317564	317311	134.26	32.35	58.15	69.55	43.75
Uttar Pradesh	10943681	2844716	2843839	1241.25	661.52	22.74	240.2	556.99

West Bengal	9726015	2818666	2816526	599.09	225.97	84.18	199.35	288.94
Chhattisgarh	3459536	1257896	1257750	576.23	93.48	201.91	287.89	280.84
Jharkhand	3526748	964024	963661	400.3	59.75	166.41	129.54	174.14
Uttarakhand	857543	244645	241151	68.79	18.47	2.62	28.38	47.69
Manipur	333698	364327	364115	145.21	0.98	112.67	51.03	31.56
Meghalaya	364461	223291	222063	47.81	0.3	46.51	20.41	1.01
Mizoram	178625	178625	178625	77.58	0	74.69	27.23	2.89
Nagaland	316568	315998	306194	151.2	0	151.2	63.43	0
Orissa	5282756	515883	499010	157.87	30.59	52.03	60.32	75.24
Puducherry	14982	12067	12067	2.7	1.32	0	1.99	1.38
Andaman and Nicobar	6782	7060	6221	0.93	0	0.11	0.38	0.82
Lakshadweep	4473	1967	1967	0.51	0	0.51	0.2	0
Chandigarh	0	0	0	0	0	0	0	0
Dadra & Nagar Haveli	10139	2314	2314	0.42	0	0.42	0.36	0
Daman & Diu	0	0	0	0	0	0	0	0
Goa	13841	1641	1509	0.28	0.04	0.09	0.16	0.13
TOTAL	106400402	34416200	33630530	13590.2	4082.7	2951.16	6953.75	6556.34

Contd.

	Funds Available in Lakhs	*Central Release (Sanctioned) in Lakhs*	*Expenditure in Lakhs*	*Works Ongoing*	*Total Works*	
	10	*11*	*12*	*13*	*14*	*15*
	251044.44	0	245022	540640	158435	699075
	480.8	1059.02	302.82	86	35	121
	71153.15	31114.24	40347.54	9771	2920	12691

137775.06	42071.69	81827.39	78613	37467	116080
42855.48	33466.21	28502.23	43229	105867	149096
9500.04	3734.06	4786.37	3761	815	4576
29480.69	0	21231.22	24639	13917	38556
10714.13	5608.25	3843.54	6444	2646	9090
46123.05	0	52495.23	166924	3934	170858
31416.47	23785.23	11894.08	10713	23407	34120
341227.03	0	177687.45	335802	78197	413999
54685.35	20469.17	21639.41	12707	4658	17365
8063.76	4004.43	4776.77	4455	1398	5853
449175.41	0	364055.36	124985	38469	163454
3476.16	4385.24	2661.06	708	465	1173
167472.01	89809.63	104503.82	29368	8046	37414
39215.5	32545.7	18834.55	3179	8537	11716
358529.83	223501.82	197372.71	157713	105820	263533
102457.19	0	70102.22	44118	34432	78550
115133.92	57017.55	65347.05	35133	26006	61139
155220.46	51833.29	65636.85	82686	35606	118292
20327.6	15025.18	10483.07	11258	6863	18121
18157.18	20611.9	14639.19	2484	744	3228
9647.27	6375.12	6049.35	3630	1479	5109
13448.1	11887.25	9128.5	991	1074	2065
18424.5	20721.34	18867.59	3355	1623	4978
65382.73	0	21104.21	152114	4467	156581
255.45	0	200.47	14	476	490
1238.01	0	305.69	83	51	134
255.1	0	69.21	233	493	726
0	0	0	0	0	0

	112.08	0	88.47	30	0	30
	0	0	0	0	0	0
	746.8	0	222.09	34	68	102
	2573194.757658	699026.32	1664027.519424	1889900	708415	2598315
	112.08	0	88.47	30	0	30
	0	0	0	0	0	0
	746.8	0	222.09	34	68	102
	2573194.757658	699026.32	1664027.519424	1889900	708415	2598315

Source: NREGA 2009

transparency intrinsic to NREGA by placing all critical variables such as wage payments, number of days of employment provided and works under execution online for easy public access, encouraging the transfer of local solutions and best practices through an online knowledge network system. Currently 400 district programme coordinators are members of this network. The network also links up with Civil Society Organisations improving delivery of services such as initial experiments in the use of smart cards for wage payment to NREGA workers in remote rural villages.

Fourthly, NREGA schemes have helped the vulnerable poor in *augmenting household income, savings and investment* to escape the poverty trap by providing legal guarantee of 100 days of work in a given financial year and a basic minimum wage of Rupees 75 to Rupees 80, in 2008-09. All wage payments are made and disbursed through bank and post office accounts of the workers. Workers under NREGA are also provided with health insurance along with smart cards and biometric signatures for wage payments to workers under NREGA project.

Fifthly, NREGA has strengthened natural resource management by developing and implementing *'Pro Poor Climate Change Policies,* such as afforestation, regenerating natural resources like grasslands, drought and flood proofing, water conservation and harvesting systems and help the poor to cope with climate change impact which will increasingly affect the poor who are most vulnerable to it by reducing access to drinking water, negatively affecting the health of poor and posing a real threat to food security (Richards 2003). Among the poor, vulnerability may also vary, as some groups are lacking in the financial, social, and political means of securing alternative livelihoods less exposed to risk than other groups. Women, for example may be constrained by social and cultural structures that place them in inferior social positions, limiting their access to income, education, public voice, and survival mechanisms (MHDC 2000; Roy & Blomqvist 2004; UNDP 2009).

NREGA integrates responses to climate change adaptation measures into strategies for poverty reduction to ensure sustainable development. It strengthens capacity to cope with current climate variability and extremes and to adapt to expected future climatic conditions. Climate change policy and mechanisms can also generate income for small and marginal farmers and investment flows including transfer of technology for rural communities. It is seen that only 3-4% of carbon trading is sourced from agriculture, land use, land use change, agro-forestry and forestry. Efforts are directed in using the unique identity of NREGA workers, NREGA ongoing works, detailed documentation and records, MIS systems and advanced ICT to streamline measurement, financial flows to benefit rural communities from carbon trading. *Finally*, it has tried to implement the MDGs of sustainable development and poverty reduction and established an Untied Fund for Local Area Planning to encourage convergence for sustainable development processes through social audits. NREGA is the first ever law internationally, and its primary goal is to guarantees wage employment at an unprecedented scale to addresses causes of chronic poverty like drought, deforestation, famine and soil erosion, so that the process of employment generation is maintained on a sustainable basis (NREGA 2009; WTO 2004; PC 2008; WB 2004).

DISCUSSION AND CONCLUSIONS

The Government of India has recognised since independence that alleviation of poverty is its long-term objective. However, poverty alleviation cannot be left to five year plans alone. The various five year plans (1st to 8st-plan) have not achieved much in terms of alleviating poverty, as the unemployment programs were not well targeted; there was paucity of revenue for infrastructure programs and employment creation in rural areas and lack of political will and commitment (Dandekar 1998; Medhekar 2005).

A direct action taken by NREGA, the buzz word for Indian politicians, along with right to work and dignity of labour, participatory relationship with the government and various anti-poverty schemes and programs which are demand driven is growth inclusive. NREGA's emphasis should be on the "power of people (poor people) and the place (rural areas)" besides to ensure what is enshrined in the NREGA, that economic growth is inclusive and reaches the poorest, weakest and the most vulnerable in the society. It has given rural poor people the right to demand work, re-established their dignity and respect, ensure their economic and democratic rights and entitlements, create labour intensive infrastructure projects and finally to build human capital empower the rural poor population, which will lay the foundation for sustainable economic growth.

Livelihood and workforce participation of the marginalised groups such as: Scheduled Castes and Tribes and Other Backward Classes and Minorities groups and the Women in the society are also ensured under NREGA. A lot more needs to be done to study and evaluate the effectiveness of these programs state wise. It is important to further research NREGS and examine what works, what doesn't work, under what conditions and what are its costs and benefits, and most importantly, what lessons can be drawn from each of these programs for enhancing our understanding of the impact of NREGA, as well as its effectiveness, political will and commitment at the state level in context of its democratic, accountability and transparency processes.

Over the last two years, implementation trends vindicate the basic objective of the Act, which is to provide employment and reduce poverty. NREGA also has provided constitutional sovereignty in the form of transparency and accountability which is woven in the daily interaction of people with the government and allows any person to monitor and report the delivery of the schemes under NREGA. The total expenditure of schemes and workers 94% of total accounts is required to be posted on NREGA official website, with every transaction revealed in detail (NREGA 2009; Roy and Dey 2009).

The question is whether India will be able to follow the path of anti-poverty programmes' developed and implemented by Malaysia, Vietnam and Indonesia, where opportunities are created for the poor people to benefit from liberalisation and reform process in terms of infrastructure development and social security safety nets. Agriculture sector (land reforms) and social security (employment prospects) should be treated jointly as an anti-poverty measure, through ownership of physical assets and investment in human and physical capital for the poor. The impact of NREGA on the rural population, workforce and cost is still to be examined, in terms of energising people, mobilising resources and empowering the marginalised rural people as a group to take action and delivering the goods and services as promised under the act and much more in the future.

According to World Development Report by World Bank (2009), NREGS programs and schemes of the UPA government are a policy barrier to poverty alleviation, economic development and internal mobility, which prevents communities to fully capture the benefits of labour mobility and migration (WSJ 2009; PTI 2009). World Development Report further explains how internal mobility is essential as way out of poverty requires shifting populations from villages to cities. The process of migration should be encouraged, according to the World Bank. Migration is overlooked as a force in economic development due to negative attitudes held by the government and ignorance of the benefits of population mobility (World Bank 2009; UNDP 2009). Economic benefits of migration are not usually recognised by policymakers. NREGS has increased rural employment and watershed developments to improve agricultural productivity and development of small and medium towns mainly to reduce or prevent migration of population from rural to urban areas and cities. These policies prevent local communities to fully capture and capitalise on the benefits of labour mobility. Further in the State of Punjab and Madhya Pradesh, implementation of NREGS, job schemes have created a wage-floor for unskilled rural workers, causing a rise in agricultural wage from rupees 58 per day in 2005-06 to rupees 91 in 2009. Farm costs have increased as a result of decrease in labour supply, and glaring irregularities and corruption have been reported in the implementation of the scheme in the Bundelkhand region, state of Uttar Pradesh (EPW 2009; WSJ 2009; TIE 2009).

According to Work Bank 2009 report, decentralised scams have become the norm for NREGA scheme across the various states and the hard earned money of the poor is being siphoned off by a corrupt administration, contractors and ruling class nexus (World Bank 2009; WSJ 2009; TIE 2009). The World Bank research in 2009 reported that NREGA has not provided urban centric development as its schemes are blocking rural migration to urban cities. The WDR 2009 proposes that concentration of economic activity is inevitable and usually desirable for economic growth. NREGA thus retards rural-urban migration. Its is important to note that, this old Lewis model of growth based on a dual economy (Todaro and Smith 2008) has had its share of criticism even from within the capitalist framework—be it the human capital framework theory or from theories of market fragmentation or even the capability approach of Nobel Laureate Amritya Sen from the 1960s (Wiebke & Sen 2005; Nussbaum 2000; Nussbaum & Sen 1993). If we follow the World Bank's suggestion, then the wages will be lower in the rural areas, the rural welfare programmes will be downsized under NREGS thus allowing the rural poor to desperately migrate into the urban areas, resulting in exploitation of the urban poor. Notably, it only suggests this model for domestic markets and not for international labour markets. World Bank (2009) report also recommends to have special economic geographical transformation based on three dimensions, that is *higher density* of population for the growth of cities, which means using the scarce resources intensively; secondly *shorter distance* to where work and economic opportunities are available and lastly *fewer the restrictions and barriers* between countries economic borders, greater is the flow of goods, services, labour, capital and ideas across borders by taking advantage of economies of scale, specialisation and trade as seen in European Union (World Bank 2009) .

It's almost 6 years to the 2015 deadline to achieve the Millennium Development Goals (MDGs). However the measures to fight poverty and hunger have begun to slow as a result of the global food crises including the global financial crisis, which has resulted in a sluggish and even negative economic growth in developed countries. Despite many successes, overall progress has been too slow for most of the targets to be met by 2015 in the developing countries (UNDP 2009). Finally India's 'show case anti-poverty program' (NREGS) is not immune from this global crisis and has a long way to go, to not only guarantee employment for the first 100 days under the Act, but empowering poor people by providing them with continuous training and skilling (while not working). Elimination of poverty is not only a question of economics (raising income and investment), but is a social and political issue related to socio-political awareness of people to the causes and consequences of poverty, and how anti-poverty programs can bring awareness, with dignity and respect for the millions living in poverty, in India. One can only hope that the Indian politician's passion for renaming streets and programs after the Father of the Nation-Mahatma Gandhi will have some miraculous impact on the NREGA goal to meet the overarching MDG to end poverty by 2015.

REFERENCES

3iNetwork (2002), *India Infrastructure Report 2002: Governance Issues for Commercialization* Oxford University Press, New Delhi, India

ADB (2001), *Asian Development Outlook*, Oxford University Press, Hong Kong.

Agarwal, A.N. (1996), *Indian Economy: Problems of Development and Planning*, 22nd revised edn, Wishwa Prakashan, New Delhi.

Ahluwalia, I.J. and Little, I.M.D. (eds) (1998), *India's Economic Reform and Development: Essays for Manmohan Singh*, 3rd edn, Oxford University Press, New Delhi.

Ahluwalia, M.S. (1978), "Rural Poverty in India: 1956-57 to 1973-74", *Journal of Development Studies*, vol. 14, no. 3, April.

Ahuja, R. (1997), *Social Problems in India*, Second edn, Rawat Publications, New Delhi.

Allen, T and Thomas, A. (1997), *Poverty and Development in the 1990s*, Oxford University Press, London, United Kingdom.

Asian Development Bank (2003), Competitiveness in Developing Asia. Asian Development Outlook, (ADB), Oxford University Press, New York.

Bagachee, S. (1987, January 24), "Poverty Alleviation Programmes in Seventh Plan: An Appraisal", *Economic and Political Weekly, Bombay.*

Becker, H. (1966), *Social Problems: A Modern Approach,* John Wiley and Sons, Inc., New York.

Cassen, R and Joshi, V. (1996), *India: The Future of Economic Reform,* India, Oxford University Press, Delhi.

CFPR (1983), *Population, Poverty and Hope,* Centre For Policy Research, (CFPR) Utpal Publishing House, New Delhi.

Dandekar, V.M. (1998), *Agriculture, Employment and Poverty,* in The Indian economy: Recent Development and Future Prospects, Lucas, R.E.B. and Gustav, F.P. (Eds) Oxford University Press, New Delhi.

Dantwala, M.L. (1985), "Garibi Hatao: Strategy Option", *Economic and Political Weekly, Bombay,* Vol. No. March, 16.

DFARSA (2005), *Cape Town Ministerial Communiqué, India-Brazil-South Africa (IBSA) Dialogue Forum,* viewed 2/10/05 2005, http://www.dfa.gov.za/docs/2005/ibsa0311.htm, (cited on 9-9-09).

Dutt, R. and Sundharam, K.P.M. (1997), Indian Economy, 36th revised edition, S. Chand & Company Ltd: New Delhi.

Dutt, G. and Ravallion, M. (1998), "Farm Productivity and Rural Poverty in India", *Journal of Development Studies,* Vol. 34, No. 4, pp. 62-85.

EPW (2009), Survival of Agricultural Labour in Punjab: A Burning Questions, Economics and Political Weekly, 18 July 2009.

Elesh (1973), "Poverty Theories and Income Maintenance: Validity and Policy Relevance", *Social Science Quarterly,* Vol.

Fields, G. (1991), *Growth and Income Distribution,* Oxford University Press, UK.

Findlay, R. and Wellisz, S. (1994), *The Political Economy of Poverty, Equity and Growth: Five Small Open economies,* Oxford University press, New York.

Hirway, I. (1985), "Garibi Hatao: Can IRDP do it?" *Economic and Political Weekly, Bombay,* Vol 6, March, 30.

IFAD (2001), *Rural Poverty Report 2001: The Challenge of Ending Rural Poverty*, Oxford University Press, USA.

Jaffer, P.C. (2008), India's National Rural Employment Guarantee Scheme (NREGA): Localised Implementation in Gulbarga District of Karnataka. (http://www.solutionexchange-un.net.in/NREGA/documents/NREGA-Gulbarg.pdf (cited on 9-9-09).

Khanna, R.S. (1996), "Liberalisation and Unemployment in India", *The Indian Journal of Public Administration*, vol. XLII, July-September issue, 1996.

Lal, D. (1999), *Unfinished Business: India in the World Economy*, Oxford University Press, New Delhi.

Medhekar, A. (2005), 'Public Private Partnership for Infrastructure Development in India', *Proceedings of the 11th International Conference on Public Private Sector Partnerships: Enhancing Sustainable Development*, Lasi, Romania, May 25th – 28th: Facultatea de Economie, i Admnistrarea Afacerilor Universitatea "Al. I. Cuza". Sheffield Hallam University Press.

Mehta, H.R. (1997), *Poverty Population and Sustainable Development*, Rawat Publications, Jaipur, India.

MHDC (2000), *Human Development in South Asia 2000: The Gender Question*, Mehboob-Ul-Haq Development Centre (MHDC), Oxford University Press.

Nussbaum, M.C. (2000), Women and Human Development: The Capabilities Approach Cambridge University Press, Cambridge.

Nussbaum, M.C. and Sen, A. (1993), "The Quality of Life", (Eds), Oxford, Clarendon Press.

National Rural Employment Guarantee Act (2009), NREGA, Status Report (2009-2010), Ministry of Rural Development, Government of India, http://www.nrega.nic.in (cited on 29-9-09)

Press Trust of India. (2009), World Bank sees NREGS as a barrier to economic development in Business Standard, October 22-2009. http://www.business-standard.com/india/storypage. php?autono=351922 (cited on 8-10-09)

Planning Commission (PC) (2008), National Rural Employment Generation Scheme- (NREGS), Ministry of Rural Development, Government of India, http://planningcommission.gov.in/plans/planrel/11thf.htm (cited on 21-10-09).

Planning Commission (PC) (2009), Eleventh Five Year Plan (2007-12) Government of India, http://planningcommission.gov.in/plans/planrel/11thf.htm, (cited on 21-10-09).

Ravallion, M. (1991), "Reaching the Poor through Public Employment: Arguments, Evidence and Lessons from South Asia", World Bank Research Observer, Vol. 6, No. 2, pp. 153-176.

Ravallion, M. (1992a), Poverty Comparisons: A Guide to Concepts and Methods, Living Standards Measurement Study, Working Paper, No 38, Washington, DC.

Ravallion, M. and Subbarow, K. (1992b), "Adjustment and Human Development in India", Journal of Indian School of Political Economy, Vol. 4, No. 1, pp. 55-79.

Richards, M. (2003), Poverty Reduction, Equity and Climate Change: Global Governance Synergies or Contradictions? Globalisation and Poverty Programme; Overseas Development Institute, London.

Roy, K.C. and Blomqvist, H.C. (2004), Government's Poverty Alleviation Programs for Women's Empowerment: Some Comments on the Indian Situation, Twentieth Century Development: Some Relevant Issues, Nova Science Publishers, Inc., New York.

Roy, R. and Dey, N. (2009), NREGA: Breaking New Grounds, The Hindu June 21-09, Online Edition, http://www.hinduonnet.com/mag/2009/06/21/stories/2009062150010100.htm (cited on 8-10-09)

Sagar, D. (1990), "Rural Development Policies of India: A Historical Analysis", Indian Journal of Public Administration, Delhi, Vol. 36, No. 2.

Squire, L. (1993), "Fighting Poverty", American Economic Review, Vol. 83, May, pp. 377-382.

Solow, R. (1994), "Perspectives on Growth Theory", Journal of Economic Perspectives, Vol. 8, pp. 45-54.

Tendulkar, S.D. and Jain, L.R. (1995), "Economic Growth and Equity: India 1970-71 to 1988-89", Indian Economic Review, Vol. XXX, No. 1, pp. 19-49.

Tendulkar, S. (1998), Indian Economic Policy Reform and Poverty: An Assessment, in I. J. Ahluwalia and I. N. D. Little (eds), India's Economic Reforms and Development, Oxford University Press, New Delhi.

The Indian Express (2006), India's Employment Guarantee Scheme, (TIE) (5-1-06), http://infochangeindia.org/200603064810/Poverty/News/India-s-employment-guarantee-scheme-to-be-launched-in-February.html, (cited on 9-9-09).

The Indian Express (2009), NREGS: UP Under Scanner, TIE, 9-October-2009, by Yadav, J.P., http://www.indianexpress.com/news/nregs-up-under-scanner/526942/#(cited on 10-9-09).

Todaro, M.P. and Smith, S.C. (2008), Economic Development, Tenth Edition, Addison Wesley, Pearson Education, USA.

UNDP (2009), Millennium Development Goals Report 2009: End Poverty by 2015 (MDGs) http://www.undp.org/mdg/ (cited on 9-10-09)

Wall Street Journal (2009), NREGS and Rural Misery (WSJ) July, 2009, http://www.livemint.com/2009/07/23233056/NREGS-and-rural-misery.html (cited on 9-10-09)

Wikipedia (2009), National Rural Employment Program http://en.wikipedia.org/wiki/National_Rural_Employment_Guarantee_Act (cited on 20-10-09)

Wiebke, K. and Sen, A. (2005), Amartya Sen's capability Approach: Theoretical Insights and Empirical Applications, Springer, Berlin.

WTO (2004), Ministerial Conference on Cultural Tourism and Poverty Alleviation, Hue, Vietnam: 1-12.

World Bank (2004), World Development Report 2004: Making Services Work for Poor People, New York.

World Bank (2009), World Development Report 2009: Reshaping Economic Geography, New York, www.worldbank.org/wdr2009, *(cited on 20-10-09)*.

Impact of Rural Employment Guarantee Programme and Poverty in India

21

V. Neelamegham

POVERTY IN INDIA: A BRIEF OVERVIEW

Poverty in India has reached abnormal heights, so much so that it has become almost impossible for the country to come out of the 'poverty-trap'. The problem of poverty is not just confined to rural India; urban poverty has been one of the most disturbing truths ever since India began treading the path of development and urbanisation. In the last five years (2004-2009) the number of people living below the poverty line has increased from 270 million to 325 million. This is an increase off 55 million people below the poverty line in just five years. Among the most important causes ascribed for the high level poverty in India are its history under the British rule, large population, low literacy, societal structure including the caste system and role of women, dependence on agriculture, and the economic policies adopted after its independence.

Poverty eradication in india, is considered to be a far fetched dream. Poverty alleviation is expected to make better progress in the next 50 years than in the past, as a trickle-down effect of the growing middle class. Increasing stress on education, reservation of seats in government jobs and the increasing empowerment of women and the economically weaker sections of society, are expected to contribute to the alleviation of poverty. However, it is incorrect yo say that all poverty alleviation schemes in india have failed. Since 1950s the Indian government and non-governmental organizations have initiated several programs to alleviate poverty, including subsidizing food and other necessities, increased access to loans, improving agricultural techniques and price supports, and promoting education and family planning. These measures have helped eliminate famines, cut absolute poverty levels by more than half, and reduced illiteracy and malnutrition.

HOW POVERTY CAN CRIPPLE A NATION

The impact of poverty in India has been very grave. Poverty cripples a nation. It is a shame for a nation if almost half of its population cannot meet the basic requirements of life. It is a shame if thousands of small children do not get access to primary education. It is a matter of great dismay, if more than half of the young Indian populace sit idle without contributing anything to India's growth story, because they are illiterate and cannot find a job. There have been various schemes to eradicate poverty and its adverse impact on a nation, however, poverty alleviation in India is a long term goal as already mentioned above. With poverty being as high as in India, we will have to wait for some more decades to actually see the results of poverty alleviation measures.

Poverty in India is one of the major concerns because even though India is one of the fastest emerging countries in the world, what is really slowing down India's robust growth rate is the prevalence of very high poverty. The rural poor depend on agricultural incomes which are highly unpredictable and the urban people rely on jobs that are, at best, scarce. Even though India is expected to grow at a double-digit rate in the near future, one factor that can pull India back is poverty. If the poor people from the rural areas are trained properly and made to work, they too can contribute in their own small way to India's incredible growth story. This is where we can rely on the effectiveness of schemes like the NREGA.

NATIONAL RURAL EMPLOYMENT GUARANTEE ACT (NREGA): AN INTRODUCTION

One of the most important schemes that the Government of India adopted in 2005 to eradicate rural poverty is the introduction of the National Rural Employment Guarantee Act. The NREG Act is an act to provide for the enhancement of livelihood security of the households in rural ares of the country by providing at least one hundred days of guaranteed wage employment in every financial year to every household whose adult members volunteer to do unskilled manual work. It is the flagship programme of the UPA Government that directly touches lives of the poor and promotes inclusive growth. Enacted after a succesful struggle for an employment guarantee legislation, the NREG Act was a partial victory towards a full-fledged right to employment. The act became operational in february 2006, starting with 200 districts, and within three and a half years, has been extended to the rest of the country. NREGA is the first ever law that guarantees wage employment at an unprecedented scale. Dr. Jean Dreze, a Belgium born economist, has been a major influence on this project.

The major objectives of the act are:

- Augmenting wage employment.
- Strengthening natural resource management through works that address causes of chronic poverty like drought, deforestation and soil erosion.
- Encourage sustainable development.
- Strengthening grass-root processes of democracy by infusing transparency and accountability in governance.
- Strengthening decentralisation and deepening the processes of democracy by giving a pivotal role to the panchayati raj institutions in planning, monitoring and implementation.

AN ANALYSIS OF THE PERFORMANCE OF NREGA

Though, three and a half years is too short a period to gauge the impact of NREGA, it is worth mentioning that this important act is bringing about a silent revolution in the rual areas. This act has had repercussions at different levels, right from altering the socio-economic conditions of the affected districts to altering the social dynamics. Although well-intentioned, this act too faced the initial jitters. It received very half-hearted support from the states and the centre in implementation. A lot of debates and arguments have been doing rounds ever since this important legislation was passed. Despite this, the act has proven to be a good step towards rural poverty alleviation.

NREGA's record on the parameter of employment generation has been much better than its predecessors. Till 2008, about 25 million households have benefitted from about 857 million of person days employment generated. The act has brought about a lot of improvements in the spheres of financial inclusion and social security provision in the rural areas. Talking about financial inclusion, lets look at some numbers. As of 2008, 27.1 million bank accounts have been opened in rural areas with zero balance requirements for wage payments under the NREGA. Almost 80-90% of these are for households that have been included for the first time in the financial network of the country. Though financial inclusion was not an objective of the act, it still is an achievement. In terms of participation of the marginalized sections in the number of workdays created, more than 50% of total person days of employment generated have gone to SC and ST households.

In 2008-2009, the NREGA provided employment to almost 45 million rural people. Of those employed, nearly 50 percent were women and over 55 percent comprised of Scheduled Castes, Scheduled Tribes demonstrating the self-targeting nature of the programme. The NREGA has contributed immensely to the increased bargaining power of the agricultural labour. No longer are they prepared to settle for less than the notified wage. The average notified wage under NREGA has itself risen from Rs.65 per day in 2006-07 to Rs.87 in 2009-10. Also, there has been a commitment to provide a real wag rate of Rs. 100 under the NREGA. State governments are being encouraged to make wage payments under the programme through banks and post office accounts. Nearly 78 million such accounts have been opened till now. The government has also proposed to establish the institution of an ombudsman in every district for effective grievance redressal under NREGA.

One of the major objectives of the act has been to ensure one-third of women participation in total person days generated, the actual numbers have been close to an impressive 50%. Implementation of NREGA has contributed to very high levels of women empowerment, particularly in the following aspects.

- As the work is organized by women's groups, the gender perspective gets built in automatically.
- As women are comfortable working along with their neighbors, nearly 80% of the workers have been women.
- For the first time equal wages are really paid and this has boosted the earnings of women.
- As the wages are paid into Bank accounts the habit of thrift has further been strengthened.
- As the Bank deposits are increasing, the intra-household status of the women has also been improving commensurately as she controls substantial cash resources and withdrawal can be only on her decision.

There has been an increase in wages in almost all the indian states since the implementation of the act. Though the increase in the wage-level in rural india cannot be attributed to NREGA alone, but it would be foolish to ignore the role of this programme in the same. An ongoing study titled 'evaluation of NREGA' being conducted by the faculty of Institute of Development Studies, Jaipur, found that the act has shown great results in the rural areas in fields of economic empowerment, teamwork, has encouraged women in villages to come out of their veil and work, and has bridged the caste bias in rural india.

During 2008-2009, NREGA provided employment opportunities for more than 4.47 crore households as against 3.39 crore households covered in 2007-2008. the government is committed to provide a real wage of rs. 100 a day as an entitlement under the NREGA. In order to increase the productivity of assetsand resources under NREGA, convergence with other schemes relating to agriculture, forests, water resources, land resources and rural roads is being initiated. In the first stage, a total of 115 pilot districts have been selected for such convergence. The government of india has proposed an allocation of rs. 39,100 crore for the year 2009-2010 for NREGA which marks an increase of a mingboggling 144% over the 2008-2009 budget estimates.

CRITICAL ISSUES UNDER NREGA THAT NEEDS PROPER SURVEILLANCE

- Issue related to providing job-cards to the people on time.
- Issues related to selection of works.
- Issues related to the execution of works.
- Issues related to the measurement of the work done.
- Issues related to timely wage payments.

SOME LOOPHOLES IN THE ACT AND IN ITS IMPLEMENTATION

Though the NREGA has helped a lot of rural poor to get employed and become self-sufficient, this act and its implementation has some flaws too. Herein, we can talk about three issues.

- The first one is- why only 100 days of work? Since people do not get those 100 days fully, this proved to be an area of constant criticism. However, this year, according to the Finance minister Mr. Pranab Mukherjee, the Union government is looking to offer 50-60 more days of work to people who have already been employed for 100 days under the National Rural Employment Guarantee Act. He said funds for this could be drawn from the National Calamity Relief Fund, which has a corpus of Rs2,000 crore.

- The second issue is the rule of only one member per family being able to use it. Since poor families see themselves as a collective, splitting up is bad economics. For instance, a day's wage at a brick kiln might be less than what it is for NREG work. But even though brick kilns are brutal and exploitative, all members of a family can work there - and for more than a hundred days.
- The last issue that we can talk about is the delay in payments. Though Andhra Pradesh seems to be ahead of many other states, this continues to be a problem. There has been instances when people have actually waited for more than four months to get an amount much lesser than what was owed to them. There have been many recording errors, when people who work do not get recorded and people who haven't worked, get recorded. The planning commission has sought the reserve bank of India's intervention in streamlining the mechanism of paying wages under the NREGA. In a letter to the central bank, the commission said that the BRI should give directions to banks to ensure that payments to the beneficiaries of the NREGA are made only through banks or post offices (mentioned above).

The focus of NREGA has always been right which is- work must be provided on demand. The NREGA has always made sure that the assets created should benefit the poorest and the marginalised communities first. The work itself has created and sustained favourable conditions for providing minimum wage employment in transparent and an accountable manner. Despite all the criticisms with respect to corruption and leakages, the NREGA has actually drawn attention to the weaknesses of the delivery mechanism.

A CRITICAL ANALYSIS OF THE IMPACT OF NREGA

NREGA has given rise to a new work culture. The workers were hitherto controlled by contractors and their middlemen who knew how to extract work. Public works have now gained respectability. NREGA has suddenly increased purchasing power of the poor and there is visible local economic development. This is particularly true of Wayanad in Kerala which was ridden with farmer suicides. The peasants have managed to get substantial relief from NREGA by getting over their inhibition in working as labourers in richer farmer's lands by moving on to the now-respectable public works

It is true, however, that the achievements of the NREGA have been uneven. If we look at NREGA's state-wise impact, Andhra Pradesh has fared better than most states, thanks to the growing awareness of the people of their rights. This is one state where, some 2.7 million people applied for job-cards in the first month after the programme was announced and everyone received them. And in many states the job-cards are yet to be issued. Rajasthan is the state after Andhra Pradesh which has gained the maximum from the NREGA. However states like Maharashtra has benefitted very abysmally from the NREGA.

The act's foundations still being weak, any immediate changes must not burden the fragile success and infact must strengthen its basic structure. With all its shortcomings and failings, the limited benefit provided by the NREGA has been an important support structure for the poorest and most marginalised rural communities. Wage work has been open to all those who offer to do casual manual work on eight categories of work—most of which are designed to strengthen the natural resource base of those who are most dependent on such community assets for their livelihoods.

So, lets examine why NREGA has been more succesful than any other poverty alleviation schemes and what ensured better targeting. Unlike the other programmes which have been made toothless by anchoring them to below poverty line (BPL) cards, NREGA is a self-targeting programme. It is no wonder that the distribution of beneficiaries by social groups is almost similar to the distribution of poor obtained from the NSSO (National Sample Survey Organisation) consumption surveys. Evidently, the self-targeting inherent in NREGA has a better score in targeting the poor than the officially conducted but flawed identification of BPL households. In fact, the self-selection nature of NREGA has persuaded the finance ministry to classify workers in the programme as poor, for inclusion in the Janashree Bima Yojana. Similarly, the case of extension of Rashtriya Swasthaya Yojana to the NREGA workers.

The NREGA has ben more or less succesful in energising, mobilising, empowering and delivering to india's poorest and most marginalised rural people. It has also been somewhat succesful in providing the rural poor a measure of dignity, tangible economic benefit and a motivation to participate in local action. The NREGA stands apart from the employment and poverty alleviation programmes in many significant ways. It is the first national programme of consequence which has woven transparency and accountability into the mundane fabric of daily interaction of people with the government. It also gives an opportunity to break the feudally enforced silence of its victims. Through transparency and social audit measures, NREGA allows anyone, anywhere, to be a part of the monitoring of the delivery system. It also gives the poor an opportunity to realise the constitutional sovereignty, the power of the people, considering India is the largest democracy in the world.

CONCLUSION

Although a programme of this magnitude will take time to be of any relevance in changing the landscape of rural India, initial reports of evaluation studies by various institutions and individuals has documented the processes of revival and resurgence largely driven by NREGA as an axis of struggle by the rural poor. It has neither been claimed nor was envisaged that NREGA is the key to successful rejuvenation of rural areas. This requires many such efforts particularly towards ensuring the broken linkages of the growth process to include the rural areas as engines of growth. Nonetheless, it does offer an opportunity for the rural poor to stake claim to the fruits of the growth. Moreover, NREGA success stories provide opportunities for mainstreaming and legitimizing the struggle for other social security legislation.

Independent India has to acknowledge the critical role the NREGA has played in providing a measure of inclusive growth. It has given people a right to work, to re-establish the dignity of labour, to ensure people's economic and democratic rights and entitlements, to create labour intensive infrastructure and assets, and to build the human resource base of our country. For the first time, the power elite recognises the people's right to fight endemic hunger and poverty with dignity, accepting that their labour will be the foundation for infrastructure and economic growth. The entitlements paradigm is still to be established in many States in the country. Second generation issues like the expansion of the categories of permissible works needs to be taken up with labour and the deprived continuing to be the central focus. The improvements must be to strengthen, not divert from these basic tenets. In the midst of the current economic slowdown, there is enough evidence that this kind of commitment can work to help reduce the slowdown.

NREGA's success is as much a hope for civil society activists fighting for the rights of the poor as it is a critique of the developmentalist state in case it fails to deliver.

REFERENCES

http://nrega.nic.in/circular/Minutes_meeting7Aug09.pdf

http://www.tribuneindia.com/2009/20090918/

http://www.indiaenews.com/business/20090909/219776.htm

http://www.theindiapost.com/2009/02/08/survey-to-study-the-impact-of-nrega/

www.thehindu.com

http://www.livemint.com

22 Rural Development through the National Rural Employment Guarantee Scheme, (NREGS)

V. Darling Selvi

INTRODUCTION

The National Rural Employment Guarantee Act NREGA, also known as National Rural Employment Guarantee Scheme, NREGS is an Indian job guarantee scheme, enacted by legislation on August 25, 2005. The NREGA provides a legal guarantee for one hundred days of employment in every financial year to adult members of any rural household willing to do public work-related unskilled manual work at the statutory minimum wage. This act was introduced with an aim of improving the purchasing power of the rural people, primarily semi or un-skilled work to people living below poverty line in rural India. It attempts to bridge the gap between the rich and poor in the country. Roughly one-third of the stipulated work force must be women. Central Government shall meet the cost towards the payment of wage, 3/4 of material cost and certain percentage of administrative cost. State Government shall meet the cost towards unemployed allowance, 1/4 of material cost and administrative cost of State council.

Adult members of rural households submit their name, age and address with photo to the Gram Panchayat. The Gram panchayat registers households after making enquiry and issues a job card. The job card contains the details of adult member enrolled and his /her photo. Registered person can submit an application for work in writing either to panchayat or to Programme Officer. The panchayat/programme officer will accept the valid application and issue dated receipt of application, letter providing work will be sent to the applicant and also displayed at panchayat office. The employment will be provided within a radius of 5 km: if it is above 5 km extra wage will be paid. If employment under the scheme is not provided within fifteen days of receipt of the application daily unemployment allowance will be paid to the applicant. The scheme started from February 2, 2006 in 200 districts, was expanded to cover another 130 districts in 2007-2008 and eventually covered all 593 districts in India in 2008. The outlay was Rs. 11,000 crores in 2006-2007, and has been rising steeply, to Rs. 39,100 crores in 2009-2010.

The NREGA achieves twin objectives of rural development and employment. The NREGA programme encompasses important rural development activities such as Rural Connectivity, working towards measures of Flood control and protection such as construction and repair of embankments, etc. Water conservation and harvesting is one of the other important tasks carried out by the employed. Digging of new tanks/ponds, percolation tanks and construction of small check dams are also carried out under this scheme. Micro Irrigation work such as construction of small canals is also carried out. The scheme also provides irrigation facilities to land owned by people coming under SC/STs, beneficiaries of land reforms, Indra Awas Yojana, etc. Renovation of traditional water bodies is also carried out. This involves desilting of tanks/ponds, old canals, open wells, etc. Land development is also given importance. The employed are given work such as land leveling, afforestation, tree plantation, etc. The main aim of the programme is empowerment of laborers by making employment a right and the guarantee of employment an assurance so that the rural workers could demand employment.

The objective of 100 days of employment was not achieved in any state. However, the per district person days of employment and households provided employment were comparatively high in Madhya Pradesh (1.6 lakh households, 68 days), Chhattisgarh (1.7 lakh households, 54 days), Orissa (0.7 lakh households, 57 days) and Rajasthan (two lakh households, 83 days). In West Bengal and Tamil Nadu although three lakh and 1.2 lakh households, respectively worked under the NREGA, they could do so only for 14 and 26 days, respectively. In Gujarat and Maharashtra, only 30,000 and 40,000 households per district availed of the employment guarantee.

As per the National Bulletin data, Employment provided to households: 2.27 Crore, Person days [in Crore]: Total: 73.14, SCs: 21.21 [28.99%], STs: 17.33 [23.7%], Women: 38.05 [52.03%], others: 34.6 [47.31%], Total works taken up: 19.52 Lakhs, Works completed: 2.66 Lakhs, and Works in progress: 16.85 Lakhs

MAXIMIZING WORK OPPORTUNITIES: LIVELIHOOD SECURITY

In the words of E.F. Schumacher, primary consideration to trigger development should be to maximize work opportunities for the unemployed and under-employed to trigger development. India has a long history of wage employment and self employment programmes and capacity building. Under NREGA in 2007-08, 33.9 million households were provided employment and 1.4 billion days of work were generated. With the expansion of the programme to the entire country, upto mid August 2008, 26 million households have worked under NREGA for 952.7 million work days. Emphasis has also been laid to ensure that economic growth is inclusive and reaches the weaker sections of our society, especially the Scheduled Castes (SCs) and the Scheduled Tribes (STs), Other Backward Classes (OBCs) and minorities. NREGA has generated sufficient volumes of employment to provide the means for uplift of large numbers of the population. Workforce participation of marginalized groups has been high with 57% (SC/ST) in 2007-08 and 55% upto mid-August 2008. Women workforce participation has also surpassed the statutory minimum requirement of one third participation. In FY 07-08, women participation was 43%, which has increased to 49% upto in FY 08-09 (upto mid-August) including states like Kerala with 85% women workforce participation.

By securing livelihood, NREGA also mitigates seasonal/ distress migration which has been a significant source of employment and income for a large proportion of rural population. Employment opportunities at the village level itself, local labour availability for agriculture increases. Irrigation facilities for SC/ST farmers and land reform beneficiaries not only enhance productivity of their small holdings but enable them to be better endowed during peak farming periods.

AUGMENTING HOUSEHOLD INCOME, SAVINGS AND INVESTMENT

Low level of income continues to be the barrier for the poor to escape the poverty trap. Most of the initiatives of self employment and skill building aim to provide the safety net to the poor from the "poverty that kills". Besides the legal guarantee of 100 days of work in a financial year, NREGA households are also assured of basic minimum income3. Post-NREGA, there has been a revision of minimum wages across the country in last three years, and the average daily wage rate has increased from Rs. 75 ($1.66) to Rs 80 ($1.77) in FY 08-09 (upto mid-August) at the national level. Higher incomes are expected to raise household savings, accelerating economic diversification and household investments in human capital. The Federal Government has directed that all wage payments to be made through bank and post office accounts of wage seekers. Thus far, 33 million (upto mid-August '08) NREGA bank and post office accounts have been opened to disburse wages, largest number of accounts linked to a development programme. Agencies for wage payment are being separated from implementing agencies through accounts-based wage payment. This will not only infuse integrity in wage payment, bring the most vulnerable people in rural India into formal banking and credit system. Workers under NREGA are provided medical and health cover insurance. Initial experiments in the use of smart cards and biometric signatures for wage payment to NREGA workers in remote villages are being supported.

REGENERATING NATURAL RESOURCES- COMPLEMENTING FOOD SECURITY

Land degradation, depletion of natural resources like grass lands and forests; price shocks, and population growth are already a major concern for sustaining agricultural productivity. Time and again it has been shown that wasteland development begins with water. For instance, once a water-harvesting system is built and equitable sharing of the water evolved, the local community becomes involved in protecting and re-greening the catchments of its water system. The auxiliary objective of NREGA is natural resource base generation and addresses growing concerns of the food security with emphasis on water and soil conservation through increasing squeeze on water availability and new irrigable land for expanded crop production, facilitating 3 Minimum wage as per NREGA 2005: Wage fixed by the State Government under Section 3 of Minimum Wages Act, 1948 for agricultural laborers as applicable in that area dual cropping and crop diversity. Cultivation of bio-fuels has also been encouraged under NREGA and works relating to drought proofing and flood protection are aimed to provide resistance to climate shocks and natural disasters. Thus, NREGA can actually be seen moving towards its objective of food and livelihood security and long term sustainable development through ecological regeneration.

In the financial year 07-08, 1.78 million works were undertaken, of which 49% constituted water conservation, and in 08-09, upto mid-August, 1.72 million works have been undertaken, of which 46% relate to water conservation. Early trends indicate enhancement of agricultural productivity through water harvesting, check dams, ground water recharging, improve moisture content, check in soil erosion and micro-irrigation, stemming of distress migration, increased access to markets and services through rural connectivity works, supplementing household incomes, increase in women workforce participation ratios, and the regeneration of natural resources.

NREGA AS INVESTMENT IN CLIMATE CHANGE FOR POOR:

Climate change is happening and will increasingly affect the poor who are most vulnerable to it by reducing access to drinking water, negatively affecting the health of poor and posing a real threat to food security. Among the poor, vulnerability may also vary, since some groups are more lacking in the financial, social, and political means of securing alternative livelihoods less exposed to risk than others. Women, for example may be constrained by social and cultural structures that place them in inferior social positions, limiting their access to income, education, public voice, and survival mechanisms. NREGA integrates responses to climate change and adaptation measures into strategies for poverty reduction to ensure sustainable development. It strengthens capacity to cope with current climate variability and extremes and to adapt to expected future climatic conditions. Climate change policy & mechanisms can also generate income for small & marginal farmers and investment flows for rural communities. It is seen that only 3-4% of carbon trading is sourced from agriculture, land use, land use change, agro-forestry and forestry. Efforts may also be directed in using the unique identity of NREGA workers, NREGA works, detailed documentation & records, the MIS systems in place and advanced ICT to streamline measurement, financial flows to benefit rural communities from carbon trading.

NREGA: BEYOND WAGE EMPLOYMENT

Benefits of NREGA are not limited enhancing economic potential of supplementing income through wage earnings, savings and investments and financial inclusion. Various multiplier effects of NREGA are now emerging:

(a) *Social Capital Formation:* Entitlements have conferred on the most vulnerable group can help build capacity among them to articulate needs and negotiate their rights.

(b) *Physical Capital:* NREGA Works have close affinity with inputs for improving productivity of land and rural connectivity

(c) *Ecological Synergies:* Focus on strengthening natural resource management such as afforestation, drought proofing, flood proofing, and water conservation help cope with Climate Change stress

(d) *Democratic Processes:* Strengthens local capacity for planning & decision making: Gram Sabha, PRIs. It also infuses transparency and accountability in grass root democratic processes through social audits.

(e) *Sustainable Development:* Untied Fund for Local Area Planning encourages convergence for sustainable development.

ICT AS A GROWTH TRIGGER FOR RURAL DEVELOPMENT

Information Communication and Technology play NREGA has used technology effectively for inclusion: The National Employment Guarantee Program aims at providing 100 days of guaranteed employment Public Policy and Programs for Poverty Reduction to unskilled labor in every poor household in rural and urban areas. The program is now being implemented in 200 poor districts in the country, in the first phase, with effect from February 2006. As per the guidelines under the Act:

- Every rural household needing employment in the implementation district can register with the gram panchayat and can obtain an identification card in the names of the adult members.
- The household should be provided employment, within 15 days of application, within a radius of 5km. In case, the employment site is more distant, higher wages (by 20% will be given).

- Failure to provide employment will entitle the applicant household to an unemployment wage, which will not be less than a quarter of the minimum wage for the first 30 days and half the minimum wage for the remaining period.
- Wages are payable every week, at the minimum rates fixed by the state governments, and should be equal for both men and women.
- Each work site has to be provided with minimum facilities for land improvement, soil and water conservation, and rural roads.
- The works can be executed by the gram sabhas or by line departments, or other government and nongovernmental agencies.
- There are several provisions to ensure transparency and social audit so that the resources are spent effectively.

National Rural Employment Guarantee Act proposed by the National Advisory Council. In the "baseline scenario", whereby a nation-wide Rural Employment Guarantee Programme is gradually introduced over a period of four years, the total cost of the Programme rises from 0.5% of GDP in 2005-6 to 1% of GDP in 2008-9. The cost can be brought down, if needed, by raising the labour-material ratio, stretching the inception phase beyond four years, or taking measures to reduce the "participation ratio". However, these cost-reducing measures are best avoided. One per cent of the country's GDP is not a high price to pay to protect the bulk of the rural population from hunger, insecurity and extreme poverty - once and for all.

Fund-flow: The fund for NREGS is allocated at the ratio of 90:10 by centre and state respectively unlike other programmes where the ratio is 75:25. The Central government releases the money to the districts directly who in turn releases it to the sub-district level to be used for various works. The payment for the labourers under all works is made by the Grama Panchayat irrespective of the implementing agencies.

Funding Pattern: The cost of the scheme is shared by the Centre and the State in the ratio of 90:10. The Central Government will bear the following costs:

- The entire cost of wages for unskilled manual workers.
- 75 percent of the cost of material and wages for skilled and semi-skilled workers.
- Administrative expenses, which will include, inter alia, the salary and allowances of Programme Officers and their support staff and work site facilities.
- Administrative expenses of the Central Employment guarantee Council.

The State Government will bear the following costs:

- 25 percent of the cost of material and wages for skilled and semi-skilled workers.
- Unemployment allowance payable in case the State Government cannot provide wage employment within 15 days of application.
- Administrative expenses of the State Employment Guarantee Council.

Priority of Works: Taking into account the field conditions in Tamil Nadu, the works are being taken up in Tamil Nadu in the following priority:

- Formation of new ponds.
- Renovation of existing Ponds, Kuttais, Kulams, Ooranies, Temple tanks etc.
- Desilting of channels.
- Desilting and strengthening of bunds of irrigation tanks.
- Formation of new roads.
- Other water conservation/soil conservation measures/flood protection measures.

The performance of NREGS in Tamilnadu is briefly presented in the table, which reveals that nearly 24 lakhs households have benefited. Out of them, nearly 59% SCs, 2%

STs, and 80% are women. Out of the total fund allocated, 67% have been utilized so far with the work completion of 17%.

Table 1
NREGA Statistics of Tamil Nadu

Employment provided to households:	24.10135 Lakhs
Person days [in Lakh]:	
Total:	1019.83
SCs:	603.9 [59.22%]
STs:	18.23 [1.79%]
Women:	805.52 [78.99%]
Others:	397.69 [39%]
Total fund:	1287.08 Crore.
Expenditure:	856.41 Crore.
Total works taken up:	35272
Works completed:	6053
Works in progress:	29219

Table 2
Average Wage Paid for the Financial Year 2009-2010 as on 24-9-2009

District	*Wage Rate (in Rs.)*	*Total Amount Paid as wages (in Rs.)*	*No. of Person Days*	*Average Wage Rate*
Ariyalur	80	10387627	147568	70.39
Cuddalore	80	31560677	508549	62.06
Dindigul	80	20231346.02	276123	73.27
Kanniyakumari	80	41552773.65	564109	73.66
Karur	80	20976845	319117	65.73
Krishnagiri	80	64131515.65	892451	71.86
Nagapattinam	80	26308971.26	360213	73.04
Sivagangai	80	105616692.21	1513232	69.8
Thanjavur	80	48376216	609129	79.42
Thoothukkudi	80	20864301.46	282101	73.96
Tirunelveli	80	257677867	3525509	73.09
Tiruvannamalai	80	7546655	122342	61.68
Tiruvarur	80	51741281.86	666821	77.59
Villupuram	80	222181237	3181113	69.84
Average	80	66368143	926313	71
Total		929154006.11	12968377	71.65

The average wage rate is determined as Rs.72 in Tamilnadu. The districts Dindigul, Kanniyakumari, Krishnagiri, Nagapattinam, Thanjavur, Thoothukkudi, Tirunelveli, and Tiruvarur are able to cross the average wage rate. Among all the districts, Tiruvarur ranks first and Tiruvannamalai ranks last.

EMPLOYMENT GENERATION THROUGH NREGS IN TAMILNADU

The scheme covers 6 districts at Phase I, 4 districts at Phase II, and 20 districts at Phase III. Among them, the districts Nagapattinam, Tiruvarur, and Kanchipuram have achieved above average in giving employment opportunities to the SC/STs of the respective districts. However the average percentage of the same among all the districts stands at 34%.

Table 3
Cumulative No. of Households Issued Job Cards

Districts	*SC*	*ST*	*Others*	*Total*	*% of SC/ST*
		Phase I			
Cuddalore	125222	1620	180308	307150	41
Dindigul	66981	1052	157650	225683	30
Nagapattinam	92694	351	81326	174371	53
Sivagangai	41706	39	151074	192819	22
Tiruvannamalai	77165	10047	202375	289587	30
Villupuram	146115	7478	282943	436536	35
		Phase II			
Karur	35947	205	85113	121265	30
Thanjavur	41840	1957	94668	138465	32
Tirunelveli	73884	1521	188003	263408	29
Tiruvarur	95155	281	89814	185250	52
		Phase III			
Ariyalur	26805	1088	61429	89322	31
Coimbatore	87093	4138	105151	196382	46
Dharmapuri	34861	9011	102443	146315	30
Erode	72120	2515	101534	176169	42
Kanchipuram	82171	4645	88470	175286	50
Kanniyakumari	4280	796	83868	88944	6
Krishnagiri	25617	2476	125791	153884	18

Contd.

Districts	SC	ST	Others	Total	% of SC/ST
Madurai	47744	327	142826	190897	25
Namakkal	42749	9048	64868	116665	44
Perambalur	29020	764	43315	73099	41
Pudukkottai	41103	289	158373	199765	21
Ramanathapuram	38913	192	98766	137871	28
Salem	34485	11693	95146	141324	33
The Nilgiris	7035	1979	9292	18306	49
Theni	21579	225	56063	77867	28
Thoothukkudi	48180	514	91657	140351	35
Tiruchirappalli	54552	1745	153999	210296	27
Tiruvallur	91292	6596	116129	214017	46
Vellore	75261	5763	176654	257678	31
Virudhunagar	51730	822	113542	166094	32
Total	1713299	89177	3502590	5305066	34
Average	57110	2972.57	116753	176836	34
%	32	2	66		

Table 4
Cumulative Person Days Generated

Districts	SC	ST	Others	Total	Women	% of SC/ST	% of Women
Phase I							
Cuddalore	229367	2037	313171	544575	411441	42	76
Dindigul	88373	1107	214622	304102	266870	29	88
Nagapattinam	264549	524	133325	398398	303561	67	76
Sivagangai	347014	50	1209911	1556975	1312315	22	84
Tiruvannamalai	37545	646	114610	152801	116070	25	76
Villupuram	1193541	30475	2135836	3359852	2647645	36	79
Phase II							
Karur	121218	688	223257	345163	279743	35	81
Thanjavur	245883	11890	375303	633076	460603	41	73
Tirunelveli	1152721	20390	2434032	3607143	2960711	33	82
Tiruvarur	416634	1180	282034	699848	463854	60	66
Phase III							
Ariyalur	37654	3076	114280	155010	116414	26	75
Coimbatore	102805	2571	60877	166253	143072	63	86
Dharmapuri	23675	4465	182019	210159	183278	13	87
Erode	358943	10921	551821	921685	806692	40	88
Kanchipuram	182282	4880	145480	332642	275480	56	83
Kanniyakumari	39873	7322	536753	583948	508133	8	87
Krishnagiri	103804	5652	790140	899596	770295	12	86
Madurai	240714	4083	678493	923290	812680	27	88

Contd.

Districts	*SC*	*ST*	*Others*	*Total*	*Women*	*% of SC/ST*	*% of Women*
Namakkal	301425	88973	426986	817384	682113	48	83
Perambalur	209934	7757	342542	560233	471881	39	84
Pudukkottai	39034	159	86387	125580	104686	31	83
Ramanathapuram	211281	176	489558	701015	565608	30	81
Salem	439936	114426	1197304	1751666	1518621	32	87
The Nilgiris	2146	4509	3992	10647	7763	63	73
Theni	85159	694	315162	401015	353489	21	88
Thoothukkudi	108088	330	199647	308065	251690	35	82
Tiruchirappalli	706449	16260	1765930	2488639	2018885	29	81
Tiruvallur	309630	18099	315311	643040	553257	51	86
Vellore	11900	105	25[illegible]81	37486	29000	32	77
Virudhunagar	20768	1281	55431	77480	66129	28	85
Total	7632345	364726	15719695	23716766	19461979	34	82

On an average the combination of SC/ST consist of 34% and that of women is 82% and so it is proved that the NREGS is useful more for the women folk. Thus it is evident that the employment opportunities are enjoyed by the people of the priority sector. The districts Dindigul, Erode, Madurai, and Theni hold the highest percentage of providing employment to the women.

Table 5
Employment Status

Districts	*Employment Demanded*	*Employment Provided*	*No. of HH Working*	*No. of HH Completed 100 Days*	*% of Working*
		Phase I			
Cuddalore	36117	36009	32411	39	90
Dindigul	34983	31731	18072	10	52
Nagapattinam	24605	24402	22006	83	89
Sivagangai	68424	68174	62862	431	92
Tiruvannamalai	9261	9261	8388	22	91
Villupuram	166304	166455	157474	488	95
		Phase II			
Karur	24021	24013	17952	30	75
Thanjavur	56191	56173	43325	52	77
Tirunelveli	119737	119679	104106	1380	87
Tiruvarur	53080	53401	43917	88	83

Contd.

Districts	Employment Demanded	Employment Provided	No. of HH Working	No. of HH Completed 100 Days	% of Working
		Phase III			
Ariyalur	19270	19270	16050	2	83
Coimbatore	11279	11256	8818	36	78
Dharmapuri	12417	12416	10232	24	82
Erode	36942	36861	25301	287	68
Kanchipuram	17755	17650	15552	57	88
Kanniyakumari	15798	15793	12272	608	78
Krishnagiri	49507	49205	46097	28	93
Madurai	52875	53130	45989	173	87
Namakkal	35878	35835	21423	314	60
Perambalur	35780	35778	32459	59	91
Pudukkottai	8732	8753	8161	22	93
Ramanathapuram	45541	45488	42128	89	93
Salem	68324	68321	62033	499	91
The Nilgiris	776	772	648	0	84
Theni	24426	24413	20455	61	84
Thoothukkudi	18007	18019	14826	29	82
Tiruchirappalli	103919	103890	91273	397	88
Tiruvallur	47343	47143	45079	71	95
Vellore	2602	2601	1293	0	50
Virudhunagar	5827	5845	5330	0	91
Total	1205721	1201737	1035932	5379	86

In the first Phase, Villupuram ranks first, in Phase II, Tirunelveli ranks first, and in Phase III, Tiruchirappalli holds the first. However, the performance of NREGS in the Villupuram district is highly appreciable. In giving employment to the applied candidates, Villupuram and Tiruvallur districts are the forerunners.

The correlation between the total Cumulative Expenditure and the Cost per Person day is estimated as .12 which shows a low relationship between the two. The average cumulative expenditure form only 16% of the total availability.

With regards to the works done, Renovation of Traditional Water Bodies consist of 45%, Rural Connectivity 22%, Water Conservation 18%, Irrigation Canals 15%, and flood control 1%. Hence, on an average, 78% of the works under National

Table 6
Outlays & Outcomes During Financial Year 2009-2010

(Rs. in Lakhs)

Districts	*Total Availability*	*Total Cumulative Expenditure*	*House Hold*	*Persons*	*Person Days*	*Cost Per Person Day (in Rs.)*	*Avg. No of Laborers Per Work*	*Avg. Person Days Per Work*
Ariyalur	1779.54	109.50	19270	21911	155015	70.64	214.81	1519.75
Coimbatore	4025.47	125.65	11281	12379	166253	75.58	32.92	442.16
Cuddalore	6775.34	339.77	36009	51954	544583	62.12	199.06	2086.52
Dharmapuri	2177.92	141.36	12416	13270	210167	67.26	75.4	1194.13
Dindigul	6484.69	315.73	31812	34029	304102	73.3	97.78	873.86
Erode	4675.42	760.26	37055	41022	921687	79.14	70.12	1575.53
Kanchipuram	3145.93	195.04	17655	21875	332645	58.63	59.6	906.39
Kanniyakumari	859.26	437.05	16006	17598	583948	74.84	55.87	1853.8
Karur	1835.64	227.15	24023	26902	345165	65.81	120.1	1540.92
Krishnagiri	1952.53	647.53	49215	54455	899630	71.98	102.17	1687.86
Madurai	3866.63	546.43	53358	61802	923298	59.05	125.61	1876.62
Nagapattinam	4677.82	289.91	24403	36043	398424	72.76	172.45	1906.33
Namakkal	2291.83	702.14	36022	42858	817399	78.01	44.14	841.81
Perambalur	1127.33	326.21	35807	43876	560325	55.64	157.83	2015.56
Pudukkottai	3200.05	99.10	8753	10737	125590	78.91	132.56	1550.49
Ramanathapuram	2880.77	464.78	45611	61295	701029	66.3	94.59	1081.83
Salem	3449.67	1241.30	68415	78399	1751709	70.86	132.65	2963.97
Sivagangai	3953.96	1093.26	68225	84238	1556980	70.22	65.55	1211.66

Contd.

Districts	Total Availability	Total Cumulative Expenditure	House Hold	Persons	Person Days	Cost Per Person Day (in Rs.)	Avg. No of Laborers Per Work	Avg. Person Days Per Work
Thanjavur	2843.33	552.74	56236	73970	633256	79.58	132.09	1130.81
The Nilgiris	634.29	8.61	772	848	10647	80.84	53	665.44
Theni	862.24	256.72	24463	27909	401023	64.02	153.35	2203.42
Thoothukkudi	2203.99	227.62	18046	22729	308066	73.89	119.63	1621.4
Tiruchirappalli	4181.68	1693.77	112832	146105	2488681	66.66	128.27	2184.97
Tirunelveli	3449.06	2635.90	120181	149590	3607231	72.99	112.05	2702.05
Tiruvallur	3006.96	381.36	47166	55321	643068	59.02	96.38	1120.33
Tiruvannamalai	6449.81	94.32	9382	12208	152810	61.72	128.51	1608.53
Tiruvarur	3823.80	544.65	53402	79775	699862	77.82	140.2	1229.99
Vellore	4627.90	23.27	2601	3240	37486	62.08	140.87	1629.83
Villupuram	10274.82	2394.84	166561	243924	3360251	69.92	231.21	3185.07
Virudhunagar	2495.76	54.66	5939	6949	77482	66.83	100.71	1122.93
Total	104013.43	16930.65	1212917	1537211	23717812	69.94	112.62	1737.7
Average	3467.11	564.35	40430.57	51240.37	790593.73	69.55	116.32	1584.47

Table 7
Work Category Wise Women Employment Provided

Work Category	Worker Employed		Person Days (in Lakh.)		Amount Earned(in Rs. Lakh)		% of Women		
	Women	Men	Women	Men	Women	Men	Emp-loyed	Person days	Amount
Rural Connectivity	306898	99412	33.64	8.27	2388.87	597.37	76	80	80
Water Conservation	253824	72234	38.42	7.48	2582.85	505.61	78	84	84
Renovation of Traditional Water Bodies	638391	193021	101.58	20.76	7118.70	1465.08	77	83	83
Flood Control	8141	1922	1.07	0.18	71.18	12.37	81	86	85
Drought Proofing	125	65	0.04	0.01	2.14	0.53	66	80	80
Irrigation Canals	194159	75163	20.00	5.78	1399.91	412.39	72	78	77
Irrigation Facilities to SC/ST/IAY/LR	1102	372	0.14	0.04	11.05	3.06	75	78	78
Land development	1522	614	0.16	0.052	10.73	3.52	71	75	75
Other works	11	2	0.0002	00004	0.012	0.0024	85	83	83
Grand total	1404173	442805	195.05	42.56	13585.43	2999.94	76	82	82

Table 8
No. of Disabled Persons and Person Days for the Financial Year 2009-2010

Name of District	*No. of Disabled Persons registered in NREGA*	*No. of Disabled Persons worked in NREGA in FY2009-2010*	*Person Days Generated in FY2009-2010*
Cuddalore	1042	78	706
Dindigul	72	2	9
Nagapattinam	477	14	125
Sivagangai	160	47	846
Tiruvannamalai	137	20	181
Villupuram	1338	422	4765
Karur	119	15	165
Thanjavur	438	75	937
Tirunelveli	414	125	2639
Tiruvarur	288	50	283
Ariyalur	53	3	13
Coimbatore	77	4	26
Dharmapuri	817	8	189
Erode	117	24	613
Kanchipuram	204	25	509
Kanniyakumari	100	17	439
Krishnagiri	92	26	407
Madurai	81	14	328
Namakkal	110	29	443
Perambalur	66	27	297
Pudukkottai	148	8	78
Ramanathapuram	125	20	152
Salem	117	15	240
The Nilgiris	5	0	0
Theni	9	2	23
Thoothukkudi	137	12	202
Tiruchirappalli	291	122	1941
Tiruvallur	435	60	829
Vellore	208	0	0
Virudhunagar	15906	518	2640
Total	23583	1782	20025

Rural Employment Guarantee Scheme has been devoted for water bodies in various aspects. The percentage of women employment amounted to 76% and that of number of days of work and the amount derived out of it are 82% each respectively. Hence, the women are the most privileged beneficiaries under the scheme.

As far as the employment to the physically challenged is concerned, Virudhunagar holds first which is followed by Villupuram and Cuddalore, whereas the districts The Nilgiris and Vellore are not able to provide employment opportunities to the physically challenged.

Village Panchayat: The Panchayats at each level will be the 'Principal Authorities for planning and implementation of the Schemes. It is responsible for planning of works, registering households, issuing job cards, allocating employment, executing 50 per cent of the works, and monitoring the implementation of the Scheme at the village level. Village Panchayat must record on the Job Card about payment of wages without fail, the amount paid and the number of days for which payment has been made. In most places it is not recorded.

Preferred Works: In Tamil Nadu State, specific Schemes have listed eight works mentioned in NREGA. Tamil Nadu has identified irrigation and land development to be given priority. It is very important that States, according to their needs, fix up priority within the suggested list of works. Many experts also advocate such prioritization for improving the livelihood situation of most deprived sections of rural population.

Schedule of Rate: NREGA and Operational Guidelines provide that the State Governments should prepare Schedule or Rates on the basis of work, time and motion studies. Productivity norms should be devised in a way that normal work for seven hours results in earnings at least equal to the Minimum Wage applicable in the State. Experience from several States so far shows that DSR has not been prepared/ revised and tasks preferred under the NREGS for earning the Minimum Wage is difficult to perform and hidden portions of work is not taken into account. Thus average wage earned is less than the Minimum Wage prevailing in the State.

Persons with Disability: If a rural disabled person applies for work, work suitable to his/her ability and qualifications should be given. This may also be in the form of services that are identified as integral to the programme. Provisions of the Persons with Disabilities (Equal Opportunities, Protection of Rights and Full Participation) Act, 1995 are not implemented.

Inadequate Technical Help: It was found that lack of a Junior Engineer in the Block to provide Technical help has hampered the planning in the work to be undertaken. There is only one JE for each Block and he too is not available when required by Village Panchayats.

Facilities: If more than five children below the age of six years are present at the Worksite, a person (preferably a woman) should be engaged under REGS to look after them. Though most of the workers are women, Crèche facilities were nowhere to be seen, even at worksites with more than five children under the age of six. Drinking water is available at some places but dearth of shade is easily noticeable. In some places, they employ only women without children. There is no First-aid Box. Even if any minor accidents occur there is no immediate medical relief.

Irregularity, Corrupt Practices: In certain Districts, it was found that muster roll contained names of those people and presence was marked for those who were absent from the work, and it certain district the payment details are neither read out aloud nor made available for public scrutiny.

Lack of Adequate Human Resources: In Tamil Nadu exclusive Staff has not been appointed, and the Panchayat President along with all their other responsibilities is doing most of the work. The existing Village Panchayat Staff is overworked and is urgent need of assistance. Additional staff is also required for work measurement and payment of wages at the Block level.

Work Grievance Redressal Mechanism: Though the NREGA has a very well laid out Mechanism, in reality, the grievances of people are not addressed.

Weak Monitoring and absence of Social Audit: Fact finding data from Tamil Nadu indicate that there is no Vigilance Committee. Monitoring and Social Audit role of Gram Sabha is totally lacking, largely due to ignorance.

CONCLUSION

The National Rural Employment Guarantee Programme which was ewcently renamed as Mahatma Gandhi Rural Employment Guarantee Programme. Changing the design of schemes alone is not enough. Greater efforts are needed to build the capacity of administration and improve governance at the district level. The success of targeted poverty schemes in India is dependent upon proper identification of the beneficiaries, transparency, supervision over field staff, and social mobilization. Funds have more than tripled in the last ten years for poorer districts. And more than the capacity, one needs to examine if the States have the required will to improve themselves. Many States in India, especially the poorer ones, have lost the dynamism and capacity to undertake reforms on their own without any external pressure. These States are ruled by people who understand power, patronage, caste, transfers, money, coercion and crime. The language of professionalism, goal orientation, transparency, building up of institutions, and peoples' empowerment is totally alien to them. In these States neither politics nor administration has the capacity for self-correction, and therefore only external pressure can coerce them to take hard decisions that will hit at their money making tactics. In the Indian situation this can come only from the Centre, backed by strong civil society action. The concept of good governance should therefore be translated into a quantifiable annual index on the basis of certain agreed indicators, and central transfers should be linked to such an index.

RECOMMENDATIONS

- An 'Employment Guarantee Assistant' should be at the Village Panchayat Level.
- A Programme Officer should be appointed at the Block level with necessary support staff for facilitating implementation at the Block Level.
- A National-level Autonomous Body should be created solely for implementing the NREGA. The Body, called, says

the NREG Agency, should be fully empowered with the Financial and Implementing Authority.

- A State Level Autonomous Body should be set up to implement the Scheme.
- District level Grievance Committee should be constituted.
- Women Friendly Projects should be undertaken like Social forestation, horticulture, floriculture, and soil conservation.
- At present in the Scheme, in case the number of children below the age of six years accompanying the women working at any site is five or more, provision should be made to depute one of such women workers to look after such children. These children need nutritious food; for this the existing ICDS Centre should give supplementary food to these children
- As per the Act, wages should be paid on weekly basis.
- State Employment Guarantee Council should be constituted immediately.
- NREGA, which is being considered as an Act of the people, by the people and for the people. Therefore, the Scheme has to a large extent, to reach to the poor and needy.

REFERENCES

Himanshu (2007), Recent Trends in Poverty and Inequality: Some Preliminary Results. Economic and Political Weekly, February 10.

Sundaram K, Tendulkar SD. (2003), Poverty Among Social and Economic Groups in India in 1990s. Economic and Political Weekly December 13.

Sen A. (2004), Poverty and Inequality in India. Economic and Political Weekly September 18-24, 39 (38).

Ministry of Rural Development (2007), Government of India, New Delhi. Available from: http:// rural.nic.in, accessed on June 1.

http://finmin.nic.in, accessed on June 1, 2007.

http://planning commission.nic.in, accessed on June 1, 2007.

http://tribal.nic.in, accessed on June 1, 2007.

Government of India. Mid term appraisal of the 9th Plan (1997-2002). New Delhi: Planning Commission; 2000.Available from:http://planningcommission.gov.in/plans/mta/midch5d.htm and midch3.htm.

http://www.righttofoodinida.com, accessed on June 1, 2007.

Government of India, 2005, Evaluation of the TPDS, PEO. New Delhi: Planning Commission, http://planningcommission.nic.in/reports/peoreport/pco/peo_tpds.pdf.

NSS 61st round. New Delhi: Government of India, Ministry of Statistics and Programme Implementation; 2006.

www.nrega.nic.in

Bavadam, Lyla (2003), "Undermining a Scheme", Frontline, 2 August.

Krishnaraj, M, Pandey, P., and Kanchi, A. (2004), "Does EGS Require Restructuring for Poverty Alleviation and Gender Equality?" Economic and Political Weekly, 17 April.

Reddy, C. Rammanohar, and Vijayshankar, P. (2004), "Making Employment Guarantee a Reality", forthcoming in Seminar.

The New Indian Express, October 25, 2009

23

Women Component Plan

R. Srinivasan

In a welfare state, the overall development of all the sections of society is the primary objective of the Government but due to various socio-economic reasons, a large scale of disparity is prevailing amongst women and female child constituting about 47 percent of the total population . The Government has taken up several initiatives to reduce gender inequity for obviating the discriminatory practices towards them but their impact has been for below the expectations. Realising this, the Government has changed its approach from 'welfare during fifties' to 'Development during Seventies' and to Empowerment during the Nineties'. During the Nineties major thrust in respect of women was to make them economically independent and self reliant while in respect of children, efforts were made to ensure their survival protection and development with special focus on the girl child and adolescent girl. Constitution of India have also given support and strength to them. Both 73rd and 74th Constitutional Amendments in 1993 have empowered women by ensuring their one-third participation in the grass root democracy through the Panchayati Raj Institutions and Local bodies.

The Ninth Plan (1997-2002) made two significant changes in the conceptual strategy of planning for women. Firstly, empowerment of women became one of the primary objectives of the Ninth Plan and secondly, it attempted "convergence of existing services" available in both women-specific and women- related sectors. To this effect, a strategy of "Women Component Plan" was initiated which suggested to keep a constant vigil on the flow of earmarked funds/benefits and ensure that it brings forth a holistic approach towards empowering women.

Important achievement along with the problems and gaps in the core sectors of health, demography, education, employment, decision making nutrition and political participation are given in the following paragraphs.

Population by Sex and Sex Ratio 1991-2001

Year	*Population*			*Sex Ratio*	*Sex Ratio 0- 6 Years*
	Persons	*Male*	*Females*		
1991	13.91	7.40	6.51	876	927
2001	16.62	8.76	7.86	898	916

POPULATION

As per 2001 census, the population of U.P. stands at 16.62 Cr comprising of 8.76 Cr. (52.67 percent) males and 7.86 Cr (47.33 percent) females. The female population in the State grew at a rate of 27.5% during the decade 1991-2001 against a growth rate of 25.8% in the total population.

- Sex Ratio Sex ratio is largely attributed to lower status of women which contributes to early marriages, lower literacy levels, higher fertility and mortality levels and affects adversely progress in human development.
- The Sex ratio which was 876 in 1991 has increased to 898 in 2001, but there has been a decline in the ratio in the age group 0-6 years. It was 927 in 1991 which has declined to 916 in 2001. some of the important for this decline can be

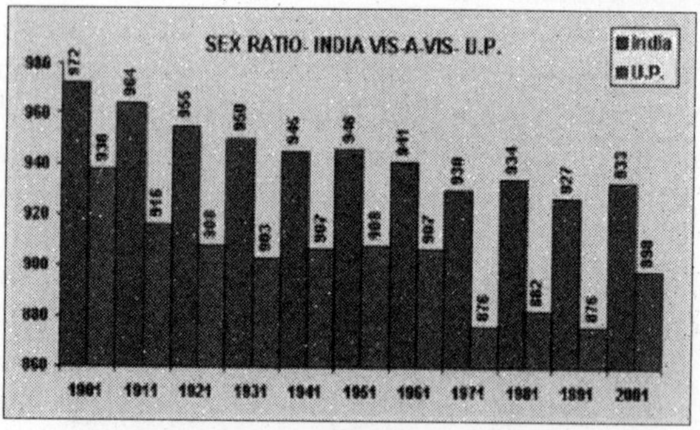

Fig. 1

— Neglect of the girl child resulting in their higher mortality at younger ages, high maternal mortality
— Sex selective female abortions,
— Female infanticide

LITERACY

According to the 2001 census, the literacy rate for the State is 56.3 percent with 68.8 percent for males and 42.2 percent for females. Corresponding rates in 1991 census were 40.71, 54.82 and 24.37 percentage respectively. There is, thus, an overall gain of 15.59 percentage points while gain in literacy for females (17.83 percentage points) is higher than that of males (13.98 percentage points). Though overall improvement in the

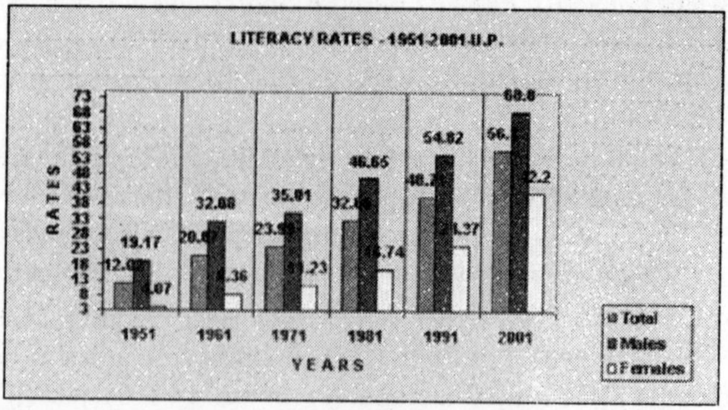

Fig. 2

literacy rate in case of males is less than females, yet the proportion of literates among males is higher than females. Census data also indicates that the discrimination is male and female literacy was nearly 15.10 percentage points in 1951 which widened to 30.45 percentage points in 1991 and than reduced to 27.35 percentage points in 2001 census. There are 37 districts which have recorded literacy rate above the State average. The Government has fixed a target of 75% literacy by the end of Tenth Plan. This target can be achieved by enrolling all the children in primary schools upto the year 2004.

WORKER POPULATION RATIO

Census data indicates that 16.3 percent of women are workers as compared to 40.74 percent of men. This is because 'work' has been defined as participation in any economic productive activity. by this definition much of the unpaid work that women do gets eclipsed. The majority of women are engaged in household duties and thus fall into the category of non workers. In organized sector the representation of women workers was only 7.8% (2-11 lakh) during 1991 which increased to 9.4% (2.39 lakh) by the end of 2001. The NSS data indicates that 4.8% of rural female labour force and 3.9% of urban female labour force were unemployed on weekly status. The corresponding rate at daily status were 5.5 and 4.8 percent respectively. The extent of under employment for females is also greater as compared to males. Therefore the focus of employment policy should be on raising the income levels of already employed through improvement of productivity and generation of additional supplementary employment opportunities. Employment programmes should be evolved keeping the employment requirement of women particularly in the rural areas.

	Worker Population Ratio%	
Census Year	*Male*	*Female*
1981	50.0	5.0
1991	49.7	12.3
2001	47.4	16.3

PARTICIPATION IN DECISION MAKING AND GOVERNANCE

The women can be empowered in real sense only when they are actively involved in decision making and adequate weightage is given to their say in the governance. In these lines decentralisation of governance through the 73rd and 74th Constitutional amendments have given political power to them through which one third of the post were kept reserved for them. As against this reservation overwhelming response from women resulted in recent elections and more than 33% women's were elected for different posts. In Panchayati Raj Institution, 53.62% females are chairperson Zila Panchayat, 37.06% member Zila Panchayat, 36.71% chairperson Kshetra Panchayat, 35.82 member Kshettra Panchayat, 35.32% Gram Pradhan and 37.95% of females member Gram Panchayat.

HEALTH STATUS

An Analysis of Reproductive Health Index (Comprising TFR,IMR, Female literacy, birth interval, medical attention at birth) reveals that U.P. stands at the bottom. The maximum RHI value is observed in Kerala (84.6) and minimum in U.P. (22.8)

Improvement in health status has been one of the major thrust areas in the social development. This can be achieved through improving the access to health services with special focus on female population. Two basic indicators namely infant mortality rate and life expectancy at birth can be used in analysing the health status.

The Infant mortality rate indicates the level of human development index in the context of education, economic condition, nutrition, poverty, mal nutrition, decline in breast feeding and lack of sanitation facilities. As per SRS 1998 for Uttar Pradesh this rate is 92.9 for girls and 78.8 for boys which is far above than the corresponding rates (73.5 and 69.8) at national level.

Life expectancy at birth or longevity is an overall indicator of economic and social well being of people. This rate is 61.1 years for women and 61.2 for men in Uttar Pradesh whereas these rates are 63.4 and 62.4 years respectively at national level.

VISION

It shall be the prime concern of the state to bolster the self confidence and esteem of women so that their undisputed identity is re-established in the society. Emphasis will be made to uplift their socio-economic status so that their contribution to the developmental process is duly recognized. To improve the quality of life of women with unequivocal and explicit emphasis on sustainable development measures and actions, emphasis shall be for :

- Female education, particularly for the girl child.
- Health and nutrition of women
- Economic empowerment
- Social and political empowerment
- Social security and protection.

REPRODUCTIVE HEALTH CARE

In reproductive health care efforts will be made to reach the following targets as fixed for women and children in the Population Policy of Uttar Pradesh 2000 :

- To reduce TFR from 4.3 in 1997 to 2.6 in 2011 and further to replacement level of facility (2.1) in 2016
- Substantially reduce unmet need for both spacing and terminal method use from 56 percent in 1998-99 to 20 percent in 2011 and to 10 percent in 2016.
- To reduce maternal mortality rate from 707 in 1997 to 394 in 2010 and further to below 250 in 2016.
- Increase antenatal care coverage from 46 percent in 1997 to 78 percent in 2011 and further to 90 percent in 2016.
- Increase institutional deliveries from 17% in 1997 to 45 percent in 2011 and further to 55 percent in 2016.
- To reduce the IMR from 85 in 1997 to 67 in 2011 and further to 61 in 2016.
- Increase complete immunization of children from 42% in 1997 to 85 % in 2011 and to all children in 2016.

STRATEGY

- Awareness generation at all levels and their confidence building Ensure effective inter-sectoral convergence. Increase the median age of marriage for women by increasing awareness about the legal age of marriage for males as well as females. Ensure that the panchayats maintain the records of all marriages in their jurisdiction.
- To reduce maternal mortality rate, increase ante-natal coverage, increase TT coverage, increase institutional deliveries, reduce mild and moderate anaemia and creating pregnancy testing facility at all PHC and CHC by 2011 AD. Strengthen the systems to identify pregnant mothers at risk and referral systems to attend to high risk cases. For this active support of the ICDS infrastructure will be extended to all the blocks of the State.
- Encourage increase use of modern contraceptives and encourage all couples with unmet need to use terminal or spacing methods based on their choice and to substantially reduce the current unmet need, increase the number of new users of sterilization services and providing spacing services to more couples. Involve NGOs and corporate sector to implement innovative reproductive health programmes.
- All efforts to be made to implement the programme of univeralisation of primary education for all and especially for girls and ensure their retention in schools upto to the secondary level. Special efforts will be conducted to make the community aware of the importance of female education.
- Added importance will be given to formation of Self Help Groups (SHGs) exclusively for women and the groups already formed will be further strengthened. Adequate training and linkage facility with banks should be provided the these groups. Voluntary Organisations with development projects funded by the Government/ International institutions will be encouraged to constitute SHGs in the project areas. Enhance women's income,

earning opportunities through improved access to credit, training , technology, market support etc and freeing them from the drudgery and time spent on household chores such as fuel, fodder and water collection etc.

- Strict implementation of the existing Pre-natal Diagnostics Techniques Regulation Act. 1994 will be ensured.
- Working Women's Hostels and Women's polytechnics will be opened in major cities in a phased manner to increase their participation in secondary and tertiary sectors.
- Panchayats will be strengthened and empowered to fulfill their role with respect to programme implementation, supervision and monitoring.

PROGRAMMES & FORTHCOMING STRATEGIES

Various economic and welfare programmes being implemented for their social and economic empowerment can be categorised under following heads:

Empowering Strategies

The erstwhile programme of Indira Mahila Yojana launched in 1995 was recasted into an integrated programme for women's empowerment renamed as *Swayamsidha* in 2001. The vision of Integrated Women's Empowerment Programme (IWEP) is to develop empowered women who will demand their rights from family, community and government, have increased access to and control over material, social and political resources, have enhanced awareness and improved skills.

The immediate objectives of the schemes are establishment of self-reliant women's SHGs, creation of confidence building and awareness among members of SHGs, their control over economic resources, improving access of women to micro-credit, involvement of women in local planning and convergence of services of Department of Women and Child Development and other departments.

Another project called *Swa-shakti* (earlier known as Rural Women's Development and Empowerment project) is being implemented in the State since October, 1998 as a centrally sponsored project. The objectives of the project are :

- Establishment of 5200 Swa-shakti groups (self-reliant women's self help groups) having 10-20 members each which will improve the quality of their lives, through greater access to and control over resources;
- Sensitising and strengthening the institutional capacity of support agencies to pro-actively address women's needs;
- Continued access to credit facilities for income generation activities;
- Enhancing women's access to resources for better quality of life, including those of drudgery reduction and time saving devices; and
- Increased control of women, particularly poor women over income and spending through their involvement in income generation activities.

In cooperative sector, Mahila dairy programme nurtures leadership amongst women dairy farmers for their economic and social empowerment besides ensuring their say in the governance of cooperative societies.

Swarn Jayanti Gram Swarojgar Yojna (SJGSY) is yet another scheme which is meant for bringing the beneficiary family above the poverty line by providing them income generating assets through a mix of bank credit and government subsidy by organising the rural poors in self help groups. It is envisaged that 50 percent of the SHGs must be formed exclusively by women.

In the field of education, efforts are made towards universalisation of elementary education which resulted in significant improvement in the enrolment of girls in school and reduction in drop-out rates at all level. Total literacy compaign, non-formal education and nutritional support to primary education programme have accelerated this process.

Employment and Income Generation

The programme of Support to Training cum Employment Programme (STEP) was launched in 1987 to strengthen and improve the skills for employment opportunities for women below poverty line in traditional sectors of agriculture, animal husbandry, dairying, fisheries, handlooms, handicrafts, cottage and village industries, sericulture, social forestry and wasteland development where women are employed on a large scale.

The scheme of Training cum Employment Production Centres was launched in 1982-83 with the assistance from Norwegian Agency for Development Cooperation (NORAD). This scheme has been renamed as Women's Empowerment Programme(WEP) from 2002-03. Under this programme, financial assistance is given to Women's Development Corporations, Public Sector Corporations, autonomous bodies and voluntary organizations to train poor women mostly in non traditional trades to ensure their employment in these areas. Some of these trades are computer programming, electronics, watch assembling, radio and television repairs, garment making, secretarial practices, community health workers, embroidery and weaving. Financial assistance is given to grantee organizations.

In order to increase women s wage employment and self employment opportunities, village and small scale industries department have also designed 'Entrepreneurial development training programmes' to develop Entrepreneurial skill, training and skill upgradation.

Welfare and Support Services

The programme of Working Women's Hostels launched in 1972-73 aims to promote reasonable rented and safe accommodation to working women belonging to low income groups who migrate to cities for employment. In some hostels, day-care centers for children of these women are also attached. Presently, 42 hostels are being run in the state.

Another programme launched by the Government of India in 1969 called Short Stay Homes for the protection and rehabilitation of those women and girls who are facing family problems, mental strains, social ostracism and exploitation and who need shelter while they adjust and cope with their personal situations. The scheme envisages for provision of services/facilities viz., medical care, psychiatric treatment, counseling, occupational therapy, education, vocational and creational activities and social facilities for adjustment.

Under the scheme of Swadhar, two ashrey sadans have been established in Vrindavan, Mathura for women 'in distress. It is also envisaged to construct a complex for them where they would be provided shelter, health facilities and vocational training. Construction of one such home is in progress at Vrindavan for which assistance has been received from Government of India.

Grant in aid of Rs. 125/- pm is given to 494585 widows having an income of less than Rs. 1000/- per month and have no one to look after them. Under widow remarriage scheme , a grant in aid of Rs.11,000/- is given to persons marrying widows.

ICDS is yet another scheme which is being implemented in 609 development blocks of the State for the purposes of development of children in the age group 0-6 years, adolescent girls and pregnant and lactating mothers. This scheme has been included in PMGY under which additional central assistance has been providing since 2000-01 for supplementary nutrition to the children in the age group 6 months to 3 years. Supplementary nutrition is also provided to school going children under mid day meal programmes.

Introduction of Kishori Shakti Yojana as an enriched version of the scheme for adolescent girls being implmented as part of ICDS to improve the nutritional and health status of girls in the age group 11-18 years. This scheme equips them with vocational skills so that they can be gainfully engaged.

Under the National Social Assistance Programme, special recognition is given to women- specific needs. Under this programme, National Maternity Benefit Scheme is launched which exclusively aims at extending financial assistance of Rs 300 to pregnant women for the first two live births. Likewise under the programme of Old Age Pension scheme, elderly women of 65 years age and above with no regular means of subsistence also received the benefit of old age pension to the extent of Rs. 125 per month. Under another scheme of National Family Benefit, women could receive financial assistance of Rs 5000 to Rs 10000 in the event of death of the prime bread earner of the family.

In order to put an end to all forms of discrimination against girl child, a specific scheme 'Balika Samridhi Yojna' have been designed under which special incentives have been provided to the mother and girl child so that birth of girt child is welcomed. Under this scheme an incentive of Rs 500 is given to mother on the delivery of girl child and annual scholarship to the girl children in class I to X.

Under the Scholarship Schemes, scholarship to the girl students belonging to Scheduled Caste/Scheduled Tribe/ OBC/ Minority living below poverty line is being provided while she is attending the school.

WOMEN COMPONENT PLAN: FINANCIAL AND PHYSICAL TARGETS AND ACHIEVEMENTS

In order to implement the above mentioned programmes a strategy of Women Component Plan is initiated to assure that not less than 30% of the funds/benefits flow to women. The total outlay allocated for the Tenth Plan is Rs.1499.83 crore. The sectorwise outlay and expenditure during the Annual Plan 2003-04 and proposed outlay for 2004-05 is given in the following table.

Women Component Plan:Outlay and Expenditure

(Rs. in Lakh)

Sectors	*Tenth Plan Agreed Outlay*	*Annual Plan 2005-06*		*Annual Plan 2006-07 Proposed Outlay*
		Approved Outlay	*Anticipated Expenditure*	
Animal Husbandry	50.00	0.50	0.50	0.52
Dairy	300.00	24.00	8.00	10.00
Rural Development	21800.00	1760.00	1629.66	1936.24
Khadi & Village Industry	150.00	50.00	46.97	52.15
Village & Small Industries	60.00	20.00	20.00	20.00

Contd.

Sectors	Tenth Plan Agreed Outlay	Annual Plan 2005-06 Approved Outlay	Annual Plan 2005-06 Anticipated Expenditure	Annual Plan 2006-07 Proposed Outlay
Elementary Education		-	-	-
Secondary Education	4600.00	1196.23	102.00	23745.60
Technical Education	5395.95	1459.23	365.00	263.00
Water Supply and Sanitation	1815.70	10.00	3.43	..
Urban Development	300.00	40.00	26.20	40.00
Welfare of Scheduled Castes	18071.95	2503.36	2133.71	5754.29
Welfare of Scheduled Tribes	1120.45	112.68	56.33	71.07
Welfare of Denotified Tribes	140.00	31.60	17.70	22.50
Welfare of Other Backward classes	20277.00	11626.12	414.65	343.54
Minority Welfare	182.00	159.00	159.00	156.00
Social Welfare	17790.00	3453.00	5136.00	5309.00
Welfare of Handicapped	225.00	233.29	210.00	278.00
Women Welfare	3000.00	1303.00	925.83	1422.18
Nutrition	77947.00	10000.00	9855.82	9229.00
Grand Total:Women Component Plan	159973.22	22774.31	20937.69	68606.55

Poverty Alliviation Programmes for Women With Special Reference to DWCRA Programme in Kurnool District

24

R. Seenivasan

INTRODUCTION

Eradication of poverty has been the overriding objective since the beginning of economic planning in India. Eradication of poverty through overall economic and social development by ensuring equitable access in resources and skills, as well as by widening the opportunities for gainful employment to the deprived sections of the society, is enunciated as the principal objective of all the rural development programmes initiated by the government. It has assumed significance more so in the context of ongoing economic reforms due to the apprehensions that the short-run impact of reforms may not be favourable for the eradication of poverty. It is known that economic growth alone is not sufficient to reduce poverty and there is a need for direct State intervention for poverty eradication.

A number of rural development schemes and programmes have been formulated and implemented from time to time as measures to attack rural poverty. But it was realized that these programmes could not deliver the desired results and suffered from a number of defects. There is also evidence to the fact that the poverty has declined due to the target oriented Poverty

Alleviation Programmes (PAPs) in the late 1980s, despite deceleration in agriculture growth (Parthasarathy, 1995; Kannan, 1995). On the other hand, there is an argument that an exclusive focus on poverty eradication programmes, in the absence of good macro-economic policies resulting in sustained growth is likely to have short-lived success at best (UNDP, 1999). Hence, it is felt that the poverty alleviation programmes should contribute for economic growth (Rao, 1992).

The defects in the prevailing policy framework, including its preoccupation with the immediate gains has resulted in the over exploitation of natural resources for achieving agricultural growth and reducing rural poverty. On account of the degradation of land and depletion of ground water resources following deforestation, it is becoming increasingly difficult to sustain agricultural growth and rural poverty reduction without imposing a heavy cost on the society and on the future generations. In order to make poverty reduction process sustainable, significant initiatives have been brought over recently to create congenial environment for poverty alleviation in terms of decentralization to strengthen panchayat raj institutions and group approach through the formation of women self-help groups. These initiatives are to ensure people's active participation in planning, implementation and post-implementation processes. There is a need to assess the impact of these initiatives on poverty eradication process. Further, though there are evaluation studies, concurrent and expost, they are focused on individual components of poverty alleviation programmes and do not take cognizance of all the components. This is required due to the fact that the focus of all the PAPs on each of the poor may increase the probability of the sustainability of poverty reduction process. Moreover, there are no attempts in the evaluation studies so far conducted to examine the poverty reduction as a process so that the contributing factors for poverty reduction can be identified. In this backdrop, the present study is proposed to assess the performance of PAPs in the State of Andhra Pradesh.

The PAPs can be grouped into five categories. They are: income enhancement programmes–self employment programmes which include IRDP, DWCRA and TRYSEM and wage employment programmes which include JRY and EAS; programmes which focus on providing food and nutritional security viz., PDS and ICDS; programmes which provide basic minimum services-housing, sanitation, health, education and income maintenance programmes viz., pension schemes, maternity benefit scheme and survival benefit scheme and natural resource management and livelihoods. Most of the PAPs are designed by the centre and implemented by the State on fund sharing basis for financing the programmes. The State of Andhra Pradesh has its own programmes.

DEVELOPMENT OF WOMEN AND CHILDREN IN RURAL AREAS (DWCRA)

Women constitute 48.1 percent of the country's population. They are playing important role in various fields such as agriculture, dairy farming, handicraft etc., but their contribution in these fields has not been viewed as economic activity. A large number of them work in the primary sector as unskilled workforce and get wages lower than men. A large number of women are illiterate, hence most of them suffer from economic subjugation, powerlessness, isolation, vulnerability, and poverty.

The issues of economic upliftment of women and their empowerment were also included in the IRDP and JRY, aimed at providing durable assets and employment generation during the lean periods. In practice however, participation of women in all these schemes remained very low.

The long term objective of DWCRA programme is to improve the survival of young children and women and the quality of their lives, and to achieve a significant growth in the income of poor women through appropriate interventions and to organize women in groups to create a demand pull on the existing delivery system along with creation of awareness to strengthen their bargaining capabilities.

Keeping the long term objective in view, the programme emphasises on strengthening the women component by raising the income levels of poor women and enabling them for organized participation in social development and economic self reliance. The programme, through formation of groups aims at improving the women's access to basic services of health, childcare, education, water, nutrition and sanitation.

PROBLEM

Several studies were conducted on the status and empowerment of women in a general way but didn't touch the impact of DWCRA Programme on the lives of rural women. Hence, on attempt is made to know how far this DWCRA programme has helped the rural women to overcome the poverty in Kurnool District of Andhra Pradesh.

Kurnool geographically is the third largest district in Andhra Pradesh and is the largest in Rayalaseema. It is one of the four ceded di9stricts, formed by the Nizam of the British in the year 1800 A.D. With the formation of the Andhra state in 1953, the Western Boundary of this district was extended by addition of Adoni and Alur Taluks of Bellary district. The District divided into 3 Revenue Divisions. They are Kurnool, Nandyal and Adoni. At present Kurnool district comprises 54 Revenue Mandals and 53 Mandals Praja Parishads with three administrative divisions. The DWCRA Programme was under Implementation in Kurnool District from 1983 and 450 women who provided assets during the period 2000-2004 were selected based on Random sampling. The scheme wise distribution of sample beneficiaries are presented in Table 1.

Out of the total women beneficiaries selected at the District Level 10.67 per cent of the women beneficiaries are engaged in Flower Vending, 5.55 per cent of the beneficiaries are engaged in Milch Animals, 4.89 per cent of the beneficiaries are engaged in Hotels, 4.44 per cent of the beneficiaries are engaged in Tailoring, 8.89 per cent of the beneficiaries are engaged in Vegetable Vending, 8.44 per cent of the beneficiaries are engaged in Ram Lamb Rearing, 6.67 per cent of the beneficiaries are engaged in Plough Bullocks, 5.78 per cent of the beneficiaries are engaged in Chappals Making, 6.22 per cent of the beneficiaries are engaged in Kirana Shop, 4.67 per cent of the beneficiaries are engaged in Bunk and Trade, 5.11 per cent of the beneficiaries are engaged in Bangle Vending

Table 1

Particulars of Scheme Wise Distribution of the Selected Beneficiaries of DWCRA in Kurnool District

Name of the Scheme	*No. of Beneficiaries in Developed Mandal*	*No. of Beneficiaries in Moderately Developed Mandal*	*No. of Beneficiaries in Less Developed Mandal*	*All Mandals/ at the Dist., Level*
Flower Vending	27(18.00)	0.00(0.00)	21(14.00)	48(10,67)
Milch Animal	25(16.67)	0.00(0.00)	0.00(0.00)	25(5.55)
Hotel	22(14.67)	0.00(0.00)	0.00(0.00)	22(4.89)
Tailoring	20(13.33)	0.00(0.00)	0.00(0.00)	20(4.44)
Vegetable Vending	24(16.00)	0.00(0.00)	16(10.67)	40(8.89)
Ram Lamb Rearing	19(12.67)	0.00(0.00)	19(12.66)	38(8.44)
Plough Bullocks	13(8.66)	17(11.33)	0.00(0.00)	30(6.67)
Chappals Making	0.00(0.00)	26(17.33)	0.00(0.00)	26(5.78)
Kirana Shop	0.00(0.00)	28(18.67)	0.00(0.00)	28(6.22)
Bunk and Trade	0.00(0.00)	21(14.00)	0.00(0.00)	21(4.67)
Bangle Vending Shop	0.00(0.00)	23(15.34)	0.00(0.00)	23(5.11)
Mulbury Plantation	0.00(0.00)	18(12.00)	0.00(0.00)	18(4.00)
Sericulture	0.00(0.00)	17(11.33)	18(12.00)	35(7.79)
Sheep Rearing	0.00(0.00)	0.00(0.00)	27(18.00)	27(6.00)
Petty Trade	0.00(0.00)	0.00(0.00)	17(11.33)	17(3.78)
Basket Making	0.00(0.00)	0.00(0.00)	16(10.67)	16(3.55)
Fruits Vending	0.00(0.00)	0.00(0.00)	16(10.67)	16(3.55)
TOTAL	150(100.00)	150(100.00)	150(100.00)	450(100.00)

Source: Primary Data from the field Survey.
(Figures in Brackets are Percentage to totals)

Shop, 4.00 Per cent of the beneficiaries are engaged in Mulbury Plantation, 7.79 per cent of the beneficiaries are engaged in Sericulture, 6.00 per cent of the beneficiaries in Sheep Rearing, 3.78 per cent of the beneficiaries in Petty Trade, 3.55 per cent of the beneficiaries in Basket Making and 3.55 per cent of the beneficiaries are engaged in Fruits Vending. It is praise worthy that beneficiaries are engaged in different categories and availed themselves loans from DWCRA in the District.

Particulars of income of the selected women beneficiaries before joining in DWCRA are presented in Table 2.

At the District Level 32.00 per cent of the women beneficiaries have income of Rs.6,000, 30.67 per cent of the beneficiaries have income in between Rs.6,001 to 8,500, 17.55 per cent of the beneficiaries have income in between Rs.8,501, to Rs.12,000, 14.23 per cent of the beneficiaries have income of Rs.12,000, and above. 5.55 per cent of the beneficiaries do not have any income.

The analysis of income of the beneficiaries after joining in DWCRA is presented in Table 3.

At the District Level 17.55 per cent of the women beneficiaries have income below Rs.6,000, 20.44 per cent of the beneficiaries have income between Rs.6,001 to 8,500, 28.89 per cent of the beneficiaries have income between Rs.8,501, to Rs.12,000, 33.12 per cent of the beneficiaries have an income of Rs.12,000, and above. In order to know whether the generated income from DWCRA is significant or not, the paired 't' test was applied.

Observed Value t = 42.21 > Table Value = 1.96

The null hypothesis is rejected at 5 percent probability value.

∴ Hence it is inferred that there is significant growth in Income Generation of Sample Women Beneficiaries in Kurnool District after the implementation of DWCRA programme.

The particulars of employment of women beneficiaries before joining in DWCRA are presented in Table 4.

Table 2

Particulars of Income of the Selected Beneficiaries Before Joining in DWCRA in Kurnool Distrct

Level of Income	*No. of Beneficiaries in Developed Mandal*	*No. of Beneficiaries in Moderately Developed Mandal*	*No. of Beneficiaries in Less Developed Mandal*	*No. of Beneficiaries at the Dist., Level*
Below 6000	56(37.33)	50(33.33)	38(25.33)	144(32.00)
6001 to 8,500	48(32.00)	48(32.00)	42(28.00)	138(30.67)
8,501to 12,000	20(13.34)	28(18.67)	31(20.67)	79(17.55)
12,000 and above	17(11.33)	12(8.00)	35(23.33)	67(14.23)
No Income	9(6.00)	12(8.00)	4(2.67)	25(5.55)
TOTAL	150(100.00)	150(100.00)	150(100.00)	450(100.00)

Source: Primary Data from the field Survey
(Figures in Brackets are Percentage to totals)

Table 3
Particulars of Income of the Selected Beneficiaries After Joing in Dwcra in Kurnool District

Level of Income	*No. of Beneficiaries in Developed Mandal*	*No. of Beneficiaries in Moderately Developed Mandal*	*No. of Beneficiaries in Less Developed Mandal*	*No. of Beneficiaries at the Dist., Level*
Below 6000	31(20.67)	24(16.00)	24(16.00)	79(17.55)
6001 to 8,500	24(16.00)	31(20.67)	37(24.67)	92(20.44)
8,501 to 12,000	42(28.00)	51(34.00)	37(24.67)	130(28.89)
12,000 and above	53(35.33)	44(29.33)	52(34.66)	149(33.12)
No Income	0.00(0.00)	0.00(0.00)	0.00(0.00)	0.00(0.00)
TOTAL	150(100.00)	150(100.00)	150(100.00)	450(100.00)

Source: Primary Data from the field Survey
(Figures in Brackets are Percentage to totals)

Table 4

Particulars of Employment the Selected Beneficiaries Before Joing in DWCRA in Kurnool District

No. of Man days	*No. of Beneficiaries in Developed Mandal*	*No. of Beneficiaries in Moderately Developed Mandal*	*No. of Beneficiaries in Less Developed Mandal*	*No. of Beneficiaries at the Dist., Level*
0 to 100 days	48(32.00)	58(38.67)	48(32.00)	154(34.22)
101 to 180 days	58(38.67)	56(37.33)	41(27.33)	155(34.44)
181 to 240 days	32(21.33)	22(14.67)	30(20.00)	84(18.67)
241 and Above	12(8.00)	14(9.33)	31(20.67)	57(12.67)
TOTAL	150(100.00)	150(100.00)	150(100.00)	450(100.00)

Source: Primary Data from the field Survey
(Figures in Brackets are Percentage to totals)

At the District Level 34.22 per cent of the women beneficiaries have employment in between 0 to 100 days, 34.44 per cent of the beneficiaries have employment in between 101 to 180 days, 18.67 per cent of the beneficiaries have employment in between 181 to 240 days and 12.67per cent of the beneficiaries have employment of 240 days and above.

The particulars of employment of women beneficiaries after joining in DWCRA are presented in Table 5.

At the District Level 14.89 per cent of the beneficiaries have employment in between 0 to 100 days, 20.89 per cent of the beneficiaries have employment in between 101 to 180 days, 27.33 per cent of the beneficiaries have employment in between 181 to 240 days and 36.89 per cent of the beneficiaries have employment of 241 days and above. To know whether the generated employment is significant or not, paired 't' test was applied.

Observed Value of t = 39.18 > Table Value = 1.96

The null hypothesis is rejected at 5 percent probability value.

∴ Hence it is inferred that there is significant growth in the Employment Generation of Sample Women Beneficiaries in Kurnool District after the implementation of DWCRA programme.

Particulars of the increase in income of the selected women beneficiaries of DWCRA at the district level are presented in Table 6.

It is clear from the table 6 that out of the 450 women beneficiaries 269 women beneficiaries could increase their income after the implementation of DWCRA programme in the district and it is significant to note that there were 25 women beneficiaries who had no income at all before the implementation of DWCRA programme and all the 25 women beneficiaries are now getting income after the implementation of DWCRA programme.

Particulars of the increase in employment of the selected women beneficiaries of DWCRA at the district level are presented in Table 7.

Table 5

Particulars of Employment of the Selected Beneficiaries After Joing in DWCRA in Kurnool Distrct

No. of Man days	*No. of Beneficiaries in Developed Mandal*	*No. of Beneficiaries in Moderately Developed Mandal*	*No. of Beneficiaries in Less Developed Mandal*	*No. of Beneficiaries at the Dist., Level*
0 to 100 days	21(14.00)	22(14.67)	24(16.00)	67(14.89)
101 to 180 days	27(18.00)	37(24.67)	30(20.00)	94(20.89)
181 to 240 days	42(28.00)	39(26.00)	42(28.00)	123(27.33)
241 and Above	60(40.00)	52(34.66)	54(36.00)	166(36.89)
TOTAL	150(100.00)	150(100.00)	150(100.00)	450(100.00)

Source: Primary Data from the field Survey
(Figures in Brackets are Percentage to totals)

Table 6
Particulars of Increase in Income of the Selected Beneficiaries of DWCRA in Kurnool District

	Before DWCRA	*After DWCRA*	
Income Level	*No. of Beneficiaries at the District Level*	*No. of Beneficiaries at the District Level*	*Difference*
Below 6000	144(32.00)	79(17.55)	65(24.16)
6001 to 8,500	138(30.67)	92(20.44)	46(17.10)
8,501to 12,000	79(17.55)	130(28.89)	51(18.96)
12,000 and above	67(14.23)	149(33.12)	82(30.49)
No Income	25(5.55)	0.00(0.00)	25(9.29)
Total	450(100.00)	450(100.00)	269(100.00)

Source: Primary Data from the field Survey.
(Figures in Brackets are Percentage to totals)

Table 7
Particulars of the Increase in Employment of the Selected Beneficiaries of DWCRA in Kurnool District

	Before DWCRA	*After DWCRA*	
No. of Man days	*No. of Beneficiaries at the District Level*	*No. of Beneficiaries at the District Level*	*Difference*
0 to 100 days	154(34.22)	67(14.89)	87(29.39)
101 to 180 days	155(34.44)	94(20.89)	61(20.61)
181 to 240 days	84(18.67)	123(27.33)	39(13.18)
241 and above	57(12.67)	166(36.89)	109(36.82)
Total	450(100.00)	450(100.00)	296(100.00)

Source: Primary Data from the field Survey
(Figures in Brackets are Percentage to totals)

The Table 7, clearly shows that out of the 450 selected women beneficiaries 296 women beneficiaries could improve their employment opportunities after the implementation of DWCRA programme and it is significant to note that the women beneficiaries who had the employment in the range of 241days and above are more in number when compared to others.

CONCLUSION

Most of the Poverty Alleviation Programmes are designed by the centre and implemented by state including DWCRA Programme. Majority of the women in Kurnool District are engaged in schemes like Flower vending, Vegetable vending and Ram lamb rearing and the income from these schemes is very low. It is evident from the study that 33.12 per cent of the women beneficiaries could generate an income of Rs.12,000/- and above. With regard to employment 36.89 per cent of the women beneficiaries could generate employment of 240 days and above. From this study one can assess the impact of this programme on women only when the programme yields the income and employment significantly and it happened in Kurnool District.

Whether NREGP is a Hot to Achieve Inclusive Growth?

25

M. Perumal, J. Mohan Raj, R. Nanda Kumar

INTRODUCTION

NREGA breaking new ground Suddenly it has become a buzz word. It stands vindicated by the mandate of the people in its most basic evaluation in a democracy - the general elections. Basking in the glory and security of post - electoral analysis, it is actually the best time for those who support the basic philosophy of the NREGA to focus on what it has done and what it has not, by its own parameters.

The first and the primary focus should be to examine its impact on the human resource base of rural India. Has it energized, mobilized, empowered, and delivered to India's poorest and most marginalized rural people? Secondly, has it provided those who were "not shining" a measure of dignity, tangible economic benefit, and motivation to participate in local action? This is the crux, for, something as vast and ambitious as the NREGA can only succeed in bringing about change if millions of workers become its true advocates and monitors.

Let us begin with the most persistent charges endemic corruption. Notwithstanding negative propaganda and the prominent reportage of corruption, NREGA stands apart from employment and poverty alleviation programmes in significant ways. It is the first national programme of consequence which has woven transparency and accountability into the mundane fabric of daily interaction of people with government. The cases of reported corruption have shocked the intelligentsia. The rural worker might often be the victim but will still offer critical support, not only because it has provided wage income, but also for facilitating disclosure, which helps identify and fight pilferage. In fact in many cases, scams have been exposed by the workers themselves. NREGA gives an opportunity to break the feudally enforced silence of its victims. Through transparency and social audit measures, it allows anyone, anywhere to be part of the monitoring of the delivery system. The other programmes appear to be clean only because no one knows what goes on! The NREGA gives a further opportunity to realize the constitutional sovereignty, the power of the people. What the political establishment would do well to understand is that the vote was not a blind endorsement, but the expression of a fragile hope of a rational participatory relationship with the government.

The NREGA has opened up a unique legal space for the poor, with a consequent, legally-mandated obligation on the administration to deliver. In fact, implementation rest on the simple philosophy that ordinary people will go to great lengths to procure their entitlements, given the space to do so. Apart from systemic corruption, we are all aware of the chronic inefficiency, unwillingness and incapacities of the bureaucratic system to deliver entitlements for the poor. The persistent argument was that in this context implementation would be impossible. The NREGA sought to create real opportunities and legal spaces, with the belief that people will begin to push to overcome bureaucratic and political resistance. The electoral endorsement over, it is a good time to begin to examine this aspect of bottom-up approach really work?

The act has a number of "trigger mechanisms" designed to activate and establish people's entitlements. One such trigger is the right to have a job card. The act mandates that anyone who applies at their panchayat for a job card must be given one within 15 days. Without a job card, people cannot even apply for work, nor corroborative the records. It is a "license" and "pan car" of the wage worker's family, with a record of days of work and wages received during the year. There are many states where large numbers of people have demanded, but not received, job cards. In many panchayats, job cards are in the control of implementing agencies. Publishing the job card as record of individual entitlements, to be updated by the authorities, and kept in possession of the workers, would ensure the NREGA is monitored by its workers.

CRUCIAL ACCOUNTABILITY

The application for work and the dated receipt are crucial to trigger the demand for work. The receipt is also the basic record for claiming unemployment allowance if the work is not provided within 15 days, but resistance to giving dated receipts has become a massive problem. No state has effectively activated this important mechanism. Nevertheless, it has worked when workers groups have got organized.

In the 30 years of existence of its precursor, the Maharashtra employment guarantee act, there is no recorded instance of payment of unemployment allowance. The NREGA has already recorded payment of unemployment allowance to large numbers of workers in chronically poorly- administered areas. The successful people's struggles for the payment of unemployment allowance–in Barwani District of Madhya Pradesh, Raichur of Karnataka, Bolangir, Navrangpur and Kalahandi of Orissa, Latehar in Jharkhand, Sitapur District of UP–has been a breakthrough in accountability, and an inspiration to other workers struggling for entitlements. Te payment of unemployment allowance emanates from an administrative lapse, and is eventually deducted from the pocket of erring officials. It is not a feebie doled out of he government exchequer. Like the right to information act, this has created an important mechanism for reinforcing the right while holding the bureaucracy accountable.

The wage under NREGA has been another and indicator of its success. The wager rate, the measurement system, and the timely payment of wages have a;; become part of the entitlement package, thanks to NREGA, minimum wages have, for the first time, become a real factor in determining the lower limit for market wages. There are many ongoing struggles for the payment of minimum wages; and adopting a transparent measurement system challenge that has thrown up many grassroots solutions.

BOTTLENECKS

Wage payment through NREGA have initiated the biggest "financial inclusion" drive with the requirement that all wage payment be made through banks and post offices have been begun to cripple the act, students and academics, working together with worker's organizations in Khunti District in Jharkhand, have operationlised the entitlement in the NREGA to get Rs.2,000/- per worker paid to over 300 workers as compensation for delayed payment under the provisions of the payment of wages act. The Khunti paymen, made last month, has once again demonstrated that the solution to the vexatious issues of late payments lies in the entitlement frame work.

The uneven implementation in different states has shown that where people's struggles have gained political and administrative respect, the NREGA has shown tangible results on a massive scale it is that battleground of struggle that could well determine the future of the political discourse in this country.

The government of India has transferred adequate money to the states and districts to make timely wage payments. Shri C.P. Joshi, the current Union minister for rural development and panchayati Raj, was reported to have talked about his partly prospects in the polls being negatively affected because of late wage payments in Rajasthan. As union minister now, if he were to exercise his administrative and political will to ensure compensation is paid to those receiving delayed wage payment, the lethargic bureaucratic system will find a way to respond. Chronic delays in wage payments during the drought in Rajasthan became a political issue, and the delays were wiped out. Innovations and mechanisms respond to a bottom-up demand, but do so best when the political establishment puts pressure.

The NREGA also assures an adequate, realistic provision for administrative expenses. At the current six percent of total costs which has been allowed for administrating costs, there is no legitimacy in citing a shortage of staff for resources for bureaucratic delay. In Rajasthan, for instance, the over 7,000 crores spent on NREGA last year amounts to a massive Rs.450 crores available for administrative expenses per year. This kind of money and resources can, in fact, help gram panchayats become properly resourced to better carry out their overall responsibilities. It can also help ensure that there is no excuse for the failure to carry out all transparency measures and put an effective grievance redressal mechanism in place.

BIGGEST CONTRIBUTION

Transparency andaccountability to the poorest and the weakest is in fact the biggest potential contribution of the NREGA to the entire governance system. The NREGA is an outstanding example of how the RTI act can be woven into the fabric of the delivery system and the whole legal and governance paradigm. The entire expenditure on works and workers - 94 percent of the total amount - is required to be put on the website of the NREGA, with every transaction revealed to 100 percent. Using this management information system (MIS), Vijayapura Gram Panchayat in Rajsamand District has begun to build a Janata information system (JIS) painted on the walls of government buildings in the gram panchayat. The boards reveal the details of the number of days work provided and payments made in the year to every job card holder in the panchayat. Also painted on the walls are list of works sanctioned, the expenditure on labour and material, and item-wise expenditure on material in each work in the panchayat, including exactly how many bags of cement, sand and trolleys of stone were procured, and at what rate in the gram panchajayat. This is like a web wall which reveals to every interested visitor all that they want to examine.

What can be done in one panchayat can be carried out in the 9,189 panchayats of Rajasthan, and the hundreds of thousands of panchayats in India. The walls in Vijayapura Panchayat provide details of 976 families given employment in 2008-09, where two thirds have completed 100 days, with anexpenditureof91 lakhs. The sarpanch is a dalit youth from a poor family, elected in a general sea, and the panchayat is proof of how well an employment guarantee programme can be implemented, in transparency measures, worksite management, and many other innovations.

LARGER IMPACT

If the million of financial transactions of the NREGA can goon there web site, there can be no justification for a not following the example and putting almost every financial transaction of government–receipt or expenditure–on the web sites of the relevant department or agency. Proactive disclosure is a requirement of the RTI act, and is a good example of the larger potential impact of the NREGA on governance.

The NREGA is India's first law to codify development rights in a legal framework, and like the RTI, it has begun to set an example in global context. Apart from the law, and a set of guidelines, there is a strong and immediate need to formulate rules to operationalise provisions in the act; which includes guaranteeing grievance redressal in seven days, social audit twice a year, and mandatory transparency and proactive disclosure. Properly incorporated and enforced, a comprehensive set of operational rules could strengthen the entitlement framework, fixing responsibility at every level. Once again, it would enable bottom-up pressure for implementation, which should be matched by a strong political mandate. Today, the NREGA has millions of workers' unresolved and un-addressed grievances and problems to be dealt with. A response system could not only radically improve the NREGA, but can impact and transform the whole face of rural governance.

Is the NREGA an administrator's nightmare or a redistribution of income and power? A social safety net or a step towards the right to work, to prevent migration and even boost local market economies? For those who cannot think beyond the pale of the free market economy and the business model manager, it is indeed a nightmare. For years, simplistic management solutions to poverty, with the poor as an input to be managed, have failed. We cannot see ordinary people as active participants and empowered citizens. That is why there is difficulty in understanding the practice and logic of democracy and difficult, therefore, to understand the realistic detailing and complexity of an employment guarantee initiative.

INCLUSIVE GROWTH

Independent India has to acknowledge the critical role the NREGA has played in providing a measure of inclusive growth. It has given people a right to work, to re-establish the dignity of labour, to ensure people's economic and democratic rights and entitlements, to create labour intensive infrastructure and assets, and to build the human resource base of our country. For the first time, the power elite recognize the people's right to fight endemic hunger and poverty with dignity, accepting that their labour will be the foundation for infrastructure and economic growth. The entitlements paradigm is still to be established in many states in the country. Second generation issues like the expansion of the deprived continuing to be the central focus. The improvements must be to strengthen, not divert from these basic tenets. In the midst of the current economic slowdown, there is enough evidence that this kind of commitment can work to help reduce the slowdown.

CONCLUSION

The political class would do well to understand that the most important solution is assertion of its will to respond to people's voices. The many wise, creative, and innovative initiatives emerging from theory and practice have a future only if they are owned by the people and implemented with justice. The NREGA can give people an opportunity to make the entire system truly transparent and accountable. Properly supported, people's struggles for basic entitlements can, in turn, become the strongest political initiative to strengthen our democratic fabric.

REFERENCES

Lakin, J. and Ravishankar, N. (2006-08-31), "Working for Votes: The Politics of Employment Guarantee in India" Paper presented at the annual meeting of the American Political Science Association, Marriott, Loews Philadelphia, and the Pennsylvania Convention Center, Philadelphia, PA.

Chakraborty, Pinaki (2007), Implementation of the National Rural Employment Guarantee Act in India: Spatial Dimensions and Fiscal Implications (July 12). Levy Economics Institute Working Paper No. 505.

Indra Hirway, Enhancing Livelihood Security through the National Employment Guarantee Act Toward Effective Implementation of the Act

Dev Mahendra (2000), 'Economic Reforms, Poverty, Income Distribution and Employment', Economic and Political Weekly, March.

Fan S., Hazell P. and Thorat S. (1999), Linkages Between Government Spending, Growth and Poverty in Rural India, Research Report No. 110, International Food Policy Research Institute, Washington.

Gaiha Raghav (1997), 'Rural Public Works and the Poor, A Review of Employment Gurantee Scheme in Maharastra', in Research and Labour Economics.

Gaiha Raghav (1997a), 'Do Rural Public Works Influence Agricultural Wages? The Case of the Employment Guarantee Scheme in India', Oxford Development Studies.

Gaiha Raghav (1998), 'Do Anti-Poverty Programmes Reach in the Rural Poor in India'? Oxford Development Studies.

Gaiha Raghav and Imai Katsushi (2000), Rural Public Works and Poverty Alleviation-The Cost of the Employment Guarantee Scheme, Maharastra, Faculty of Management Studies, University of Delhi, Mimeo.

Government of India (1997), Planning Commission, Perspective Planning Division, Estimates of Poverty, New Delhi.

Government of India (1980), Programme Evaluation Organisation and Government of Maharashtra, Joint Evaluation of Employment Guarantee Scheme of Maharashtra, New Delhi.

Government of India (2000), Planning Commission, Mid Term Appraisal of Ninth Five Year Plan, New Delhi.

Government of India (2000), Programme Evaluation Organisation, Evaluation Study on Employment Assurance Scheme, New Delhi.

Government of India (2001), Planning Commission, Perspective Planning Division, Poverty Estimate for1999-2000, New Delhi.

Gupta S.P. (2000), Trickle Down Theory Revisited, Annual Conference of Indian Society of Labour Economics, Mumbai.

Hirway Indira (2001), How Far Can Poverty Alleviation Programmes Go? The Case of Gujarat, Interim Report, Centre for Development Alternatives, Ahmedabad.

Raghav, G. (1997), 'Rural Public Works and the Poor: the case of the Employment Guarantee Scheme in India, Research in Labour Economics.

Rao C.H. Hanumantha (1992), 'Integrating Poverty Alleviation Programmes with Development Strategies: The Indian Experience', Economic and Political Weekly.

Rao C.H. Hanumantha (1994), Agricultural Growth and Rural Poverty in India: Emerging Trends and Perspectives, Dharm Narain Memorial Lecture, Institute of Economic Growth, New Delhi.

Impact of Rural Employment Guarantee Programme and Poverty in India

26

G.H. Nagaraj

Development and utilization of human resources and the improvement in the overall quality of life of the people are central to any development planning. There are, however, two -way linkages between human development and overall economic progress sustained high economic growth is a necessary condition and a significant driver of human development, on the other hand , if people are healthy, educated and adequately skilled they can participate fully and contribute more to economic development process. The Tenth Five Year Plan recognized these linkages while laying down monitorable targets for human development for the plan.

UNDP's global human development report (HDR) for 2005 ranks India at 127 out of 177 countries of the world in terms of the composite human development index (HDI) for 2003 (Table 10.1) Between 2000 and 2003, while the absolute values of HDI and gender Development Index (GDI) consistently improved for India, its ranking remained invariant at 127 consecutively for three years in a row. on the other hand, some of India's neighbours not only improved their HDI and GDI values, but also improved their relative ranks. Central Government also provides assistance to the state for social sector development in the form of central assistance to states plan, centrally sponsored schemes (CSS), special central assistance and additional central assistance. Expenditure of the central government on social services including rural development increased from Rs 18,240 crore in 1995-96 to Rs. 70, 910 crore in 2005-06

NATIONAL RURAL EMPLOYMENT GUARANTEE ACT 2005

The National Rural Employment Guarantee Act was noticed on September 7, 2005 and the scheme launced on February 2, 2006. The on-going programmes of Sampoorna Grameen Rozgar Yojana (SGRY) and national food for work programme (NFFWP) will be subsumed within the NREGS in the 200 districts identified in the initial stage, all the districts in the country will be covered under the scheme within five years.

The objective of the Act is to enhance the livelihood security of the people in rural areas by generating wage employment thorough works that develop the infrastructure base of that area. The choice of work suggested addresses the causes of chronic poverty like drought, deforestation and soil erosion. The objective behind suggesting certain key activities/works is to rejuvenate the natural resources of the area to stimulate the local economy enabling those who work for wage employment in creating an assest to tale adavantage of it to engage in productive ways of self -employment and augment their income. Implementation of the Act calls for the formulation of NREGSs by the State Governments. Section 4 of the Act provides that within six months from the date of commencement of the Act, every state government shall, by notification make a scheme for providing not less than 100 days of guaranteed employment in a financial year to every household in the rural areas covered under the scheme and whose adult members volunteer to do unskilled manual work subject to the conditions laid down in the Act.

Oflate, it has been well established fact that in our country is that al-though GDP growth has accelerated, it has not been accompanied by a com-mensurate increase in employment leading to a worsening in the employ-ment situation. These considerations have led to a demand for greater at-tention to the employment objective in the Eleventh Plan document. There is also a concern on youth and educated unemployment as increase in it will lead to waste of human resources and social tensions. If these factors are not properly understood and solved in time, it could jeopardize all the developmen-tal activities and can nullify the gains achieved so far. Particularly, the employment generation strategy can-not be distinguished from the broader policy thrust for growth and structural changes in the economy as a whole (Gol, 2001).

STRUCTURAL CHANGE

The most striking feature of the structural change in the Indian economy in recent decades has been the pre-eminence of services sector as the major contributor to growth, raising its share rather sharply in the national output but unable increase employment opportunities commensurately. On the other, Industry, particularly manufactur-ing, which has been observed histori-cally to be the main contributor of growth, at least in the initial period of economic development, is playing only a minor role in India's, economic growth in recent years. While the developed countries entered the phase of predominance of services in their economies, after going through a phase of industrialization, and industry having attired a share of 50 percent in the economy, and thus India on the other way becoming a post-industrial 'service economy', without industrialization.

The share of agriculture in GDP declined from around 60 percent in 1950-51 to 24 percent in 2003-04. That of industry increased from 13 to 25 per-cent and of services from 28 to 51 per-cent. This pattern of shifts has been continuous throughout the period of over half a century, but the speed of the shift has been faster since 1990-91. The first forty years saw a decline in the share of agriculture from 59 percent to 35 percent, the next 13 years from 35 to 24 percent. Share of services in-creased from 28 to 40 percent in the first 40 years and from 40 to 51 percent in the next 13 years. Share of industry has grown slowly but has stagnated since 1990-91.

Two propositions have been general-ly advanced to explain such a swift and a historical transition of an economy directly from an agricultural to a service economy, bypassing industrial develop-ment. One, it is argued that technologi-cal advancements over the past few decades have led to increasing demand for services even at a relatively low level of per capita income and also the distinction between products and 'services has become rather blurred. Development of communication tech-nologies and movements of people across countries have produced "demonstration effect" creating similar pattern of demand in developing countries as in the developed countries leading to larger demand for and, consequently, production of services (Pandhamukhi, Nambiar and Mehta, 1986). As a result, elasticity of demand for services has become greater than unity even in countries with relatively low per capita income levels (Sabolo, 1975), thus leading to a rise in the con-tribution of services in national product.

Second, the classical model of struc-tural changes with economic develop-ment was based on the experience of nations with more or less autarkic regimes with little international trade, a situation in which, domestic product structure of each country has to reflect its demand pattern, With increasing openness of economies and trade play-ing significant role in them, changes in demand pattern can be met through trade and countries can have a product pattern, very different from the pattern of consumption demand, largely based on comparative advantage.

ANTI-POVERTY, EMPLOYMENT GENERATION AND BASIC SERVICES PROGRAMMES

Pradhan Mantri Gram Sadak Yojana (PMGSY)

Launched in December 2000 as a 100 per cent CSS, PMGSY aims to provide all-weather connectivity to all the eligible unconnected rural habitations. Bharat Mirman, envisages connectivity by 2009 to all the habitations with a population of 1000 or more in the plains, and of 500 or more in the hilly, desert and tribal areas. The systematic upgradation of the existing rural road network also is an integral component of the scheme, funded mainly from the accruals of diesel cess in the Central Road Fund, with support of the multilateral funding agencies and the domestic financial institutions. Up to December 2005, with an expenditure of Rs.12,049 crore, a total length of 82,718 km. of road works had been completed.

Indira Awaas Yojana (IAY)

IAY aims to provide dwelling units, free of cost, to the Scheduled Castes (SCs), Scheduled Tribes (STs), and freed bonded labourers, and also the non-SC/ST BPL families in rural areas. It is funded on a cost-sharing basis in the rates of 75.25 between the Centre and the States. Under (AY, the ceiling on construction assistance is Rs.25.QOO/- per unit in the plains and Rs.27,5007- for hilly/difficult areas; and Rs. 12.500/- on upgradation of unserviceable kutcha house to pucca/semi pucca house for all areas. Up to January 30, 2006, about 138 lakh houses had been constructed/upgraded with an expenditure of Rs.25,208 crore.

Swarnjayanti Gram Swarozgar Yojana (SGSY)

SGSY, launched in April, 1999 after restructuring the Integrated Rural Development Programme and allied schemes, is the only self-employment programme for the rural poor. The objective is to bring the self-employed above the poverty line by providing them income-generating assets through bank credit and Government subsidy. Up to November 2005, the Centre and States, sharing the costs on 75:25 basis, had allocated Rs.8,067 crore, of which Rs. 6,980 crore had been utilized to assist 62.75 lakh self-employed.

Sampoorna Grameen Rozgar Yojana (SGRY)

SGRY, launched on September 25, 2001 to provide additional wage employment in the rural areas, has a cash and food grains component, and the Centre bears 75 per cent and 100 per cant of the cost of the two with the balance borne by the States/ UTs. In 2004-05, 82.23 crore persondays were generated with the Centre releasing Rs. 4,496 crore as cash component and about 50 lakh tonnes of foodgrains to the States/ Uts. Besides, under the special component of.the SGRY, with the States/ Uts meeting the cash components, Centre released 26 lakh tonnes of foodgrains to the 13 calamity affected States. In 2005-06 up to November, 2005, the number of persondays generated under SGRY was 48.75 crore, while the Centre's contributions in terms of the cash and foodgrains components up to January, 2006 were Rs. 4651 crore and 35 lakh tonnes, respectively. Under the special component, about 11.65 lakh tonnes of foodgrains have been released to the 11 calamity-hit States in the current year

National Food for Work Programme (NFFWP)

The NFFWP was launched as a CSS in November 2004, in the 150 most backward districts to generate additional supplementary wage employment with food security. States receive food grains under NFFWP free of cost. The focus of the programme is on works relating to water conservation, drought proofing (including aforestation /tree plantation), land development, flood-control/protection (including drainage in waterlogged areas), and rural connectivity in terms of all-weather roads. In 2004-05, allocation of Rs 2,020 crore and 20 lakh tonnes of food grains generated 7.85 crore persondays of employment. In 2005-06, of the allocation of Rs 4,500 crore and 15 lakh tonnes of food grains (Revised), Rs.2,219 crore and 11.58 lakh metric tonnes of food grains had been released up to January 27, 2006. About 17.03 lakh person days were generated up to December 2005.

DPAP, DDP and IWDP

Drought Prone Areas Programme (DPAP) was launched in 1973-74 to tackle the special problems faced by those areas constantly affected by severe drought conditions. Desert Development Programme (OOP) was launched in 1977-78 to mitigate the adverse effects of desertification. Integrated Wastelands Development Programme (IWDP) has been under implementation since 1989-90 for the development of wastelands.

Swarna Jayanti Shahari RozgarYojana (SJSRY)

In December 1997, the Urban Self-Employment Programme (USER) and the Urban Wage Employment Programme (UWEP), which are the two special components of the SJSRY, substituted for various programmes operated earlier for urban poverty alleviation. The SJSRY is funded on a 75:25 basis between the Centre and the States. In 2003-04, the centfal allocation of Rs. 94.50 crore plus Rs. 10.50 crore for North-/ Eastern Region including Sikkim was fully utilized. Even 2004-05 saw the release of the entire budgetary allocation of Rs. 122.00 crore. In 2005-06, out of an allocation of Rs. 160.00 crore, Rs. 84.52 crore had been utilized until November 30, 2005.

Valmiki Ambedkar Awas Yojana (VAWIBAY)

VAMBAY, launched in December 2001, facilitates the construction and up-gradation of dwelling units for the slum dwellers, and provides a healthy and enabling urban environment through community toilets under Nirmal Bharat Abhiyan, a component of the Scheme. The Central Government provides a subsidy of 50 per cent, with the balance provided by the State Government.

Since its inception and up-to December, 31 2005, Rs. 866,16 crore had been released as Central subsidy for the constructlon/upgradation of 4,11,478 dwelling, units and 64,247 toilet seats under the Scheme. For 2005-06, out of the tentative Central allocation of Rs. 249 crore, up to December 31, 2005, an amount of Rs.96.4 crore had been released covering 60,335 dwelling units and 381 toilet seats.

INCREASING ASYMMETRY

Further, there is an increasing asym-metry between the sectoral shares of GDP and employment with strong likelihood of growing inequality in in-comes among sectors, groups and in-dividuals. With shrinking share of agriculture in GDP without a commen-surate decline in its employment share, the income gap between agriculture and non-agricultural workers is rapidly increasing. With a 50 percent share in GDP and 74 percent share in employ-ment, the ratio of per worker agricul-tural to non-agricultural incomes in 1960 was 1:3 ; now with 60 percent workers and 21 percent GDP in agricul-ture it is close to 1:6. Ratio between agriculture and services is 1·7 and be-tween agriculture and industry 1:4. With increases in the share of services, this gap will certainly increase unless the growth is accompanied by an increase in the employment share of services.

NATIONAL RENEWAL FUND (NRF)

With the introduction of structural ad-justment and liberalization policies in nineties, the government had initiated several measures to take care of their adverse implications for workers and vulnerable sections of the population. The pronounced policy of the govern-ment was to effect closures or retrench-ments only as a last resort, after all avenues of reviving the units were ex-hausted. And where these measures were inevitable a National Renewal Fund (NRF) was constituted in 1992-93 to enable enterprises to pay reasonable benefits and assist the workers rendered redundant by their retraining and redeployment.

Another important objective of NRF was to find the approved programmes for employment generation. However, although a large amount of money has been spent on NRF, the expenditure—about 93 percent—has been mainly on voluntary retirement scheme (VRS) and other aspects have been almost completely ignored. Several studies have shown that displacement of a .large section of the workforce though VRS without equipping them with adequate skill and training to re-enter in the job market, has resulted in huge loss of productive manpower.

The government of India and state governments also expanded and restructured the existing poverty-alleviation and employment generation programmes to deal with the possible adverse effects of stabilization measures on the poor. The Public Distribution System was also restructured strengthened which played an impor-tant role in mitigating food security. IT is widely believed that the existence of a large-scale programmes of poverty-alleviation in India helped in minimizing to some extent the adverse impact of liberalization and globalization. How-ever, some disquieting trends in the' labour market and economy particularly! the slackening of the employment: growth and deterioration in the quality of employment in the wake of increas-ing pace of globalization, call for appropriate policy responses.

(a) water conservation and water harvesting

(b) drought proofing

(c) irrigation canals including micro and minor irrigation works

(d) provision of irrigation facility to land owned by households belonging to Scheduled Castes and Scheduled Tribes, beneficiaries of land reforms, or beneficiaries of Indira Awas Yojana

(e) renovation of traditional water bodies including desalting of tanks

(f) flood control and protection works including drainage in water logged areas; and

(g) rural connectivity to provide all-weather access. All these activities improve rural infrastructure and increase agricultural productivity.

REFERENCES

Bhagavati, J. (2001), "Growth, Poverty and Reforms". *Economic and Political Weekly,* March 10.

Chaterjee, B. (2003), "Poverty Studies and Poverty Alleviation in India", in R.K. Sen (ed.)., Economic Reforms and Development, Deep & Deep Publications (p) LTd.. New Delhi.

Datt, Ruddar (2003), Lockouts in India, Indian Society of Labour Economies and Institute for Human Development, New Delhi.

Dev, S. (1995), "Experience of India's (Maharastra) Employment Guarantee Scheme: Lesson for Development Policy", *Development Policy Review,* Vol.14, No.3.

Dev, S. Mahendra (1996), "Employment Guarantee Scheme", *Economic and Political Weekly,* March 2.

GOI (2001), "Report of Task Force on Employment Opportunities", Planning Commission, Government of India.

27 Rural Poverty Drops in India

G. Paramasivan, J. Sacratees

INTRODUCTION

Poverty is one of the main issues, attracting the attention of sociologists and economists. It indicates a condition in which a person fails to maintain a living standard adequate for a comfortable lifestyle. Though India boasts of a high economic growth, it is shameful that there is still large scale poverty in India. Poverty in India can be defined as a situation when a certain section of people are unable to fulfill their basic needs. India has the world's largest number of poor people living in a single country. Out of its total population of more than 1 billion, 350 to 400 million people are living below the poverty line. According to the a 2005 World Bank estimate, 42% of India's falls below the international poverty line of $1.25 a day (PPP, in nominal terms Rs. 21.6 a day in urban areas and Rs 14.3 in rural areas); having reduced from 60% in 1980. According to the criterion used by the Planning Commission of India 27.5% of the population was living below the poverty line in 2004–2005, down from 51.3% in 1977–1978, and 36% in 1993-1994. While poverty rates in India are high, they are not on a par with what neighbouring Pakistan and Bangladesh experience.

Poverty in India is reducing but it is still a major issue. Rural Indians depend on unpredictable agriculture incomes, while urban Indians rely on jobs that are, at best, scarce. Since its independence, the issue of poverty within India has remained a prevalent concern. According to the common definition of poverty, when a person finds it difficult to meet the minimum requirement of acceptable living standards, he or she is considered poor. Millions of people in India are unable to meet these basic standards, and according to government estimates, in 2007 there were nearly 220.1 million people living below the poverty line. Nearly 21.1% of the entire rural population and 15% of the urban population of India exists in this difficult physical and financial predicament. An estimated 260.3 million are below the poverty line, of which 193.2 million are in the rural areas and 67.1 million are in urban areas. More than 75% of poor people reside in villages. Poverty level is not uniform across India. The poverty level is below 10% in states like Delhi, Goa, and Punjab etc whereas it is below 50% in Bihar (43) and Orissa (47). It is between 30-40% in Northeastern states of Assam, Tripura, and Mehgalaya and in Southern states of TamilNadu and Uttar Pradesh.

POVERTY REDUCTION PROGRAMMES

Since the 1970s the Indian government has made poverty reduction a priority in its development planning. Policies have focused on improving the poor standard of living by ensuring food security, promoting self-employment through greater access to assets, increasing wage employment and improving access to basic social services. Launched in 1965, India's Public Distribution System has helped meet people's basic food needs by providing rations at subsidized prices. The largest credit-based government poverty reduction programme in the world, the Integrated Rural Development Programme (IRDP) provides rural households below the poverty line with credit to purchase income-generating assets. Launched in 1979, the programme has supplied subsidized credit to such groups as small and marginalized farmers, agricultural laborers, rural artisans, the physically handicapped, scheduled castes and scheduled tribes. Within this target population, 40% of the beneficiaries are supposed to be women. Although the programme has reached 51 million families, only 27% of the borrowers have been women. The programme has significantly increased the income of 57% of assisted families.

Other programs include the Integrated Rural Development Programme, Jawahar Rozgar Yojana, Training Rural Youth for Self Employment (TRYSEM) and to the credit of the government, other on-going initiatives. Government has introduced a number of antipoverty programs since independence to alleviate poverty. These include various employment guarantee programmes such as National Rural Employment Programme, Rural Landless Employment Guarantee Programme etc. Recently, Government has initiated National Rural Employment Guarantee Program (NREGP). As per NREGP, the government will provide 100 days of employment per year to whosoever is willing to work. NREGP is considered as a landmark program in poverty alleviation measures. One of the major problems with poverty alleviation programs is their implementation. Rajiv Gandhi once said that out of 100 paisa allocated for poor only 14 paisa reaches them. But in spite of their weaknesses, poverty alleviated program can be credited for their success in alleviating poverty to an extent. Greater public-private partnership and committed and efficient bureaucratic machinery is required to tackle poverty. In 1982-83, Development of Women and Children in Rural Areas (DWCRA) was launched as a sub-scheme of IRDP. The focus of DWCRA was on economic activities for rural women to be taken up in groups. The concept of the group was to enable women to take a larger amount of loan, so that by pooling their individual loans they could start viable non- farm activity. DWCRA too met with limited success.

RURAL POVERTY REDUCTION THROUGH NGOS AND SHGS

Poverty, particularly rural poverty, has been one of the enduring policy challenges in India. Surely the most important objective of the reforms process would have been to make a significant dent on rural poverty. It is from this that a program of accelerated growth must draw its rationale. Since the 1970s, numerous Non Government Organizations (NGO) had begun experiments in micro financing to address poverty issues and create self-employment for women. Official interest in informal group lending took shape during 1986-87 when National Bank for Agriculture and Rural Development (NABARD) supported and funded an action research project on, 'Savings and Credit Management of Self Help Groups' of an NGO in Karnataka. Following a survey of 43 NGOs in 11 states in India to study the functioning of SHGs in 1988-89, NABARD impressed upon the Reserve Bank of India to come out with a circular on July 24, 1991 advising the commercial banks to extend credit to the SHGs under the pilot project of NABARD. The results of the pilot project run by four NGOs extending credit to 1706 SHGs were found to be quite encouraging. The RBI constituted a working group in 1994 to review the functioning of NGOs and SHGs and accepting the recommendations advised the banks that lending to the SHGs should be considered as an additional segment under priority sector advances. The SHGs, thus, became a component of Indian financial system.

In 1999, the Ministry of Rural Development restructured the numerous programs and introduced the new self-employment program called Swarnajayanti Gram Swarozgar Yojana which is implemented through SHGs. Following the decentralisation initiative in Kerala, SHGs called Kudumbasree are being formed to implement poverty alleviation programs. The emergence and rapid multiplication of Self Help Groups (SHGs) based on micro credit is a phenomenon that is gaining increasing importance in the development scenario. Today there are seven million SHGs in the country. Nearly 90% of the groups are women only groups. SHGs have been viewed by the State as a strategy for both women's empowerment as well as poverty reduction. SHGs are a conduit for routing a wide range of government sponsored development messages and schemes. NGOs have increasingly been adopting SHGs as a strategy to bring women together, at a faster pace and larger scale than the collective building processes adopted by them earlier.

The experience of SHGs has shown that although they have provided improved access to credit it is not affordable credit. Poor women pool in their resources and access credit for crisis and consumption (mostly food, health and education). Although participation in SHGs has meant opportunities related to mobility and a legitimate space in the public realm for leaders of SHGs, the overall picture is one that raises several critical concerns related to gender justice and livelihoods that the 11th Five Year Plan process needs to address. These concerns draw upon the understanding of equity and gender justice of concerned social activists, the intensive engagement of practitioners who have implemented SHG programmes as well as several research studies. By projecting the SHGs involved in savings and credit activities as the most effective way to deal with poverty the onus of poverty removal falls on women.

The major form of microfinance in India is that based on women's Self Help Groups (SHGs), which are small groups of 10-20 members. These groups collect savings from their members and provide loans to them. However, unlike most Accumulating Savings and Credit Associations (ASCAs) found in several countries, these groups also obtain loans from banks and on-lend them to their members. By 2003, over 700,000 groups had obtained over Rs.20 billion (US$425 million) in loans from banks benefiting more than 10 million people. Delinquencies on these loans are reported to be less than 5%. Savings in these groups is estimated to be at least Rs.8 billion (US$170 million). Despite these considerable achievements, sustainability of the SHGs has been suspect because several essential services required by the SHGs are provided free or at a significantly subsidized cost by organizations that have developed these groups. A few promoter organizations have, however, developed federations of SHGs that provide these services to the SHGs and others that SHG member's need, but which SHGs cannot feasibly provide.

Over the last decade, cumulatively more than 700,000 SHGs have obtained approximately Rs.20 billion (US$425 million) in loans from banks under a program of the National Bank of Agriculture and Rural Development (NABARD). Since the average membership of SHGs is around 15, in cumulative terms over 10 million people may have thus benefited from such loans. The on-time repayment rate on these loans has been over 95 percent. In addition to the NABARD program, several other financial institutions2 lend to NGOs for on-lending to SHGs. By a conservative estimate, savings in SHGs are at least Rs.8 billion (US$170 million). The program, started in 1992 as a pilot project and upgraded to a regular banking program in 1996, has expanded rapidly since then. NABARD's refinance has however been falling in proportion–possibly because of the prevailing low interest rates, high level of liquidity in banks, and not the least, because of the banks starting to see the program as a profitable proposition. Of the Rs.10.2 billion (US$212 million) lent by banks in 2002-03, they only requested Rs.6.2 billion (US$130 million) in refinance (NABARD, 2003). NABARD's original goal of supporting one million SHGs under this program by 2008 seems easily surpassable. A Microfinance Development Fund, created at NABARD with a start up fund of Rs.1 billion (US$21 million) using contributions from the Reserve Bank of India, NABARD and other commercial banks, is to be used to consolidate and further expand the program.

In India, Self Help Groups or SHGs represent a unique approach to financial intermediation. The approach combines access to low-cost financial services with a process of self management and development for the women who are SHG members. SHGs are formed and supported usually by NGOs or (increasingly) by Government agencies. Linked not only to banks but also to wider development programmes, SHGs are seen to confer many benefits, both economic and social. SHGs enable women to grow their savings and to access the credit which banks are increasingly willing to lend. SHGs can also be community platforms from which women become active in village affairs, stand for local election or take action to address social or community issues (the abuse of women, alcohol, the dowry system, schools, and water supply).

SHGs represent an opportunity for social action and empowerment through women's involvement in considering, addressing and participating in issues that affect their members and their communities, including issues that affect women in particular. The extent to which this happening is perhaps less than hoped for–although a beginning is being made. One reason is the huge challenge involved in women having the right to speak out and take a stand in still very traditional, patriarchal, societies.

Women from different social and economic levels are joining SHGs, including the poor, and some very poor. This process continues as the numbers grow. However, the barriers to entry for the poor are high–not only do they have lower incomes (by definition), but their incomes are usually more variable. To reduce barriers for the poor means allowing more flexibility to cater to varying and seasonal cash flows, for example allowing varying deposit amounts and frequency, perhaps with a specified annual minimum. The same principle applies to access to credit and repayment, again within specified minimum norms.

CONCLUSIONS

SHG-based microfinance in India has significant achievements: over 10 million people reached, Rs.8 billion (US$170 million) in savings mobilized, Rs.20 billion (US$425 million), and over 95% on-time repayment rate on these loans. However, the financial sustainability of SHGs has not been clear because several of their costs are subsidized by organizations that had promoted them, and because of less than market cost paid by SHGs on loans from banks. Similarly, their organizational sustainability has been suspect because of their small size, which limited the financial and human capital available to them, and thereby the services they could provide themselves.

NABARD has played a crucial role in the development of the SHG microfinance program. It has been focusing, perhaps justifiably given the slow initial progress of the program, on increasing the outreach of SHGs and strengthening their linkage with the banking system. However, given the exponential increase in the program in the recent years and similar trends observed in other microfinance programs around the world (including that of Grameen Bank) (World Bank 2003), the focus needs to shift to sustaining the benefits provided by SHGs.

Despite the considerable achievements of the SHG-bank linkage program, sustainability of SHGs has not been clear. The extent of sustainability and factors determining sustainability are not known. Knowledge on impact is also inadequate. The need to investigate these issues is long overdue. Factors those are likely to make the benefits of SHGs sustainable need to be identified. Fundamental questions such as whether SHGs need to be sustainable for the program benefits to be sustainable need to test. This study assumes the SHGs need to be sustainable and suggests that SHG federations have the potential to contribute to this. This suggestion needs to be tested further. These services help the SHGs gain economies of scale, obtain value-added services, reduce transaction cost, and enhance empowerment, thereby contributing to organizational sustainability of the SHGs. The financial analysis conducted for two federations indicates that both SHGs and SHG federations can be financially viable even when all costs, including those subsidized by the promoter agency, are accounted for.

REFERENCES

Andhra Pradesh Mahila Abhivruddhi Society (APMAS), Self Help Groups in India- A study of the lights and shades, EDA Rural Systems Pvt Ltd in association with CRS, USAID, CARE, GTZ/ NABARD, EDA Rural Systems Private Ltd Gurgaon 122001, India.

Dasgupta, R. (2001), An Informal Journey through Self-Help Groups. Indian Journal of Agricultural Economics. 56(3): 370-386.

Madheswaran, S., & Dharmadhikary, A. (2001), Empowering Rural Women through Self-Help Groups: Lessons from Maharastra Rural Credit Project. Indian Journal of Agricultural Economics. 56(3): 427-443.

Mohiuddin, A., et.al. (2001), Activities for Women under Cluster Approach and their Capacity Building: SGSY- An Evaluation Study. Orientation Programme on SGSY for District Level Officials. National Institute of Rural Development, Hyderabad.

Namboodiri, N.V., & Shiyani, R.L. (2001), Potential Role of Self-Help Groups in Rural Financial Deepening. Indian Journal of Agricultural Economics. 56(3): 401-409.

World Bank (2003), Microfinance in India: Issues, Constraints, and Potential for Sustainable Growth. Washington, DC.

www.apmas.org
www.edarural.com

Index

S